AI VALLEY

ALSO BY GARY RIVLIN

AI
VALLEY

Microsoft, Google, and the Trillion-Dollar
Race to Cash In on Artificial Intelligence

GARY RIVLIN

HARPER
BUSINESS
An Imprint of HarperCollins*Publishers*

HarperCollins books may be purchased for educational, business, or sales promotional use. For information, please email the Special Markets Department at SPsales@harpercollins.com.

FIRST EDITION

Designed by Michele Cameron
Title page image © Shutterstock
Heart image (shutterstock_2307576345.jpg) on page 84 © Shutterstock

Library of Congress Cataloging-in-Publication Data

Names: Rivlin, Gary, author.
Title: AI valley: Microsoft, Google, and the trillion-dollar race to cash in on artificial intelligence / Gary Rivlin.
Description: First edition. | New York: HarperCollins Publishers, [2025]
Identifiers: LCCN 2024043017 (print) | LCCN 2024043018 (ebook) | ISBN 9780063347496 (hardcover) | ISBN 9780063347502 (ebook)
Subjects: LCSH: Artificial intelligence—Environmental aspects.
Classification: LCC HC79.I55 R567 2024 (print) | LCC HC79.I55 (ebook) | DDC 338.4/70063—dc23/eng/20241026
LC record available at https://lccn.loc.gov/2024043017
LC ebook record available at https://lccn.loc.gov/2024043018

25 26 27 28 29 LBC 5 4 3 2 1

To Daisy, Oliver, and Silas,
with love

CONTENTS

PREFACE

Elon Musk was no doubt late because he was invariably late for any appointment. Reid Hoffman took a seat in a private dining room at Fuki Sushi in Palo Alto, California, not far from Stanford University's campus. Hoffman, the founder of LinkedIn, is certain he dined there with Musk on that fateful night in early 2015 because "that's where Elon always wants to meet," he said. For Musk, the restaurant's main selling point was its private tatami rooms, with doors that slide shut. Billionaires prefer to meet where people who aren't billionaires won't stare.

Musk cuts a much higher profile than Hoffman in the wider world but not in Palo Alto or the rest of Silicon Valley, where Hoffman is every bit Musk's equal. The two, who had first met at the end of the 1990s, when both worked at PayPal, occasionally got together to share a meal as each grew in stature within the tech world. Some dinners between the two have been friendlier than others. There was much that Hoffman admired about Musk. He praised Musk as a "polestar"—a guiding light—for other entrepreneurs. Despite the Valley's reputation for bold thinking, the typical founder pursued incremental improvements or niche applications rather than transformative ideas. Musk, in contrast, was a long-term thinker who ignored the naysayers and took big swings that might actually move the needle on humanity. Yet Hoffman has also dismissed Musk as a "sole-preneur"—a man incapable of working alongside others. Musk, Hoffman said, "has instincts for the good," but suffered a "God complex." Everything will be okay—so long as Musk is the one in charge.

There was something inherently transactional about their encounters. "It's always what new things are you thinking about, what can I learn from you during this dinner," Hoffman said. When the two met on that chilly night in 2015, Musk brought up artificial intelligence almost immediately. Hoffman waved him off. Hoffman had practically majored in AI as an undergraduate at Stanford in the late 1980s. One of his advisors was a towering figure in the field; the summer internships he secured had him working on artificial intelligence. Yet researchers back then were teaching computers to distinguish between a circle and a square or a cat and a dog. And Hoffman was eager to have an impact on the world, not play pre-K instructor teaching shapes and animals to a machine.

"I saw firsthand what AI was doing, and I thought it was juvenile," Hoffman said. AI has been disappointing humanity since the term "artificial intelligence" was first coined in the 1950s. Before Hoffman sat across from Musk at that dinner, nothing he had come across gave him reason to consider returning to his AI roots.

"I know about this stuff," Hoffman said dismissively. But Musk pushed back. He had recently returned from Puerto Rico, where eighty or so researchers had gathered to talk about AI. So rapidly was the field progressing that a new group, the Future of Life Institute, had formed to address concerns about AI's potential to harm humanity. Google was pouring hundreds of millions of dollars into the race to deploy AI. So too were Facebook, Microsoft, and Baidu in China.

Musk mentioned DeepMind, an AI startup Google had recently purchased for $650 million. Rather than create "expert systems" based on a preprogrammed set of instructions like previous generations of computer scientists had written, DeepMind was building so-called "neural networks"—programs that mimic the workings of the human brain. A DeepMind algorithm had taught itself how to play a variety of videogames at superhuman levels. They were just games, but Musk, who had been an investor in DeepMind, had seen a demo. The speed with which a machine learned was mind-bending. DeepMind's engineers would introduce one of its models to a new game in the morning. By lunchtime, a superior player might still beat the machine.

But by late afternoon, no human stood a chance. Together, Musk and Hoffman imagined the possibilities if machine learning could be applied to other areas.

"This is happening," Musk told him. "You need to be ready." Hoffman didn't have to be told twice. "My way is to find smart people and learn from them," he said. On the spot, Hoffman decided to set about learning what he could about AI.

"I don't have hobbies," Hoffman said. "I'm not someone who likes laying on the beach. Most of what I like doing is spending time with really smart people who are doing stuff."

Trillion-Dollar Ambitions

I n the fall of 2022, just before the world was upended by the release of ChatGPT, I received an email from Reid Hoffman, whom I have known since shortly after his company, LinkedIn, launched in the early 2000s. I had first written about him for *Wired* and then later while covering Silicon Valley for the *New York Times*. At some point he must have added my name to a list, because for years I've been receiving group emails from him at a pace of around two per annum. They were cheery, upbeat missives that included a mix of links to pieces that he had written, articles he found interesting, and thoughts he described as "top of mind." Typically, they addressed some sweeping trend in tech, though in more recent years he also shared his thoughts on politics. On a different day, I might have hit delete without reading it.

"Dear Friend," Hoffman's missive began. His personal chief of staff confirmed that I was one of more than two thousand friends that Hoffman, who has been called the best-connected person in Silicon Valley, has collected over the years. "ICYMI," read the subject line: In Case You Missed It. Indeed, I had missed the news. Earlier that year, Hoffman had cofounded an artificial intelligence startup, his first since launching LinkedIn two decades earlier. Inflection AI, he called his company.

I'll confess that before reading Hoffman's email, a long time had passed since I had given much thought to artificial intelligence. Like a lot of kids who grew up watching shows such as *Star Trek* and *Lost in Space*, I had fantasized about friendly robot companions and all-powerful supercomputers that ran the world. But covering tech in the 1990s and 2000s, I had never given any thought to AI. Upon reading Hoffman's email, though, I was immediately taken by the animating idea that gave rise to his company. Since the start of the computer age, humans have needed to create and learn new machine languages to communicate with a device. But Hoffman's aim, and that of his cofounders, was machines that understand our language. Finally, we would be able to talk to computers in our own native tongues—speaking human rather than conversing in symbolic code.

Hoffman has long been one of the Valley's bigger thinkers and steps ahead of most everyone else. He had practically invented the social media sector in the 1990s when he cofounded a startup called SocialNet. He holds a share of twenty-one patents in the field. He was early in online payments as a key employee at PayPal and had a hand in the rise of photo sharing, digital music, social gaming, and the sharing economy. He also stood out as one of the Valley's savviest investors. The $37,500 he gave Mark Zuckerberg to help him finance Facebook was worth roughly $400 million after the company went public in 2012. His first investment after becoming a venture capitalist for Greylock Partners in 2009 was in Airbnb, a $5 million bet that generated a payout of not 10x or even 100x but a 1,000-fold return. Eleven times, *Forbes* named Hoffman to its annual "Midas List" of top VCs. Eventually, he would make his share of political enemies as a Democratic megadonor who, by 2024, had spilled several hundred million dollars opposing Donald Trump.

Yet despite a net worth in the billions, Hoffman is cut differently than most who inhabit that economic stratum. Another serial entrepreneur, Joseph Ansanelli, who joined Greylock several years after Hoffman, was struck by the modesty of the by-then-Silicon-Valley-famous Reid Hoffman. Hoffman didn't drive a fancy car but rather a metallic green Acura that he had owned for years. He dressed as if shopping out of a Kmart bargain bin and had his regular crew with whom he played Settlers of Catan, a favorite board game among the geek set. "Here's this guy who's hanging out at the White House with the Obamas until two in the morning but remembers the names of my kids and asks how they're doing," Ansanelli said. "He's really just a normal person who's wildly successful and hasn't let it go to his head." He was a billionaire you wouldn't mind rooting for.

Hoffman is a large, unkempt bear of a man with unruly brown hair. If Elon Musk had Robert Downey Jr. playing him on the silver screen, at least when Musk was younger (and slimmer), Hoffman would have been played by John Candy. Hoffman is less arrogant Master of the Universe and more the rumpled, affable guy behind the counter at the automotive supply store. When we met, his shirt would be misbuttoned, or a blot of food stain would scream from his shirt throughout the meal. As I learned during breakfast with Hoffman in 2012, he was not above scooping up whatever bit of food had landed on his clothes and popping it in his mouth. He has a quick smile and a habit of nodding vigorously, puppy dog–style, eager to show his assent. Chris Yeh, a fellow Valley entrepreneur who has coauthored two books with Hoffman, described what happened when he asked his writing partner a question that caused him to think hard. "He'll close his eyes for a count of two or three seconds," Yeh said. "Sometimes it might be a count of three of four. Then he'll open his eyes and give a nod and start talking." Initially Yeh sat there feeling awkward, but he came to see it, he said, "like rubbing the lamp of the genie. The man just fizzes with intellect."

I had tried my hand at coding when I was younger, but I never was much of a programmer. I had earned a bit of acclaim among my peers in a high school computer club when I crashed the district's main computer. The matrix of possibilities I had laid out in a program that I sent to the district's sole machine, which we were granted access to for a few hours per week, was too large for the system to handle. In college, I studied Fortran and felt flummoxed trying to learn this rudimentary early computer language. Mainly what I remember of those months was the anguish of using punch cards to communicate with the machine. It would be late into the night at the Vogelback Computing

Center, a bleak and oppressive, low-slung bunker on the campus of Northwestern University. I'd hand to a clerk a rubber-banded batch of beige punch cards and wait—and an hour later, be heartbroken when the machine spit out a solitary page indicating an error. I had introduced a typo or made some small syntax error and I'd need to start all over again, search for my mistake in one of dozens of cards, fix it, and then get back in queue. A computer that let a person code using plain English would have been a gift from the gods.

I started writing about tech in 1996, near the dawn of the internet era. At that point, Hoffman was a junior product manager at Apple. Early on, I interviewed a prominent venture capitalist who had recently invested in a tiny bookseller named Amazon.com. Amazon would be much more than a bookstore, he told me, but I took that to mean the company might one day also sell CDs and DVDs. I met the founders of Google when theirs was maybe a forty-person startup and few gave them a chance at knocking off AltaVista, the dominant search engine at the time. In my social circle then was a quirky, female-companionship-starved guy named Craig Newmark, who created an eponymous site he called Craigslist.

The first time I met Hoffman was in 2003, while writing for *Wired* about a budding field people were then calling social networking. Later that year, the *New York Times* hired me to cover Silicon Valley. LinkedIn remained a good story and Hoffman a valuable source. In 2005, over dinner in Palo Alto at an elegant Indian restaurant popular among the tech crowd, Hoffman told me that when he was younger, he dreamed of becoming a college professor. But he dropped out of Oxford University, where he been working toward a PhD in philosophy, once he understood that success would mean writing books that maybe a few dozen of his fellow academics would read. "I imagined myself having more of an impact than that," he said. Instead he would serve as Silicon Valley's philosopher-king, thoughtful and reflective where his peers tended toward thoughtless and oblivious. In a locale where the typical denizens barely saw beyond their own narrow interests, Hoffman was politically engaged. He would even have his cameo on the national stage when it was revealed that he had funded E. Jean

Carroll's defamation and sexual assault suit against Trump, prompting the former and future president to call Hoffman a "disgusting slob."

• • •

MUSTAFA SULEYMAN, A fellow founder and friend of Hoffman's, had come up with the idea for Inflection and roped in Hoffman for help getting the company off the ground. Because Hoffman was involved—and because the idea was born in Silicon Valley—I knew even before I reached out to Suleyman that what the pair had in mind, should they succeed, would result in a product used by tens of millions of people, if not hundreds of millions. Suleyman's ambitions were every bit as oversized as Hoffman's. He sought to create a chatbot that had not just high IQ but also EQ: emotional intelligence.

"It's a new class of thing," Suleyman wrote in a founding memo for Inflection he shared with me. Forget the limited range of an Alexa or a Siri, with their scripted responses. He was imaging an engaging conversationalist that "will spark your interest and keep you asking questions." People might turn to the empathetic, ever-patient bot Suleyman had in mind for advice or use it to work through difficult issues, as if speaking with a life coach or therapist.

"It's there for you when you want to vent at the end of day," Suleyman wrote. "It makes you feel heard but it gives you feedback. Periodically, it might challenge you."

Yet a synthetic companion that seemed as if ripped from the movie *Her* was just the start. Ultimately, Suleyman's plans had him creating an AI-powered personal assistant that learns a user's likes and preferences in the way a famous person's real-life personal assistant gets to know them. As Suleyman laid it out, this digital agent would make reservations on a user's behalf, pick out gifts for the kids, and set up lunches with friends. "We believe everyone in the world is going to have their own personal intelligence," said Suleyman, who served as Inflection's CEO. The goal was a company worth in the tens of billions, if not eventually in the trillions, like other Valley giants.

The ambition rather than the feasibility of the business plan was primary when talking about the prospects of a Silicon Valley startup. "The game as an entrepreneur and an investor is to have these massively audacious hopes that far outstrip what any rational person would be thinking," Hoffman said. "You have to believe beyond all conception. Sometimes it even works out." More often than not, it does not. Hoffman has had some spectacular misses along with those big hits, including the central role he played in a Seattle-based startup called Convoy. Convoy, which was supposed to be Uber for trucks, instead burned through nearly $900 million before shutting down in 2023. Only a tiny fraction of venture-funded startups end up attaining the lofty aims their founders laid out in their initial business proposal. In the case of Inflection, there was also the competition to consider. Other venture-backed startups were working on a chatbot, as were Goliaths such as Google and Microsoft. Inflection was a long shot because every startup is a long shot.

Inflection also placed Hoffman and Suleyman in the center of the debates over AI. The companies provoking widespread unease in 2023 specialized in "generative AI," the catch-all term for models that, in response to a short prompt, create new content, whether text, images, video, or sounds. These were the systems that wowed many in the public and inspired flights of fancy among industry leaders, who made grandiose pronouncements likening the arrival of AI to the invention of electricity and even the discovery of fire. Yet a technology that could seem almost human frightened some and raised a host of philosophical and ethical questions. The bot Suleyman had in mind, for instance, would express sympathy. Yet was this really empathy if spit out by algorithms parsing human language patterns? Generative AI made mistakes that even its creators couldn't explain, and there were the potential risks posed by models projected to improve exponentially each year. Some grappled with the existential question of what it might mean if humans lost our apex status. Both Hoffman and later Suleyman positioned themselves at the forefront of this discourse, preaching a third way that neither imagined all of humanity being ruled by laser-eyed robots (the "doomers") nor sided with those who oppose any attempts to slow or regulate its advancement (the "accelerationists," as they came to be called). "The rise of powerful AI will either be the best or the worst thing ever to happen to humanity," Stephen Hawking had said in 2016. "We don't yet know which." Both Hoffman and Suleyman argued the same: that AI can be an incredible force for good—if humans are deliberate and don't squander the moment.

As someone who has been writing on and off about Silicon Valley since the mid-1990s, a different existential question also interested me: What might AI mean for the Valley itself? The essence of the Valley always had been the startup: specifically, the company founded in a garage or a friend's living room that grew into tech's next Google or Facebook. Yet AI called into question whether it was even possible for a startup to win the race in an area like generative AI, which was voracious in its demand for resources even as it promised a huge payoff. Generative AI required bottomless reservoirs of data, which a Google, a Facebook, or a Microsoft could amass or access, but which were out of reach for some dorm-room startup. There was also the massive amount of computer time required to train and operate these models—what insiders simply refer to as "compute." A startup would need millions of dollars of compute just to train one of these giant models, and eventually billions more if what they created found a wide audience. AI also impacted a startup's ability to hire talent. The old way had an employee taking a relatively modest salary in exchange for an equity stake and the chance at a large windfall. That no longer worked in the AI era. Engineers with AI experience still expected shares in the company but that was on top of large signing bonuses and salaries that could exceed $1 million a year. If cashing in on AI were a contest, the game seemed rigged in favor of today's tech titan.

Even Hoffman—a creature of the Valley and one of its best-known boosters—harbored his worries. "The economics of AI have changed the equation for startups in the Valley," he said. More than the cradle of technology, Silicon Valley was a startup factory—what James Currier, a serial entrepreneur who founded NFX, an early-stage venture fund, jokingly referred to as the "startup industrial complex." Yet what chance would any startup have if table stakes required a bankroll in the hundreds of millions of dollars, if not the multiple billions? Not long after my arrival back in Silicon Valley in the winter of 2023, I picked up on the anxiety of founders and others who were part of the startup ecosystem. Every period in tech has created a new set of giants, but now the question people were asking was whether the AI age was different. Their fear was that the same behemoths that dominated tech in the 2010s— Google, Facebook, Microsoft, Apple, a few others—would ultimately dominate artificial intelligence, blocking the birth of a next generation of tech powerhouses.

If any newly minted startup could prove that AI wouldn't be an extinction-level event for the Valley's startup culture, that company seemed Inflection. There seemed something can't-miss about their endeavor, despite the competition. Hoffman brought with him all the connections a company would need plus a track record for creating giants. Suleyman himself was a star within the AI world. The London-born son of a Syrian cabdriver, he had cofounded DeepMind, the startup that Elon Musk had been raving about over sushi. DeepMind was AI's first truly successful startup. Inflection's third cofounder, Karén Simonyan, had served as DeepMind's principal scientist and was a top researcher in the field.

Money didn't appear to be a problem for Inflection, at least not with Hoffman on their team. The founding trio seemingly had access to as much money as they might need. Hoffman's firm wrote a $100 million check to get the company started in the spring of 2022—the largest check in the nearly sixty years of Greylock's existence. Hoffman threw $40 million of his own money into the kitty and hit up friends for more. Bill Gates was an investor in Inflection, as was Eric Schmidt, the former CEO of Google. So too were Ashton Kutcher and will.i.am, both of whom Hoffman had gotten to know over the years. With all that cash, Suleyman was able to assemble what he described as a "dream team" of talent. He poached people from DeepMind and other parts of Google; with his promise of a different kind of chatbot, he lured people from OpenAI and other AI labs. In June 2023, Inflection raised another $1.3 billion—a preposterous pile of cash for a small, fifteen-month old startup that had yet to generate any revenue.

There were plenty of other startups joining the race to capitalize on this AI moment—more than ten thousand in 2023 alone, according to the count by one AI-focused website. But most were much more modest efforts. Only a small subset of startups were started with the same outsized, trillion-dollar ambitions as Inflection's. For them, there was a ticking clock. Shortly after starting this project, I caught up to a talk that the venture capitalist James Currier had given at the Stanford Graduate School of Business in early 2023. Currier had always struck me as one of the smarter, more honorable people I came across during my time covering tech, and his crisp analysis of the moment didn't disappoint. The internet arrived in 1994, giving rise to a new generation of tech giants. Fourteen years later, in 2008, the smartphone took off and launched a new generation of large enduring tech companies. "Now we've got generative AI," he told the assembled students. He pinpoints its start to mid-2022—again, fourteen years later.

"This is the moment," he said, but then added a warning. "Basically, you get eighteen months to cash in, twenty-four months tops."

AI VALLEY

CHAPTER 1

The Creators

Expectations were high as academics and industry researchers arrived on the campus of Dartmouth College in the summer of 1956. They were gathered at the invitation of Dartmouth's John McCarthy, a young mathematics professor who had recently coined the term "artificial intelligence." There, on the top floor of the building that housed the college's math department, a group of around twenty pursued an ambitious agenda. "An attempt will be made," McCarthy and several collaborators wrote in advance of their eight-week conclave, "to find out how to make machines use language, form abstractions and concepts, solve kinds of problems reserved for humans, and improve themselves." The Dartmouth Summer Research Project on Artificial Intelligence marked the start of AI as a field of research—and established a pattern of lofty, unrealistic goals that fell far short of expectations.

"At the time, I believed if only we could get everyone who was interested in the subject together to devote time to it and avoid distractions," McCarthy later said, "we could make real progress." Attendees predicted, for instance, that within the decade, a machine would beat the world's reigning chess champion. Instead, more than thirty-five years passed before a machine bested a champion-caliber player at checkers, and then more years before one was able to beat a chess master.

Unfettered optimism proved the fatal flaw of many of AI's earliest believers. One pioneer who predated McCarthy was Alan Turing, the English mathematician who famously cracked Nazi codes during World War II (he is played by Benedict Cumberbatch in the 2014 film *The Imitation Game*). "I propose to investigate the question as to whether it is possible for machinery to show intelligent behaviour," Turing wrote in a 1948 paper he titled "Intelligent Machinery." Two years later, he proposed a test for determining whether a machine could think. What he called the "imitation game" came to be known as the Turing Test: Could a computer imitate conversation so adroitly that it fooled humans? Turing predicted that a computer would pass his test by the year 2000—a forecast that was off by more than two decades. That encapsulated the story of artificial intelligence through its first sixty or seventy years as a discipline: a technology that has hovered tantalizingly just around the next bend, forever a decade away.

• • •

FRANK ROSENBLATT HAD only just completed a PhD a few weeks before the Dartmouth conference and wasn't among those invited to Hanover, New Hampshire, to talk about the budding field of artificial intelligence. Yet Rosenblatt, who taught at Cornell University, was infected by this same propensity for overpromising and underdelivering. The year after completing his PhD in psychology, he released a research paper laying out his idea for what he called "the Perceptron."

"Since the advent of electronic computers," Rosenblatt wrote, "an increasing amount of attention has been focused in the feasibility of constructing a device possessing such human-like functions as perception, recognition, concept formulation, and the ability to generalize from experience." His area of research, the human brain, would serve as his template. It was in the late nineteenth century that scientists discovered that the brain wasn't a single, continuous network of nerves, as believed, but a complex structure based on interconnected neurons. Rosenblatt aimed to mimic the human brain by creating a network of artificial neurons. The Office of Naval Research was among the institutions that funded Rosenblatt's idea.

Later, the industry invented the term "vaporware" to describe products that companies announce and heavily market even when they don't quite exist. Rosenblatt was not the first to sell the world on a half-baked technology nor would he be the last, yet he was among the more audacious. He had not actually built a new electronic brain when he began talking up his idea among reporters and others during a trip to Washington, D.C., in 1958. Instead he used an IBM mainframe borrowed from the U.S. Weather Bureau to show what his invention could do. His demonstration was a modest one: a computer was able to learn on its own to distinguish a card with a marking on the left from one with a marking on the right. But apparently Rosenblatt was persuasive in laying out the possibilities.

"New Navy Device Learns by Doing," read the headline over an article in the next day's New York Times that began, "The Navy revealed the embryo of an electronic computer today that it expects will be able to walk, talk, see, write, reproduce itself, and be conscious of its existence." A writer for the New Yorker was equally impressed. "It strikes us as the first serious rival to the human brain ever devised," according to a "Talk of the Town" item the magazine ran about Rosenblatt and his invention. Some were more alarmist in their pronouncements, like the headline from an Oklahoma newspaper: "Frankenstein Designed by Navy That Thinks."

In photos from the time, Rosenblatt looks more buttoned-down company man than mad scientist. He wore his hair short and favored the thick, black-framed glasses that were fashionable at the time. He dressed in Oxford shirts and skinny dark ties. One historian described him as a "true Renaissance man who appears to have been an expert in everything from music and astronomy to mathematics and computing." Rosenblatt was a brilliant, charismatic figure who won people over with the boldness of his vision. "He made these wild claims about computers that can think that turned out to be a lot of hype and not much reality," said Chris Manning, director of the esteemed Stanford

Artificial Intelligence Laboratory, a research center that dates to the early 1960s. "But Frank Rosenblatt pioneered this idea of a brain-like computer we now call a neural net. He invented it." Machine learning, it would come to be called: rather than being explicitly programmed for every scenario, a computer improves its performance on a given task through learning and through trial and error.

Yet it was as if Rosenblatt could not help himself. A year after he made headlines with his idea for a thinking machine, Rosenblatt wired together a contraption he called the Mark 1 and inked deals with the U.S. Postal Service (for help sorting the mail) and the Air Force (to read aerial photographs). Back in Washington to meet with his backers, he again made the rounds among reporters. Over coffee with one, he declared the Perceptron "the first machine which is capable of having an original idea." It may never be able to feel love or joy, he said, but it would learn in the fashion of a human and have insights and convey thoughts.

"My colleague disapproves of all the loose talk one hears nowadays about mechanical brains," Rosenblatt said of his collaborator at Naval Research. "But that is exactly what it is."

• • •

ROSENBLATT'S ACADEMIC PEERS were less impressed than reporters or Perceptron's funders. The scientists who had traveled to Dartmouth in the summer of 1956 had explored the idea of neural networks, but a consensus formed around an alternative path to AI called rule-based computing. Theirs would be a more brute-force approach to artificial intelligence that had human coders laying down specific instructions. Rather than creating a neural net that learns in the fashion of a human, they would hand-code knowledge and reasoning capabilities into a machine. Also called symbolic AI and later expert systems, its main proponent, or at least its fiercest champion, was a Massachusetts Institute of Technology professor named Marvin Minsky.

Minsky was an archetype I would come to recognize once I started writing about tech: arrogant and imperious even if wrong about more or less everything. There was no doubting his prominence in the field. He had been one of the main organizers of the Dartmouth meeting and later cofounded, with John McCarthy, the Artificial Intelligence Project at MIT. Minsky had experimented with neural nets as a graduate student but concluded that it was a dead end. By the mid-1960s, Minsky had embraced a rule-based approach to AI. Soon most in the field were following that same path. "Within a generation," Minsky declared in 1967, "the problem of creating 'artificial intelligence' will be substantially solved." Herbert A. Simon, another pioneer who embraced the rule-based approach, predicted that machines, by the mid-1980s, would be capable "of doing any work a man can do."

Minsky, by all accounts, was a contentious figure with a bully's streak and a flair for the dramatic. In that way he seemed a perfect forerunner to some of the figures who would come to create and define Silicon Valley. Minsky went out of his way to ridicule Rosenblatt. In *Genius Makers*, his history of artificial intelligence, Cade Metz tells of a small AI conference held in Puerto Rico in 1966. A researcher stepped to the podium to talk about the neural network he and his colleagues were building using a Mark 1. When it was time for questions, Minsky chose to taunt the young presenter. "How can an intelligent young man like you waste your time with something like this?" he asked, The audience laughed as Minsky mocked claims that Perceptron mirrors the human brain. "The performance was typical of Minsky, who enjoyed stirring public controversy," Metz wrote. Not long afterward, Minsky cowrote an entire book documenting the shortcomings of neural networks. Its title, *Perceptrons*, left no doubt of its target. "This is an idea with no future," Minsky said of neural nets. Government dollars shifted to rule-based efforts. Machine learning fell out of favor among researchers.

"For a long time, Marvin Minsky was one of the giants of our field," Stanford's Chris Manning said. Manning himself had adopted a rule-based approach to AI earlier in his career but acknowledged that Minsky's contributions ultimately added up to nothing—except to demonstrate to people the futility of the path he had chosen. Programmers could never devise enough rules to handle the complexity of the real world.

"His was such a different approach that it was no help to what people are doing now," Manning said. "It's completely irrelevant. And the fact is his dominance held back all these things that could have happened."

• • •

THE LIMITS OF computers helped explain the lack of progress in AI. Machines couldn't store enough information or process it fast enough to accomplish much of substance. One researcher decades ago likened their dilemma to a team designing a jet engine before anyone had discovered the fuel needed to propel a plane into the air. "Computers are still millions of times too weak to exhibit intelligence," he offered. The Mark I computer that Rosenblatt built to run Perceptron took up most of a room but could handle only 400 artificial neurons. The human brain, in contrast, is made up of around 86 billion neurons.

Still, there would be more fantastic claims made in the name of AI, and more puffery. One heavily ballyhooed project was Shakey, a six-foot-tall robot on wheels developed during the 1960s. Shakey wasn't the world's first robot, but it was the first designed to act autonomously. Ask it to fetch an item and, like a human, it would reason out a course of action—in theory. The actual Shakey was more of a filing cabinet on wheels, outfitted with sensors and a TV camera (for vision) and antenna (to hear instructions). It could barely make it from point A to point B and ran out of juice within minutes. Yet in the pages of *Life* magazine, Shakey was the world's "first electronic person." At an AI conference in the late 1960s, a speaker offered that soon intelligent robots like Shakey would be in people's homes, picking up their dirty laundry. Shakey's mapping software serves as a foundation for today's navigation apps. Its DNA lives in the technologies used to process human language. Yet overinflated claims ensured that Shakey was viewed as a disappointment rather than a promising first attempt at creating an autonomous robot.

Eliza, unveiled in the mid-1960s, endures as one of AI's more interesting early creations. It, too, inflated people's expectations around AI, though less because of the claims of its creator and more because of the desires of the people who used it. An MIT computer scientist named Joseph Weizenbaum created Eliza to parody some of the more outlandish claims made in the name of AI. Specifically, the superficiality of a computer's capacity for conversation. This chatbot, named in honor of Eliza Doolittle from *Pygmalion*, did little more than parrot back someone's words using a simplistic pattern matching program. ("I'm feeling sad today" "Why are you feeling sad today?") Yet rather than laugh with Weizenbaum at his little thought experiment, many spoke to it as if it were a therapist or friend. In a book Weizenbaum wrote a decade later, he described himself as shocked at people's reaction to Eliza. Even his secretary, who was in on the joke, would ask her boss to leave the room when she interacted with Eliza.

A big freeze descended on AI in the 1970s—what those in the field came to refer to as "AI winter." The Pentagon had funded Shakey through its Defense Advanced Research Projects Agency, or DARPA, the government agency that spearheaded the creation of the internet. Yet where the military was anticipating robot soldiers that could do reconnaissance or at least stand sentry duty, they instead were hearing reports that, millions of dollars later, a computer could barely distinguish left from right. Government funding for AI dried up, as did other research dollars. This first of two AI winters, academics agree, started in 1974 and lasted through 1980.

"The AI problem," a chastened Marvin Minsky declared in 1982, "is one of the hardest science has ever undertaken." Minsky came to regret the success of *Perceptrons* and acknowledged that there was promise in neural net technology. However, no apology would ever reach Rosenblatt, who drowned in a boating accident on his forty-third birthday, just two years after the publication of *Perceptrons*.

• • •

INTEL, BASED IN Santa Clara, a town forty-five miles south of San Francisco, stamped out the silicon-based semiconductors—chips—that gave rise to the personal computer and also the area's indelible nickname. "Silicon Valley" was coined in 1971 by a reporter with a computer trade magazine looking for a clever way of referring to the Santa Clara Valley, an area just south of San Francisco that once had ranked as a leading fruit-producing region. With the PC revolution, the center of gravity in the tech industry shifted west. Apple went public in 1980 and word spread about the venture capitalists who saw a return of more than 200x on their investment, drawing more VCs to the area. Speculators bulldozed apricot, plum, and cherry orchards and in their place built office buildings and industrial parks.

The East Coast had dominated the early decades of AI. Yet the groundwork for a westward shift had been planted in the 1930s when Stanford's then dean of engineering, Frederick Terman, pushed for a marriage between university research and commercial enterprise. In 1939, two of Terman's disciples, Bill Hewlett and Dave Packard, launched their electronics company in a Palo Alto garage. Propelled by that same impulse to encourage entrepreneurism, Stanford, just after World War II, established a nearby industrial park for graduates and faculty interested in creating a tech startup. In the early 1960s, John McCarthy, the man who had coined "artificial intelligence," left MIT to help create the Stanford Artificial Intelligence Laboratory. There, in a semicircle-shaped wooden building tucked away in the hills above campus, researchers worked on everything from robotics to machine-generated music to computers that could see and speak. Over the decades, IBM, Xerox, Lockheed, and General Electric were among those established electronics giants that set up shop within a few exits of Stanford. By the 1980s, Stanford stood as the world's preeminent AI center.

There was another burst of interest in AI at the start of the 1980s. The hype this time was around "expert systems," which was little more than a new name for Minsky's rule-based AI. The idea, championed by a Stanford professor named Edward Feigenbaum, was that the specialized knowledge of an expert could be captured and programmed into domain-specific systems. Stationing a safety officer on every oil rig so as to monitor a crew's actions is expensive. But what if machines hard-coded with an expert's knowledge could do the job? One interesting project from that era aimed to bolster the investigative powers of the Securities and Exchange Commission (SEC) by programming an expert system to find irregularities in the paperwork that publicly traded companies filed with the agency.

This second wave was fueled less by government grants and more by the venture capitalists and corporations that saw vast money-making potential in AI. Much like would happen in 2023, rivers of money flowed to any company offering a plausible story for cashing in on AI. Hardware companies formed as if the secret to making AI work was specialized equipment maximized to run LISP, a programming language created by John McCarthy and favored by AI researchers. (A joke among programmers: LISP stood for Lots of Idiotic Stupid Parentheses.) Texas Instruments and Xerox were among the business machine makers peddling LISP machines. Similarly, companies large and small sought to capitalize on the popularity of Prolog, another favorite language among AI researchers. A slew of startups formed to peddle expert systems for a particular "vertical": automakers, retailers, lawyers. Other startups were founded to sell the digital tools companies would need to build and operate an AI system.

Analysts predicted that expert systems would give rise to a multibillion-dollar industry. "With all this money flowing into the field, people were forgoing an academic career to start a company," said Jerry Kaplan, who had recently earned his PhD at Stanford. "I was doing a post-doc on Stanford's campus when the whole startup, Silicon Valley thing was heating up. So I decided to start a company." He went into business with Feigenbaum, who had been one of his professors on campus. The two made sales calls together on behalf of a startup they called Teknowledge, where Kaplan watched his former mentor tell prospective buyers whatever they wanted to hear. If meeting with an oil executive, Feigenbaum spoke of the many ways his not-yet-built expert systems could help with exploration and drilling. "There was a little bit of Rosenblatt and Minsky in Feigenbaum," Kaplan said.

"There were tons and tons of companies created," Kaplan said. "But most of them were complete garbage." Teknowledge would go public in 1985, making it one of the era's few winners, but Kaplan did not stick around much longer. He had lost faith in expert systems and, by extension, rule-based AI generally. Adding line after line of code to train a computer increased a system's complexity but never seemed any closer to proving useful in a business setting. "I concluded that something like this would never work," Kaplan said.

Kaplan was hardly the only one making that determination. The money stopped flowing and, without funding, progress slowed. This second AI winter hit in 1987 and would be longer in duration. "Not much would be going on with AI through the end of the nineties," Chris Manning said.

"It was very lonely," said James Manyika. Manyika, who had grown up in Zimbabwe, had started work on a PhD in artificial intelligence at Oxford just as the second AI winter was settling on the field. "All of us were being advised not to use the word 'artificial intelligence' in our thesis because no one will take you seriously," Manyika said. He received similar advice when pursuing postdocs after graduating.

"If you were looking for research grants," Manyika said, "you were told to say you're working on machine intelligence or machine learning. Anything but AI."

CHAPTER 2

Lonely Boy

Silicon Valley is populated largely by people from somewhere else. Reid Hoffman, however, was born at Stanford Hospital. William Parker Hoffman, his father, and Deanna Ruth, his mother, had met at Foothill College, a small community college in the hills above Silicon Valley. Reid Garrett Hoffman was born in Palo Alto in August 1967—the Summer of Love. The couple married while Bill Hoffman was attending Stanford Law School and separated not long after their only child was born. Reid mainly lived with his father.

"To have your parents get divorced at a young age, there's a lot of turbulence," Hoffman said. "It was intense, vibrant, sometimes oppressive. I felt I was very much in a world of my own."

Hoffman was a precocious kid. His father told of reading his five-year-old son *The Lord of the Rings* and noticing the bookmark had advanced since the previous night. Hoffman didn't really play sports and did not join the other kids on the block when they ran around in the street. "The nice way to say it was that Reid spent a lot of time by himself," said Ben Olander, who lived down the street from Hoffman and his father. The not-so-nice way to put it was that Hoffman was a child who had no friends. "I was very lonely," Hoffman confessed. He sought refuge reading about futuristic worlds in books he found at his local public library. "I would just pull the next book off the science fiction shelf and read it," he said.

When he was nine years old, a babysitter taught him the game Dungeons & Dragons. Taking up this game built around the imaginary adventures spun out by a dungeon master gave Hoffman a way to connect with other like-minded enthusiasts, including Olander. "The strongest memory I have of Reid is him wanting desperately to belong," Olander said.

Hoffman was eleven when a new game called RuneQuest was released. RuneQuest was another role-playing game but more rules-heavy than Dungeons & Dragons and with a danger element alluring to a kid Hoffman's age. Hoffman learned from a classmate at his middle school that Chaosium, the company that created RuneQuest, had an office in the neighboring town of Emeryville. Hoffman showed up unannounced one Friday after school.

An awkward, chunky kid with braces, glasses, and a mop of brown hair that rarely saw a comb, he arrived at Chaosium's offices carrying a marked-up copy of one of their game manuals, with suggestions for improving the game written in red. A follow-up memo he wrote so impressed the game's designer that he invited Hoffman to test their games and write reviews for a magazine the company published. Years later he still remembered the precise amount of his first check: $127. If nothing else, the money quieted his father's complaints about his incessant game play.

"My dad thought that I was going to be a social outcast," Hoffman said. "But after I brought home that first check, he was like, 'Oh, maybe you'll be okay.'" Board games were another obsession and especially Tactics II, one that simply pitted red against blue and has been described as military chess. When years later Hoffman got to talking about Tactics II on a podcast, his interlocutor asked him about his level of play. A sheepish Hoffman confessed he couldn't remember ever losing a game.

• • •

HOFFMAN WAS IN the ninth grade when, without mentioning it to either of his parents, he applied to a boarding school in Vermont called the Putney School. "I was kind of bitten by the independence bug rather early," Hoffman said, "and Vermont was the furthest place from California I could imagine that still seemed feasible."

Putney was different from other elite boarding schools—a less traditional, progressive institution with a granola-crunchy, holistic approach to learning. The school stressed both independent study and the merits of manual labor. There was a working farm on campus ("outdoor experiential education is just as important as what happens behind a desk," according to the school's promotional materials) and classes in carpentry and blacksmithing that appealed to the teenage Hoffman. He learned to milk a cow and tap a maple tree for syrup and, if he didn't exactly master the art of driving a team of oxen, he learned a critical life lesson ("Partner with someone who knows what they're doing," Hoffman joked when talking about the experience on a podcast). A profile of Hoffman the *Putney Post* ran in 2009 cast him as "socially awkward" but obviously smart without being condescending. His faculty advisor described him as "way beyond his years intellectually." Hoffman, for his part, praised the school for the quality of education he received but also called out the bullying endemic on campus. Some classmates seemed deliberately cruel as a means of demonstrating their dominance over others.

"It was kind of like *Lord of the Flies*," Hoffman told the *Putney Post*.

The loneliness that plagued Hoffman in Berkeley followed him to Putney. "Frankly, it wasn't always easy for me to find friends who shared my interests," he said. He was an overweight, nerdy kid not into sports and something of a straight arrow. He didn't drink or smoke marijuana at a school where the pressure to do both could be intense.

Hoffman ultimately found his people on campus—in the school's small computer room. Eventually he managed to neutralize his tormentors by remembering his game logic. "The way you deal with bullies is you change their economic equation," Hoffman explained. "Make it more expensive for them to hassle you." He told his chief assailant that if the harassment continued, "I will break everything you own," and the bullying stopped. Hoffman graduated from Putney in the spring of 1985 and returned to the Bay Area to start Stanford that fall.

• • •

EVEN THEN, STANFORD was at the center of so much that was going
on in Silicon Valley. One of the area's highest-profile companies then
was Silicon Graphics, which helped to transform the film industry
(the makers of *Jurassic Park*, *Forrest Gump*, and *Terminator 2: Judgment
Day* used its technology to power then cutting-edge special effects).
Silicon Graphics had been born on campus in the early 1980s. So
too had Sun Microsystems (Sun was short for Stanford University
Network), which made a class of computers more powerful than PCs
called workstations, and Cisco Systems. Both Sun and Cisco played
pivotal roles in the rise of the Internet.

Hoffman loved his time on campus. He was among the first ten
people at Stanford to pursue a newly minted major called Symbolic
Systems, which, just like the field of artificial intelligence, melded
computer science with linguistics, psychology, and other disciplines.
On campus, computer science majors dismissed Symbolic Systems as
"C.S. lite" but the intellectually curious Hoffman valued the opportunity
to take a wide array of classes across campus. Life was finally as he had
fantasized it when he was younger, surrounded by like-minded souls
who shared his thirst for learning and desire for late-night debates on
vital issues.

One of those late-night debate partners was Peter Thiel, who would
play a critical role in the development of artificial intelligence. The two
made for an unlikely pairing. Where Thiel had been raised in a deeply
religious conservative family, Hoffman was a product of the counter-
culture sixties. Family lore put Hoffman on his father's shoulders at
demonstrations opposing the Vietnam War that sometimes turned
tumultuous. "Apparently, I was running from tear gas even before I
could walk," Hoffman said. The two met during their sophomore year
in a philosophy class called "Mind, Matter, and Meaning."

"I'm pretty sure he saw me as a bleeding-heart pinko commie,"
Hoffman said. "And I'm absolutely certain I saw him as a libertarian
wacko who seemed to have sprung out of Ayn Rand's book, *The Foun-
tainhead*, fully formed." The two argued for well over an hour after their

first class together and pretty much continued that debate for several decades, until Thiel gave more than $1 million to Donald Trump's first campaign and they decided, for the sake of their friendship, to avoid politics. As upperclassmen, the two ran for Stanford's student government on a joint ticket. Hoffman was the left-winger, Thiel the right-winger. Both won.

The second AI winter hit just as Hoffman arrived on campus, but the kid who had worked his way through shelves of science fiction at the local library was excited for a real-life glimpse at what machines could do. "I was not alien to the notion of robots and artificial intelligence," Hoffman said. He secured a summer internship at the legendary Xerox PARC (Palo Alto Research Center), which gave the world the mouse and icon-driven computing, among other cornerstone contributions. There he became so engrossed in the AI-related research project he was assigned that he took a semester off to continue his work. The next summer, he worked on expert systems at IBM. As an upperclassman, Hoffman worked with David Rumelhart, a giant of the AI world who had pioneered "parallel distributed processing models," an approach that accelerated the speed by which a neural net could process information. Rumelhart served as Hoffman's advisor through much of his time at Stanford.

Yet his front-row seat on AI left Hoffman unimpressed. As he would tell Musk years later over dinner, he viewed the technology as if it were just a toddler. An AI winter meant less money for research but, even if cash had been flowing, computers were still not powerful enough. "The networks were so small they wouldn't do anything other than toy problems," Hoffman said. A major breakthrough while he was still at Stanford was a computer that could reliably read numbers printed on a check.

"I concluded AI was not going to happen anytime soon," Hoffman said. "So I just went off to do other things." An exceptional student, he applied for and won a coveted Marshall Scholarship, which provides free tuition and living expenses for American citizens pursuing a graduate degree at a university in the United Kingdom. In 1990 he moved to England to pursue a doctorate in philosophy at Oxford University.

There, at the oldest university in the English-speaking world (Oxford was founded in 1096), he imagined himself "grappling with the big questions of values and ethics and who we should be as a society," he said. Instead he learned that his teachers were "hostile to the idea of academics being public intellectuals. The professors there seemed to only want to talk about esoteric theories without any interest in actual people. I very quickly realized that wasn't me." Hoffman stuck it out long enough to earn a master's in philosophy from Oxford's Wolfson College. With no savings and no job prospects, he returned to his homestead to figure out what he would do next.

• • •

HOFFMAN MOVED IN with his father back in Berkeley. His father, who had been a crusading lawyer earlier in his life, had settled into a career as a real estate attorney. During Hoffman's second week home, his father asked him: You're going to get a job, right?

"I'm researching my options," Hoffman told him.

His father's retort: Why don't you research why you need to get a job?

Hoffman had taken several computer science courses at Stanford but did not have the background or training he needed to secure a programming job in Silicon Valley. But plugging into the substantial network of friends he had built during his four years in Palo Alto, he learned about a team inside Apple developing a new online service called eWorld. They needed a contractor who could produce design mockups using Adobe's Photoshop. Hoffman had never used Photoshop, but his contact there handed him a manual and told him to be ready to start the following week. "Locking myself in a room for a weekend, I became a Photoshop ninja," Hoffman said. Soon he was working as a full-time junior product manager, overseeing the design and launch of eWorld's international offerings. Hoffman had imagined himself as a public intellectual who penned essays and books on the day's big issues. Instead he was helping Apple find a way to cash in on the internet.

• • •

THE PC HAD given rise to Silicon Valley, but the internet lit the area on fire. The match was Netscape Communications' IPO in August 1995. A Brit named Tim Berners-Lee had invented the World Wide Web, along with its first browser. But it was the team behind Netscape, founded around the time the second AI winter was coming to an end, who figured out how to get rich off the idea. Its user-friendly, feature-rich browser both provided tech novices an easy on-ramp to the internet and allowed developers to create dynamic, interactive web pages featuring images and clickable icons.

The company went public only sixteen months after it had incorporated, sparking a frenzy among traders. The company had yet to turn a profit, but that didn't make a difference when so many people were hungry to own a piece of the future. Netscape's debut was one of the more remarkable in Wall Street history. Its stock price more than quadrupled its first day of trading. For venture capitalists, the moment became what they would call a proof point. Near-instant riches were possible if they invested in the right internet company. For countless entrepreneurs, the Netscape IPO proved an inspiration. The dot-com era was born, and with it, as John Doerr, a prominent venture capitalist whose 1990s hits included Netscape, Amazon, and Google, memorably described it, "the greatest legal creation of wealth in the history of the planet." The area's central role in bringing the internet to the world solidified the Valley's reputation as the globe's capital of tech innovation.

Hoffman's story was no different than that of any number of would-be entrepreneurs who saw the internet as their chance to hit it big. Shortly after Netscape's IPO, Hoffman and Thiel made the 150-mile drive north from Palo Alto to Gualala, the enchanted seacoast town where Hoffman's paternal grandparents owned a home. Hoffman was about a year into his job at Apple. Thiel was working as a derivatives trader at an investment bank. The two, Thiel said, spent a weekend "brainstorming how to start internet companies." Thiel laid out a plan for starting his own venture fund. Hoffman, in contrast, voiced a desire to start his own business. "That was the way Reid was going to have an impact," Thiel said. Through Thiel and other Stanford connections, Hoffman set up meetings with several venture capitalists. His mother, who had also earned her law degree, worked at Wilson Sonsini, one of the Valley's top law firms. She introduced him to one of the Valley's best-known VCs.

"I wasn't at the stage yet of 'Here's my business plan, give me money,'" Hoffman said. "It was more like, 'How does this dance work?'"

Apple discontinued eWorld in early 1996. Apparently, there was no great demand for a Macintosh-only internet service provider that struck reviewers as an AOL copycat except more expensive. The timing would have been perfect for starting a company—if Hoffman had a concrete idea for one. Through his network, Hoffman learned about WorldsAway, a virtual reality project that Fujitsu, the Japanese electronics giant, was developing. He was hired as the product manager in charge of the look, feel, and features of this service that let multiple players interact through avatars in the online worlds Hoffman and his team created. Game administrators were called wizards and dressed in long white robes. The avatars were playful cartoon characters that could wave, take a bow, and take on different moods (happy, angry, sad). Hoffman had recently read *Snow Crash*, Neal Stephenson's 1992 novel about a futuristic California where people, after the collapse of the government, take refuge in what Stephenson called "the Metaverse." With WorldsAway, Hoffman had a hand in building an early version of the metaverse.

The gig seemed a dream come true for a science fiction nerd who had grown up on role-playing games like Dungeons & Dragons. Yet Hoffman was also a man in a hurry. Each week, he heard about founders cashing the multimillion-dollar checks the venture capitalists had given them in exchange for a piece of their startup. In 1994, five Stanford students founded Excite, a web "portal" that included search along with news, sports, and other content. Two years later, Excite went public, and soon each founder, all of them under twenty-five, had a net worth in the tens of millions. More than 150 tech startups had gone public in 1996. Another 100 IPO'd in the first six months of the next year.

"By the summer of 1997, I was getting nervous," Hoffman said. "The internet market was getting really hot. . . . and I thought there is going to be a limited time here."

Hoffman had been working on WorldsAway for around twenty months when he was asked to demo the product for a man named Patrick Ferrell. Ferrell had worked as an executive at video game pioneer Atari until leaving in the late 1980s to create *GamePro*, a magazine covering the interactive gaming industry that Ferrell sold to a larger publisher and grew into a 175-person company. A year before meeting Hoffman, Ferrell had set up a one-man consulting shop. Fujitsu was looking to spin out WorldsAway and an executive there had enlisted Ferrell for advice.

Hoffman, as Ferrell remembered him, was his usual disheveled self, dressed in a polo shirt and jeans. "Let me walk you out," he said to Ferrell when the meeting was over. Standing by the elevators, Hoffman was cryptic. "He says to me, 'Hey, I've got this idea and you seem very entrepreneurial. Maybe I can bounce it off of you?'" Intrigued, Ferrell invited Hoffman to his house for dinner. "He was just getting his career going but you could just tell that he was over-the-top brilliant," Ferrell said.

• • •

FERRELL LIVED ON the western edge of Silicon Valley, in Los Altos Hills, in the foothills of the Santa Cruz Mountains. Los Altos Hills was the town where founders bought a home after their company went public or sold for an eight- or nine-figure check. David Packard of Hewlett-Packard lived there back in the day, as have many other tech luminaries over the years. Jerry Yang lived down the street from Ferrell. While at Stanford, Yang and his classmate David Filo created a directory they called "Jerry and David's Guide to the World Wide Web" before renaming it Yahoo and going public in 1996. Google was founded on Stanford's campus a little later. Google cofounder Sergey Brin bought a home in Los Altos after his company went public.

Ferrell grilled steaks and uncorked a bottle of red wine. It was the summer of 1997 and if anyone was talking about social networking, they were likely academics studying human connections in real life, not describing online interactions. "Social media" was more than a decade away from entering the lexicon, and even pioneers in the field such as Friendster and MySpace were several years into the future. Nineteen ninety-seven was the year Mark Zuckerberg had his bar mitzvah. Yet sitting at Ferrell's kitchen table, Hoffman laid out his idea for a social networking company. He quoted Metcalfe's law, which was tech pioneer Robert Metcalfe's maxim from the 1980s about the power of networks. Each additional member of a network increases the value of that network not by one but exponentially. Hoffman explained that once enough people were on the internet, they would seek one another out online just as they did in the physical world. They might look to make business connections or romantic ones or just search out potential tennis partners. His idea: a digital town square where people would make these connections. They would start with a business networking site and expand from there. "He basically laid out all of social networking over dinner," Ferrell said.

The VCs Hoffman had approached, however, had not been impressed. Later, I'd hear the same from early AI founders, who voiced the oft-repeated Valley maxim that being too early is as bad as being too late. "He'd say, 'I have a business networking idea,' and they'd hang up the phone or they just wouldn't return his call." There were more late nights at Ferrell's home that sometimes stretched past midnight and more bottles of cabernet sauvignon. "He had very deeply held ideas he was very intense about it, but he would listen to my point of view," Ferrell said of Hoffman. "He's the kind of guy you can disagree with but have a civil argument." Ferrell agreed to throw some money into the new venture. A few weeks after that first dinner, Hoffman gave notice at Fujitsu.

Hoffman wanted to call the company relationship.com. But Ferrell convinced him the name made it sound like a dating site. "So Reid and I sat with our wine and brainstormed," Ferrell said. They had been using the term "social networking," so they mushed the words together and chopped off the end. SocialNet, they would call the company. Ferrell took on the title of CEO. Hoffman was vice president. "We knew we had to have titles, but we felt strongly we were equal partners," Ferrell said. Hoffman was responsible for engineering and product development. Ferrell handled the business side of things, including finances and sales. With the seed money Ferrell had put up, they hired a few engineers to start building the site. Each drew a minimal salary of around $400 a week to cover their living expenses, along with a small ownership slice in the new enterprise. To keep expenses low, the house Hoffman rented served as the company's first headquarters.

"It was a total shithole," said Ferrell, who chose to work out of his own home. "There were pizza boxes everywhere and card tables with computers. It was a true startup." Hoffman drove a beat-up Toyota. "Reid would show up at my house with a bag of dirty laundry whenever he ran out of clean clothes," Ferrell said. They would talk SocialNet business while Hoffman used his washer-dryer.

Ferrell thought raising money would be as simple as taking a series of meetings up and down Sand Hill Road, where most of the Valley's top venture capital outfits had offices. He had hit what he described as a "home run" with his first venture, and of course there was the ease with which so many untested greenhorns were raising millions for their half-baked ideas. Yet VCs, despite a reputation as bold risk takers, generally run with the pack. Most conform to a groupthink that has them only investing in whatever sectors everyone agrees are hot—and the VCs, not knowing what to make of this notion of social networking, put SocialNet in the same bucket with every other startup aiming to help potential romantic partners meet over the internet. Ferrell, or Ferrell and Hoffman, would pitch their idea and immediately a VC would start talking about everything that was wrong with online dating. Yahoo Personals was a cesspool. Other sites were nasty back alleys frequented by creepy men. Eventually the pair found a lesser-known venture outfit in St. Paul, Minnesota, to lead an "A round," as a first round investment is known in VC circles, of $5 million. A board of directors was formed that included Hoffman, Ferrell, and the VCs who put in the most money. At the start of 1998, Hoffman, Ferrell, and their small team moved into offices they found in Mountain View.

Building a website in 1997 was a lot harder than it is today and far more expensive. There were few drag-and-drop widgets, so most everything had to be hand-coded in HTML. Particularly grueling was the process for translating a designer's layout, including color schemes and font sizes, into a functioning web page. Adding to their challenge was that Hoffman and Ferrell were essentially building four websites: one for those interested in business networking, a second for those seeking roommates or an apartment rental, a third for activities such as tennis or golf, and a fourth for dating.

There were hundred-hour workweeks, especially in the early months of SocialNet. "But it didn't feel like a grind because it was a passion project with people you loved working with," said Allen Blue, whom Hoffman hired as the company's director of product design. No one put in more hours than Hoffman. "He's always been a working animal. Always," Ferrell said. "I'll love him to death but that's where we're different. I want to take off for a weekend or go to Hawaii. But Reid's brain needs to be constantly nourished. For him a ton of fun is going to a conference."

Hoffman did some things right in his maiden voyage as an entrepreneur. SocialNet's website was handsome and well designed, especially for the time. Its offerings were generally well reviewed. But he made his share of mistakes. People used aliases on SocialNet, which was fine for dating but not a business networking site. Only too late did he come to appreciate that to build a community where people felt safe and enjoyed spending time, Hoffman said, its users had to be "based on real identity." In retrospect, he said, the company spent too much time perfecting the product when they should have shared it earlier to collect user feedback. The company launched its products, and only then did they start working on a plan for attracting users. "The cadence of learning at a startup—" Hoffman said, then cut himself off to offer this assessment: "fucking intense is an understatement."

The venture capitalists forced out Ferrell in the fall of 1999, two years after the founding of the company. Adopting the role of team player, Hoffman helped the VCs find a new CEO and raise the next round of funding. Yet he would be gone before they closed on a "B round" of $17 million. "I was reading the paperwork, which is how I learned that I would no longer be on the board," Hoffman said. "It was all very passive-aggressive." Still, he confessed to feeling relieved. More than anyone else, he recognized how much work they had in front of them. He would be the captain who went down with the ship, "but not if you dismissed me from the bridge," Hoffman said.

One year earlier, Thiel had asked him to join the board of directors of his first startup, a payments company called Confinity. In January 2000, two and a half years after he founded SocialNet and in the final days of the dot-com boom, Hoffman joined this company that would soon be renamed PayPal.

• • •

THIEL HAD NOT set out to start a company. True to the plan he had laid out for himself in Gualala, he sought to establish himself as a venture capitalist. He raised money from friends and family, hired an assistant, and rented a literal broom closet on Sand Hill Road, so he could claim a prestigious address for what he called Thiel Capital. But shortly into his tenure as a Valley VC, he met a Ukrainian-born computer whiz kid named Max Levchin, who was trying to solve the problem of digital payments. Despite the rise of what everyone called ecommerce, only one in every ten online transactions at the end of the 1990s was conducted digitally. More typically, a buyer sent a check in the mail to consummate a deal. Thiel put up the seed money to get Levchin started but, recognizing the great opportunity should Levchin succeed, put his VC dreams on hold. Thiel joined Levchin as the CEO and cofounder of Confinity at the end of 1998.

Confinity worked out of an office in downtown Palo Alto. By co-incidence, another digital payments company, founded by Elon Musk and called X.com, leased a suite down the hall. The venture capitalists arranged a shotgun wedding between the two startups that placed Musk in charge. Musk lobbied to keep the name X.com because he thought it was the "coolest URL on the internet" but the decision was made to rename it PayPal, which Confinity had named its service. Musk, of course, would revive the name X years later.

The VCs were not pleased when Thiel proposed that they hire Hoffman as the company's chief operating officer. The company was hemorrhaging cash and needed a disciplinarian. They viewed Hoffman as too nice a guy for the role. But Thiel trusted that his college friend could do the job and even offered him a small ownership stake in the company. Among Hoffman's first acts: help them deal with the despotic rule of Musk as CEO. Not long after he joined the company, Hoffman joined a small cabal of conspirators who dethroned Musk—while Musk was on a long-delayed honeymoon with his first wife. Thiel was installed as PayPal's chief executive, and it fell to Hoffman to assuage any hard feelings among those employees loyal to Musk.

The AI startups that would blossom in 2023 would confront the same financial reality that almost did in PayPal: the need to control its "burn rate," the expression in the startup ecosystem for the cash founders spent each month on salaries and other expenses. The company had raised tens of millions of dollars in venture funding but it was paying millions each month in credit card fees and millions more on promotions. It was losing millions because of fraud. "If we were standing on the roof of our building," Hoffman said, "throwing wads of hundred-dollar bills over the side, we'd be spending money less quickly." In September 2000, PayPal had a monthly burn rate of $12 million and roughly $65 million in the bank.

By then, the tech-heavy Nasdaq was in the midst of a precipitous slide that saw it shed more than 80 percent of its value. In place of speeches about pursuing more market share, the VCs were delivering lectures about profligate spending. The same venture capitalists who only months earlier were overpaying to own a small slice of some copycat startup with no clue of how it might ever make money now announced that they were reluctant to write a check to a company unless it could show a clear path to profitability. The days of easy money were over.

A core group of PayPal executives gathered in Gualala for a three-day retreat at the weekend home Hoffman's grandparents owned.

"The question was, 'What the fuck do we do?'" Hoffman said. Adding to their woes: almost all their transactions were through eBay, whose sellers used PayPal as its preferred method of payment, yet the auction site was promoting a competing service it had bought. They devoted day one of their retreat to laying out their challenges. Day two was for brainstorming solutions. Day three was set aside to give people a chance to discuss what they might do should PayPal go down in flames.

The company managed to get a handle on expenses and fend off eBay's copycat product. When PayPal went public at the start of 2002, tech was still in the midst of a deep freeze and Wall Street was dubious of any enterprise connected with Silicon Valley. Yet its stock rose by more than 50 percent on its first day of trading. Five months later, eBay bought PayPal for $1.4 billion. Presumably, Musk's $200 million payday on the sale helped to assuage any bad feelings about being booted from his own company.

While Hoffman was at PayPal, a German online dating company bought SocialNet. The original investors saw a 10–20 percent return on their investment, and Hoffman pocketed between $40,000 and $50,000. His stake in PayPal, however, was worth roughly $9 million when he cashed out. "I did notice that after PayPal, people who weren't returning my calls were calling me to ask to meet me for dinner," Hoffman said. "Now suddenly I had this legitimacy."

Said Patrick Ferrell: "I don't know if Reid'll be pissed at me that I told you this but after eBay bought PayPal, he says to me, 'Pat, I finally got my F-U money.'" Hoffman had his fuck-you money. "And what he meant by that," Ferrell continued, "is he had enough money to launch his next company without having to kowtow to the VCs." At least for the moment.

• • •

THE FIRST THING Hoffman did after the sale of PayPal was travel. After years of working hundred-hour weeks, he was exhausted and needed a break. His first stop was Australia, where he spent time with a friend from Oxford. There Hoffman told his former classmate about Friendster, a social networking startup kicking up a stir in Silicon Valley. Just as Friendster was helping people enjoy a richer social life, Hoffman said, he had in mind a business networking site that could help them achieve a more satisfying career. His friend only repeated to him what Hoffman knew, that a founder could not wait six months or a year before jumping in. Hoffman's break was over barely before it had started.

Back in the Valley, Hoffman rented a modest one-bedroom apartment in downtown Mountain View. There, from his living room, he launched LinkedIn. "I basically sketched out what I thought the product would be, assembled the business model, and then started hiring people," Hoffman said. Among them: Allen Blue, the designer he had worked with at SocialNet and a LinkedIn cofounder. Blue's most vivid memory of his visits to Hoffman's place were the Amazon boxes stacked everywhere. Hoffman would buy something that caught his interest—a book, a game, some new tech toy—but then was too busy or too distracted to even open the packages that piled up. "It was the apartment you would expect of somebody who spends almost no time there," said Blue. Except that Hoffman both worked and lived there.

"Nuclear winter" is the way some in Silicon Valley describe the time after the dot-com collapse. That's just an evocative way of saying that, in the smoldering remains of the dot-com era, the area's venture capitalists went into deep hibernation for several years, cutting their investments by 80 percent between 2000 and 2003. LinkedIn was started while Silicon Valley was still in a deep freeze. So was Tribe, a social networking site founded by Mark Pincus, who would become one of Hoffman's closer friends. "It was a quiet, dark, sad place here," Pincus said of the Valley in the early 2000s. Pincus and Hoffman initially connected around politics but then bonded over their shared frustration that the Valley felt so bleak for anyone working on a consumer internet company. "Nobody was interested in investing," Pincus said.

Pincus had founded two startups in the 1990s. The first he sold for $38 million seven months after it was launched and the other had gone public in 2000. He had millions to throw around as an angel investor. Hoffman and Pincus invested in Friendster and Six Apart, another social networking site popular in the early 2000s. They also invested in one another's startup. They thought of swapping a 1 percent stake in each other's company, as Pincus had done with another friend, but Pincus was worried about bad feelings getting in the way of their budding friendship. "I had this feeling that LinkedIn was going to be worth a lot more than Tribe," Pincus said.

"Our relationship is like when you go out with good friends and you're fighting over who pays the bill," Pincus said. In this case, however, demurring on a 1 percent swap meant missing a later payoff in the hundreds of millions of dollars.

Hoffman self-funded LinkedIn in the early months. By doing so, he saved himself the trouble of convincing venture capitalists of the merits of the idea before he and his founding team had a chance to refine it. Waiting also allowed him to hold on to a larger percentage of his company and gave him greater leverage when he was ready to seek outside funding. The early success of Friendster, a precursor of Facebook founded in 2002, convinced the VCs that there was money to be made investing in a social networking site. In 2003, Hoffman closed on a $4.7 million A round led by Sequoia Capital, a storied Valley firm (a firm whose greatest hits include Apple, Electronic Arts, Atari, Cisco, Oracle, Yahoo, PayPal, Instagram, and Google). That allowed LinkedIn to move into offices not far from Hoffman's apartment. One year later, LinkedIn closed on a B round of $10 million, led by Greylock Partners, another venerated tech venture firm.

Josh Elman, who joined LinkedIn around the time the company raised its first round of funding, was surprised the first time he met the famous Reid Hoffman for his job interview. Hoffman wore baggy pants and an ill-fitting polo under a tan jacket that looked as if it had been picked up at a Salvation Army store. Elman did not know what to think until Hoffman began laying out his vision for the company. "Reid is so energetic and passionate and incisive," said Elman, who served as LinkedIn's first product manager. "You talk to him and within ten minutes, you know this guy is absolutely brilliant. He had this aura."

Hoffman was a phantom in the offices of LinkedIn, so much so that his coworkers had a life-sized cardboard cutout of him made. "More or less every photo we have after we hit some membership milestone or some other group picture has paper Reid in it," Allen Blue said. Only sometimes did Hoffman's trips or get-togethers have anything to do with LinkedIn. "Reid was always working on so many things at once," Blue said. Despite the intensity of running a fast-growing startup, Hoffman remained one of the Valley's more active and successful angel investors.

"It's mind-boggling the way he's doing a thousand things when I'm doing a hundred and feeling overwhelmed," said David Sze, a partner at Greylock and a member of LinkedIn's board of directors.

Hoffman had been working on LinkedIn for two years when he met a twenty-year-old Mark Zuckerberg, who was looking to raise seed money for a company then called TheFacebook. "He's very articulate now," Hoffman said of Zuckerberg. "But back then there was a lot of staring at the desk and not saying anything." Hoffman knew immediately that he wanted to invest but introduced him to Thiel. Hoffman was running his own social networking site and worried about appearances. He let Thiel lead the round (as the person who invested the most amount of money, the lead typically sets the deal terms). Thiel wrote a check for $500,000 and Hoffman and Pincus split the remaining $75,000 Zuckerberg raised.

Facebook was only the most incredible investment on a long list of Hoffman's hits. By the time he started investing in AI startups, he was viewed as a man with a golden touch. His first angel investment after PayPal was in IronPort, which Cisco bought for $870 million. Early in his angel career, he invested $75,000 in Nanosolar, a solar panel company that would be worth in the multiple billions. A $100,000 investment in an early music-streaming service earned him a payout of $6.6 million when CBS bought the company the following year. He was one of several angel investors who funded the photo-sharing app Flickr, which sold barely six months later to Yahoo for a reported $35 million. Zynga (Mark Pincus's gaming company) and Groupon are among his investments in startups that would go public. And, of course, there was his seed investment in his own startup. LinkedIn went public in 2012 and was bought in 2017 by Microsoft for $26.2 billion—then the largest deal in the software giant's history. Even disappointments such as Friendster, Digg, and Six Apart were groundbreaking, if not financially remunerative.

"You have to consider him one of the great angel investors of all time," David Sze said. "I can't think of anyone who's done what he did in that ten-year span of history."

It seemed inevitable that Hoffman would become a venture capitalist. Recognizing that he needed to replace himself with a chief executive more adept at growing a company than building one from scratch, Hoff-man in 2009 stepped down as CEO of LinkedIn. He remained with LinkedIn as its executive chairman but joined Sze at Greylock Partners. "There's something about helping entrepreneurs grow their company that I find invigorating," Hoffman said.

Hoffman's new colleagues wondered if maybe they had made a mistake when their newest partner brought them a startup struggling to build a business around regular folks inviting strangers to sleep in their home, as if they were bed-and-breakfast hosts. This was long before anyone was talking about Uber or throwing around terms like the "sharing" or "gig" economy. "I'm on record as having been very skeptical about investing in Airbnb," Sze said. Another partner was blunter: "All of us thought the guy was insane." Yet they invested, despite their doubts. Hoffman's first investment as a venture capitalist earned the firm a payout of nearly 1,000x on their initial wager—the single best return in the history of a firm that dates back to 1965. "I'm hoping for that kind of massive outcome with Inflection," Sze said.

CHAPTER 3

The True Believers

"The Zachary effect," I would dub it. In 1995, while Reid Hoffman was still toiling away on eWorld inside Apple, I was living in Oakland and met G. Pascal (Gregg) Zachary, a tech reporter at the *Wall Street Journal.* In retrospect, the timing of his call seemed kismet. I had just come out with a book that used the story of a single drive-by shooting to tell the wider story of the gun violence overwhelming our cities. I was broke and eager to sink my teeth into something new.

I was paying attention to the internet out of a corner of one eye. I had bought a modem and joined CompuServe in 1994 so I could "surf the web," as everyone said back then, and then moved to America Online, or AOL, mainly because CompuServe assigned you a string of numbers for your online name rather than allowing you to pick your own alias. Those were the days of Listservs, online forums, message boards, and web directories such as Yahoo. Netscape had recently gone public, which was hard to miss living in the Bay Area.

Yet listening to Zachary talk, the race to cash in on the internet made me think of the great Oklahoma land grab. The Netscape IPO had been the crack of a gun going off that sparked the latest rush for easy riches, like oil in the 1970s or junk bonds and leveraged buyouts in the 1980s. Zachary had written a book, *Showstopper*, about Microsoft's attempt to create an industrial-grade version of Windows good enough to convince large corporations to use it to run their operations.

Yet Netscape going public threatened Microsoft's dominance over the personal computer and gave rise to hundreds of startups. I didn't need much convincing that this should be my next topic once he told me what the tech trade publications were paying—triple what I made writing articles about politics or a social issue. Some headed to Silicon Valley for riches. I was going there to climb out of credit card debt.

• • •

SILICON VALLEY IS both a place and an idea. It's a geographic area south of San Francisco that stretches down around forty miles to San Jose. But it's also a stand-in phrase for tech generally. It's akin to saying "Wall Street," which is a stretch of asphalt in New York City but more a catch-all figure of speech to talk about the power of big money in our world. Later, when I went to work for the *Times* as a Silicon Valley correspondent, the companies for which I was responsible included Amazon, which is headquartered in Seattle, and Dell, just outside of Austin, Texas.

Physically, the Valley is not much to look at. It has a birthplace: the garage where Bill Hewlett and Dave Packard built their first product (an audio oscillator that Walt Disney Studios used to test its sound systems for the film *Fantasia*) and gave rise to Hewlett-Packard. Sand Hill Road—the "Wall Street of Silicon Valley," as it has been called—is a broad thoroughfare lined with low-slung, personality-less buildings whose two greatest attributes are its proximity to Stanford and easy access to a backdoor highway to San Francisco. A TV producer might choose a shot of Stanford's distinctive Hoover Tower as a visual icon for Silicon Valley, or maybe the Apple or Google logo outside its headquarters. But in fact the area is an endless suburb crisscrossed with highways and dotted with indistinguishable office parks. There was no real there there.

I wrote my first article about tech in 1996 for a trade publication called *Upside*, a Silicon Valley–based magazine backed by venture money (naturally). Logging on to an online service such as CompuServe or AOL meant connecting over a phone line. Yet the phone company's twisted wires could not carry nearly as much data as a cable company's fat pipes, explaining why it could take minutes to download even a single page of text. The assignment: figure out what the big cable companies were thinking about the internet. My first interview was a sit-down with Eric Schmidt, then the chief technology officer of Sun Microsystems but later the CEO of Google and Valley superstar. I might even have understood half of what my second interviewee, Paul Saffo, then a forecaster at the Institute for the Future, said as he laid out the technical challenges the cable companies faced. But I certainly remembered Saffo's admonition that we tend to overstate the short-term impact of any new technology and understate its long-term impact. Among those I also interviewed for that first article was John Doerr, the VC who later declared the internet the greatest wealth creator of all time. Doerr, a VC at Kleiner Perkins, basically laid out the future for me. Thick pipes meant music and movies over the internet. Increased bandwidth would "allow people to buy and sell things." In a few months, Doerr and his partners would invest several million dollars in a company called Amazon.com. Led by Doerr, Kleiner would also be the first venture money (along with Sequoia Capital) in Google.

The trade publications invariably wanted me to write about the tech juggernauts—what the internet will mean for Microsoft, or Sun, or the cable giants—but I was attracted to the startup ecosystem, where everyone dreamed of building the next Netscape. The founders fascinated me. So too did the venture capitalists, who were the gamblers financing this high-stakes game. The VCs knew from experience that failure was far more likely than success, but they also knew that one big strike could more than make up for the losses. I took a meeting with any startup founder willing to sit down with me. I embedded for a month with a VC firm for a feature article for *San Francisco* magazine. Similarly, I shadowed a couple of the younger VCs at Kleiner Perkins as they sped up and down Highways 101 and 280, the twin cement spines that run the length of the peninsula and stretch from San Francisco south to San Jose. "Kiss enough frogs, you'll find a prince," one said to me, snapping on the neon smile I saw him use with the founders he sought to win over. Multitudes were descending on the Valley, not to take jobs with the large incumbents that editors wanted me to write about, but to get in on the ground floor of a hot, venture-backed startup. "To ride the rocket ship," as I heard more than one of them say.

Yet in the second half of the 1990s, writing about startups meant writing about Microsoft. The giant to the north in Redmond, Washington, loomed over virtually every conversation. The company came up at almost every pitch meeting where I played a fly on the wall. A founding team would lay out what seemed a promising idea, but then the first question out of a VC's mouth: What if Microsoft decides to compete in that space? Usually that possibility was enough to scare off most venture capitalists. Even people with companies that had some traction spoke incessantly about Microsoft. It was no wonder, given the cautionary tales making the rounds. Someone from Microsoft would reach out to a Silicon Valley startup, ostensibly to discuss a partnership deal or a possible acquisition. A team dispatched by Microsoft would glean what they could from founders eager to impress this deep-pocketed giant of the software world. Its real aim became clear six months later when Microsoft announced it was entering the same market with a product of its own.

Microsoft was a constant source of complaint. The company released buggy, crash-prone products long before they were ready for release, as if its customers were beta testers. Its people ran roughshod even over its closest partners. They stole ideas from others and behaved like arrogant bullies.

Often, the ire was aimed at Bill Gates, the public face of Microsoft. Someone's laptop would crash during a demo and they'd say, "Thanks, Bill Gates," and everyone would laugh. Gates was often spoken about as if he were the actual culprit, when it had been a junior product manager who supposedly had stolen their code. Petulant, haughty, driven, successful: Gates was the embodiment of Microsoft's success and, by extension, a villain to most of Silicon Valley.

• • •

"A COMPUTER ON every desk and in every home, running Microsoft software": that had been Microsoft's motto since practically its founding, in 1975, when Gates was a squeaky-voiced nineteen-year-old sophomore at Harvard. Yet even a mission as grandiose as that didn't quite capture Gates's intention to dominate every aspect of the software business. By the 1990s, Microsoft Windows had cemented its place as the default operating system on most of the world's personal computers. That would serve as the foundation from which Microsoft built itself into a multitrillion-dollar company.

Microsoft's hordes of programmers first attacked rivals that had written the software packages that ran on top of Windows. At the start of the 1990s, Lotus 1-2-3 was the dominant spreadsheet and WordPerfect the top word-processing program. Yet Microsoft had financial resources that independent software publishers lacked. It offered an Office Suite, which included Microsoft's own spreadsheet, word processor, and presentation software, and priced the bundle so it was much cheaper than buying products separately from competitors. There were also advantages in building the underlying operating system. More than once, Microsoft was accused of tweaking Windows in ways that harmed a rival or helped one of its own product teams. Eventually Lotus and WordPerfect would be history and Excel, Word, and PowerPoint would become as dominant as its OS.

Microsoft had already begun its assault on the high-end corporate market by the time I started covering tech. The company enlisted hundreds of programmers and eventually thousands to build the industrial-strength business applications on which large organizations depended: database programs, server software, and other packages that run back-office operations. Rather than consumer software packages that cost $99 a pop, they aimed at customers like International Harvester, Mobil, Georgia Pacific, and other corporate giants able to pay millions.

Microsoft was slow to recognize the potential of the internet, and people in the Valley grew giddy. The internet, it seemed, would hobble Microsoft, just as happened to IBM during the PC era. Traditionally, the new eat the old in tech; yesterday's Leviathan is tomorrow's dinosaur. But in mid-1995, around the same time I started regularly crossing the Dumbarton Bridge to spend time in towns like Palo Alto, Mountain View, and Menlo Park, Gates wrote a memo titled "The Internet Tidal

Wave." This would be his call to arms. He was done arguing about the internet's importance, he wrote in a memo addressed to his top executive team that eventually was shared with the company's rank and file. "I assign the internet the highest level of importance," Gates wrote. At a meeting of journalists and financial analysts later that year, Gates proclaimed, "We are hard core about the internet."

Netscape, the Valley's pride and joy, was nimbler than Microsoft. Its people were as talented and its high-profile cofounder, Marc Andreessen, as arrogant and brash as Gates. Netscape, Andreessen declared, would reduce Windows to a "slightly buggy set of device drivers." But Microsoft's operating system came preinstalled on every new PC. Its answer to the Netscape Navigator web browser was to bundle Internet Explorer with every copy of Windows. Users could download Navigator or another competing browser, but it seemed simpler to use what came with the machine. By the second half of 1997, Internet Explorer had more users than Navigator. The following year, Netscape waved the white flag and sold to the Dulles, Viriginia–based AOL. By the early 2000s, Internet Explorer had captured 95 percent of the browser market. (It renamed its browser Microsoft Edge in 2015.) As much as I might have wanted the story to be about startups, it was about the giants, and Microsoft in particular.

With Netscape's surrender, resentment over Microsoft's power turned into anger. "They are like the Chinese army," Schmidt said of the company. "They send wave after wave of soldiers at you, all of them expendable." One prominent Valley CEO—Schmidt's then boss at Sun, Scott McNealy—routinely called Microsoft the "Death Star." Most simply referred to the company as the "Evil Empire," which of course cast the Valley as the rebel alliance, risking everything to save the world. In 1996, Kleiner Perkins created a $100 million fund expressly to seed efforts built on a platform that wasn't Windows. Among those throwing money into the kitty were Netscape, Sun, Oracle, and IBM, who were the highest-profile members of what reporters started calling the "ABM movement"—Anyone But Microsoft.

Yet resistance was futile. One startup founder I had spent time with around that time didn't want to sell his company to anyone, let alone to Microsoft. But he did end up selling to them because he had to grudgingly admit it was either accept its terms or watch the Death Star enter the market and probably wipe out his creation. He asked me not to use his name because he had seen the reaction when a company sold to Microsoft for a big payday (Hotmail for $450 million, Link-Exchange for $265 million). Their founders were derided as traitors. Maybe Microsoft wasn't the Death Star from *Star Wars* but "the Borg" from *Star Trek*, a relentless collective that travels through the universe seeking to absorb every species it encounters and reprogramming every life entity so that its fidelity is to the ship's central brain.

In 1999, I published *The Plot to Get Bill Gates*, a book about Gates and all those who resented this smarty-pants mop top with oversized nerd glasses who always seemed to win. He was gobbling up the software world, and his competitors seemed helpless in their quest to stop him. I offered an unflattering portrait of Gates, who was monomaniacal in his pursuit of market share, but also wove in the stories of the CEOs he had bested and those still fighting to fend off him and his minions. The "Captain Ahab's Club," I called this group obsessed with revenge against the great white whale that had caused them so much pain. They were by and large as arrogant as Gates, and a prideful crew forced to grapple with the reach and might of a despised foe. That was the real indignity driving those still in the fight: Microsoft was so dominant that they had no choice but to work with them. Envy no doubt played a role too. By the end of the 1990s, Gates had a net worth of $60 billion.

I'd make several visits to Redmond while working on the book. It was hard not to be impressed, if not also a little horrified, watching Microsoft's methodical and machinelike approach to growth. Its people didn't wear suits like their corporate counterparts. In what would soon become a cliché in tech, its people came to work each day wearing T-shirts and jeans, unless it was warm and then they arrived in shorts. But despite appearances, these baby-faced engineers and nerd-kings were as sharklike and ruthless as the people running any high-growth Fortune 500 company. They were fast copycats who had no qualms about dropping a half-baked, imitative product on the market. Meanwhile, its teams worked virtually around the clock adding features and making other improvements. Elsewhere in the company, others did what they could to ensure that the competition had no chance. By offering PC manufacturers a deeply discounted price on Windows, Microsoft indirectly paid PC manufacturers not to preinstall competing software products. PC makers needed access to Windows more than Microsoft needed the business of any single PC maker, and Microsoft's people weren't above reminding them of that if they thought of bundling Netscape Navigator or some other competing product on their machines.

Microsoft hit the peak of its power in 1999, the year my book came out. The U.S. government sued the company while I was working on it, as did twenty state attorneys general, charging the company with using its monopoly in the operating system market to build its budding internet browser business. In March 2000, the Nasdaq began its great fall, precipitating the dot-com crash and harming virtually every tech company, even Microsoft. A few weeks later, a federal judge ruled that the company violated the country's antitrust laws by bundling Internet Explorer with Windows. It was too late to help Netscape, but the judge ordered that Microsoft be broken into two. There would be one Microsoft for operating systems and another for the rest of its software products.

The breakup order was overturned on appeal, but the damage was done. Inside Microsoft, people talked about the lost months while the judge's breakup order hung over the company. A settlement agreement with the government required them to share their programming interfaces with third parties, taking away one of Microsoft's competitive advantages. The company also agreed to create an internal antitrust compliance committee. That meant an extra layer of bureaucracy that slowed decision-making in an industry in which speed was critical. The fearsome, brutish Microsoft of the 1990s was dead. In its place was a weaker, chastened giant operating under federal oversight.

• • •

MY TIMING FOR a book about Microsoft was good. The producers at all the big news shows had me on speed dial, at least for a few minutes. By then I had taken a job at the *Industry Standard*, a buzzy new magazine covering the business side of the internet. Gates, who obviously no longer needed the grief, stepped down as CEO several months after the book's release and replaced himself with Steve Ballmer, his close friend and number two. That day, I hit a kind of media trifecta with quick hits—interviews—on CNN, MSNBC, and Fox. Each studio used the same iconic shot of the San Francisco skyline as a faux backdrop as I spoke to an anchor back in New York, except it was sunny in one and a foggy in the other two.

Each interviewer asked me the obvious question about Gates's choice of Ballmer to take his place. I'll confess I didn't know what to say. I brought up Ballmer's intensity (he had shouted so loud for so long at one companywide meeting that he needed surgery to repair his shredded vocal cords) and spoke of his success at running key units of Microsoft. He had headed the company's operating system division early on, and then oversaw the company's business software efforts, which was its largest growth area. The two had been working side by side since the start of the 1980s, when Gates convinced Ballmer to drop out of business school to help him with the nuts and bolts of running Microsoft. But did he have what it takes to keep the company ahead of everyone else? My intention for the book was a fun romp through the software wars of the 1990s. I just repeated the conventional wisdom as I was hearing it. He was smart, talented, and committed to the cause. But he didn't have a technical background, which some believed was mandatory if running the computer industry's dominant software company.

I figured I was done reporting on tech. With the dot-com crash, I saw my role evaporate. I had been a skeptic—the "skunk at the garden party," as one editor teased me—surrounded by enthusiasts. Most reporters bought into the hype and inflated valuations, along with the platitudes of underage CEOs promising to change the world. I remembered Paul Saffo's warning about our tendency to overstate a technology's potential short-term impact, even one as transformative as the internet. Companies disappeared and fortunes were lost, and there was no more talk of IPO'ing in eighteen months. No one needed my contrarian voice anymore. The market made cynics of us all.

I left San Francisco in 2002. The plan was to casino-hop my way east to New York, where I'd start work on a book about the rapid spread of casinos from two states to more than thirty in barely a decade's time. But before I reached New York, where I had grown up, *Wired* made me an offer I couldn't refuse. I was again a tech writer. Soon after, in 2003, the *New York Times* hired me to cover Silicon Valley. Back in San Francisco, I continued to cover the rise of social media, including a small startup called TheFacebook.com, and other ideas bubbling up, including "software as a service," or SaaS (pronounced "sass"), that threatened to disrupt the entire business software market.

Hurricane Katrina hit the Gulf Coast in 2005, and the *Times* moved me to New Orleans to cover that city's efforts to rebuild after flooding that damaged most of that city's homes and almost all of its businesses. That ended a decade focused on Silicon Valley. I'd go back to writing about issues like race and politics, and only occasionally find myself writing about tech until pulled back in by the arrival of AI.

• • •

IF THE PHRASE "artificial intelligence" came up during my decade covering Silicon Valley, I don't remember it. The second AI winter had supposedly thawed around 1993, but that impacted universities and research labs, not the venture capitalists and entrepreneurs I was spending time with. Besides, the typical AI researcher teaching at a big-name university was still rejecting this notion of neural networks created to mimic the workings of the brain. Rule-based AI still dominated. At Stanford, Chris Manning focused on teaching computers to speak as fluently as a human: natural language processing. He was building enormous tree banks of diagrammed sentences, hoping he could drill the rules of a language into a machine. Researchers at MIT and Berkeley and Carnegie Mellon were experimenting with a rule-based approach to sentiment analysis that programmed predefined linguist rules into a machine. AI was still a long way from being relevant to most real-world applications.

Yet the world was shifting, even if largely out of sight, with the increasing influence of the second coming of Frank Rosenblatt in Geoff Hinton. Hinton was forged by the same institutions that gave rise to a generation dismissive of neural networks. He had studied at Cambridge University in the late 1960s and did his graduate work at the University of Edinburgh, which had recently established a Department of Machine Intelligence and Perception. At Cambridge, a professor sparked his interest in machines that were programmed to learn for themselves, like biological systems do. His professors at Edinburgh then did what they could to beat that belief out of him. They reminded him that Minsky and others had debunked this approach. But Hinton had read Minsky's book and had not found it persuasive. He was convinced that Rosenblatt was on the right path. Hinton forged ahead despite the naysayers.

Hinton had the right lineage to serve as prophet. His great-great-grandfather was the English mathematician George Boole, who developed a system for logical thinking, called Boolean algebra, that is fundamental to the workings of a computer. A great-great-grandmother was Mary Everest, a prominent mathematician in her day (and the niece of George Everest, the Mount Everest namesake), and Lucy Everest was the first woman elected to the Royal Institute of Chemistry. A cousin, Joan Hinton, worked on the Manhattan Project. His father, Howard Everest Hinton, was a prominent entomologist who taught at the University of Bristol.

Geoff, however, did not seem destined for anything great. He meandered through his course work at Cambridge, jumping from major to major. He tried chemistry, physics, philosophy, and art history before deciding to focus on the brain and experimental psychology. Hinton seemed especially ill-suited for a role as an artificial intelligence pioneer. He was not a programmer. He was not a mathematician, though math and especially linear algebra are foundational to AI. Hinton quotes his own father as telling him, "If you work twice as hard as me, when you're twice as old as I am, you might be half as good."

Timing also worked against Hinton. He graduated from Edinburgh with a PhD in artificial intelligence in 1978, as AI was in the throes of its first deep winter. The British government had released a report while Hinton was in graduate school concluding that research into AI had added up to little more than twenty-five years of disappointments. There were no teaching positions to be found in Great Britian and academic jobs were scarce in the U.S., especially for a newly minted PhD believer in neural nets.

Hinton's break came when he landed a postgraduate fellowship at the University of California, San Diego (UCSD), where he found what one member of the clan called "the neural network underground." He was listed as the second-named author on a landmark paper by David Rumelhart, Hoffman's Stanford advisor, that served as a critical breakthrough for those believing in neural nets. By that time, Hinton had joined the computer science department at Carnegie Mellon. There he and a colleague created what they dubbed the Boltzmann machine. This creation, named in honor of a nineteenth-century physicist, represented a giant leap forward in the field of neural networks. Unlike Rosenblatt's Perceptron, which had only a single layer of artificial neurons, the Boltzmann machine was a multilayered network that began to more resemble the workings of the human brain. With a multilayered approach, a machine could tackle more complex problems, much like how our brains use layers of neural connections to process information and formulate abstract thoughts. Like Perceptron, the Boltzmann machine learned from the data it consumed rather than spitting out an answer based on a specific set of instructions. Yet like its predecessor, it still couldn't do much, preserving Hinton's status as a fringe player in the field.

• • •

IT WAS A science experiment called Cyc, also announced in the mid-1980s, rather than the Boltzmann machine that drew people's attention. Cyc, which was short for "encyclopedia," was the creation of a young Stanford professor named Doug Lenat. A disciple of Ed Feigenbaum, the father of expert systems, Lenat left the university in 1984 to pursue a dream of what he called a "common sense machine." Humans possess intuition. They are guided by truisms and commonsense learnings that aren't written down so much as innately understood. A five-year-old understands that she must chew most foods but not all foods before she swallows; that people can't be in two places at once; and that animals see with their eyes and hear with their ears. Lenat and the people he was able to hire with venture backing would teach machines rule by rule, observation by observation, even if it took them millions and millions of lines of code to do so.

Yet rather than pointing the way to the future, Cyc seemed to underscore the herculean nature of a rule-based approach. The systems they were creating grew impossibly complex as their creators spelled out exceptions and, line by line, attempted to program a near-infinite number of possibilities. Driverless cars were another example of the Sisyphean nature of their task. Researchers had devoted years to hand-coding every rule of the road into the computers controlling autonomous vehicles yet had made little progress. They were thwarted by simple things such as debris in the road or bad weather, let alone police officers manually directing traffic or the unpredictability of fellow drivers. People learned through experience, not by following lists of rigid instructions. Even Lenat seemed to recognize the futility of his pursuit. Two years into the project, he confessed that he figured it would take as many as two thousand human years of labor to finish his project. Fifteen million lines of code later, Lenat was still not close to done when he died in 2023.

Rule-based AI had its successes in the 1990s. An early chatbot named ALICE, released in 1995, drew thousands of people from around the world interested in chatting with a program the *New York Times* described as "so eerily human that some mistake it for a real person." The creator of ALICE (Artificial Linguistic Internet Computer Entity), Richard Wallace, who had earned a PhD in computer science at Carnegie Mellon, was inspired by Eliza and its simple call-and-response construction. ALICE programmed responses to thousands of the most common things people say in conversation. "What's up?" someone might ask, and its preprogrammed response might be, "Not much, nice to meet you." But the answers it gave were the same scripted responses, whether someone was sharing a deep fear or chatting about a friend.

Eventually, rule-based computing also impressed with its chess-playing skills, as Marvin Minsky predicted it would. In 1997, world chess champion Garry Kasparov squared off against an IBM super-computer dubbed Deep Blue. Games had been a proving ground for AI since the 1950s, when a PhD student at Cambridge programmed a computer to master tic-tac-toe (or noughts-and-crosses, as it is known in Great Britan). Later in the decade, IBM's Arthur Samuel, the man who coined the term "machine learning," wrote a checkers-playing program because, he explained, teaching a machine to play a game gave researchers a structure for solving other hard problems.

"The Brain's Last Stand," a headline in *Newsweek* declared ahead of the match between Kasparov and Deep Blue; another headline cast Kasparov as the "defender of humanity." Apparently, humanity lost when Deep Blue prevailed, in just nineteen moves, in the final and decisive game of the match. The machine at times "played like a God," Kasparov famously said of his silicon rival. The loss launched a torrent of think pieces about humanity's inferiority complex, laced with doom-talk about a reshuffling of our place atop the globe's hierarchy of intelligence. Columnists wondered, if a machine could best the top chess player on the planet, what else could it do in our place?

Yet in hindsight, Deep Blue's triumph stands not as a dark day for humans but a high point for rule-based computing. In 1997, IBM's feat was viewed with a mixture of awe and fear. Looking back twenty-five years later, however, tech journalist Clive Thompson, writing in the *MIT Technology Review*, cast the moment as a "kind of death knell" for "the laborious handcrafting of endless lines of code." He compared Deep Blue to a lumbering dinosaur not knowing it was about to be wiped out by an asteroid.

• • •

HINTON NEVER WAVERED from his belief in neural networks, despite the hostility of colleagues. "It wasn't really faith—it was just completely obvious to me," Hinton said. (In 2024, Hinton would share a Nobel Prize for his pioneering work on neural nets.) Yet in the 1990s and into the 2000s, the academic establishment and, more importantly, the government agencies that funded AI research still viewed neural nets as a dead end. A peer of Hinton's and fellow outcast, Yoshua Bengio, wrote in the 1990s what in hindsight is a groundbreaking PhD thesis about using a neural net to teach a machine to talk. "I was looked at like I had very strange, misguided, crazy ideas," Bengio said. Attending a conference in Boston in the early 2000s, Andrew Ng, another early believer in neural nets, was giving a talk arguing that they were the future—and a prominent UC Berkeley professor interrupted his presentation to tell him what he was saying was nonsense. Ng's PhD advisor viewed him as a traitor to the AI cause because of his views.

Those who saw merit in neural networks sought alternative words for describing their work. Some preferred "machine learning," while AI researchers used the term "connectionism" to describe the models they were building that, inspired by the human brain, aimed to create a vast number of interconnected faux neurons. Those and other phrases, including "statistical learning theory," were embraced by academics seeking euphemisms to avoid saying "neural nets." Hinton preferred "deep learning," which Rina Dechter, a professor of computer science at the University of California, Irvine, had coined in a paper she published in 1986. Soon "deep learning" was the preferred term for describing this approach to AI—a "cunning piece of rebranding," wrote Cade Metz.

Whatever it was called, neural nets were showing promise. The team working on self-driving vehicles inside Carnegie Mellon's AI lab scrapped the code they had painstakingly written over years in favor of a system based on neural nets. The new model learned to drive processing visual data, much like humans do. In 1995, their autonomous vehicle (a modified Chevy) successfully navigated the 125 miles from Pittsburgh to Erie, Pennsylvania, with no human intervention.

An acolyte of Hinton's named Yann LeCun would advance the cause of computers that could see with a program that outperformed hard-coded efforts. LeCun was working on a PhD in computer science when he first met Hinton in the mid-1980s. He worked with Hinton, who by this time had moved to the University of Toronto, on a breakthrough algorithm modeled on the visual cortex, the part of the brain that processes what we see. He trained his invention on thousands of hand-addressed envelopes from the U.S. Postal Service. By the mid-1990s, a device LeCun and his colleagues at Bell Laboratories had developed was being sold to banks to read handwritten checks.

Another pioneer of what insiders call "computer vision" was Fei-Fei Li, a young Princeton computer science professor. "What if the secret to recognizing *anything*," she wondered, "was a training set that included *everything*?" Li revived an abandoned project called ImageNet, a neural net she trained by having it ingest nearly nine million labeled images sorted into ten thousand–plus categories. Soon ImageNet was outperforming computer vision that relied on hard-coded rules for detecting objects and scenes.

Speech was another realm in which neural nets were demonstrating potential. Terry Sejnowski, who had collaborated with Hinton on the Boltzmann machine, created NETtalk. Sejnowski connected an electronic speech box to a computer so it could read children's books aloud. At first the machine spoke a mechanical-sounding babble, but within the day, NETtalk was uttering words. After one week of training, it could read full sentences. Microsoft and Google were among the established tech companies experimenting with neural nets and speech in the 2000s.

Yet these were the kind of baby steps that impressed academics, not investors and corporate executives. A vehicle had driven itself from one city to another, but that had been a straight shot on a highway in ideal conditions. Yes, a computer could distinguish a schnauzer from a pit bull or read a children's book in a halting, mechanized voice. But Bell Labs disbanded Yann LeCun's team, and his check-scanning project was discontinued because higher-ups didn't see it as a profitable venture. Investors seemed to have little interest in AI, and who could blame them after the financial losses brought on by the second AI winter? The decades of overpromising and unfulfilled expectations had taken their toll.

"There was enough of a legacy that people in the 2000s still weren't taking artificial intelligence very seriously," Stanford's Chris Manning said. Even a true believer such as LeCun, who by then was a professor at New York University, wondered if computers would ever have the power required to train a large enough neural net to make them useful. Said Hinton: "No one ever thought to ask, 'Suppose we need a million times more [power]?'"

• • •

THE 2010S MARKED a turning point. It helped that computers had grown far more powerful. Nvidia, a chip maker based in Santa Clara, California, pioneered the Graphics Processing Unit. The GPU, as everyone called it, was originally created for better video game play but proved perfect for training a neural network because it enabled parallel processing and was therefore able to perform billions of calculations per second. The faster the computer, the deeper, more sophisticated a model a research team could build. With the rise of the internet, there was exponentially more data available for training a model.

Hinton, LeCun, Bengio, and their fellow neural net rebels now held center court at AI conferences. By then, Minsky, who died in 2016, was a diminished figure. Chris Manning was among the converts. For twenty years, Manning, a linguist by training, was known for using statistical prediction models to improve a computer's ability to understand a given language. Statistical machine learning, as this approach is called, was more mathematically precise. Researchers could prove their theorems were correct before actually constructing a model. "There were a few crazy neural network people doing this not very rigorous stuff," Manning said. "But they kept beavering away." Manning joined them around 2010.

The field was still minuscule then. Manning remembered attending a deep-learning workshop in 2010 or 2011. "About forty people showed up, yet it felt like that was two-thirds of the people around the world who were doing neural networks," he said.

"It wouldn't really be until 2013 or 2014 when the floodgates opened and everyone was using neural nets for almost everything at the research level," Manning said. The "Golden Decade," some researchers would dub the period that followed, given the great strides they made in artificial intelligence.

CHAPTER 4

DeepMind

Mustafa Suleyman was feeling lost in 2010. He had recently stepped away from an intense job as a conflict-resolution mediator that had left him feeling cynical about the wider world and was casting about for what he might do next. "I was rather passionate about poker," he said. For a time, he let himself get hooked on the multi-table player games made possible by its migration online. He would play eight games simultaneously and consistently win. He was also a regular at "the Vic," as locals call the Victoria Casino in London, which held regular poker tournaments. The stakes were never very high—a prize of maybe 250 pounds—but Suleyman relished the chance to best the hundred or so players who typically showed up for one of the Vic's midweek tournaments.

Somehow it seems appropriate that AI's first truly successful startup, DeepMind, was born in a casino. The cards were not falling for Suleyman on a spring night in 2010, and he was bumped early from a tournament at the Vic. Another regular tournament player, Demis Hassabis, had also been knocked out early. Both Hassabis and Suleyman had grown up in North London, where Suleyman was best friends with Hassabis's younger brother George. The two retired to the Vic's restaurant to commiserate. "We're sitting there eating chocolate cake and vanilla ice cream and Diet Cokes. Obviously, we're supercool," Suleyman said in a plummy British accent.

Suleyman is a slim six-footer with a head of black curly hair, brown eyes, and a watchful, laid-back demeanor. Back then, he wore a scruffy dark beard and a small earring in one ear. Over their cake and Diet Cokes, they began "whinging about our bad bets," Suleyman said—complaining about the hands that knocked them out—but soon fell into a conversation about robots and the future. Robots seemed a long way away, both agreed, but Hassabis, who had a PhD in cognitive neuroscience, made the case that the world seemed tantalizingly close to machines that could learn. "Like surely a machine could learn to play poker, a machine could learn a set of heuristics and then produce those patterns," Suleyman said. Not that many months later, Suleyman, Hassabis, and a third man, Shane Legg, formed DeepMind.

"It all seems kind of insane looking back, talking about machines that learn in 2010," Suleyman said. "It certainly felt pretty far out at the time." Said Hassabis: "Most people thought we were completely mad to be embarking on this journey."

• • •

SULEYMAN'S FATHER WAS born in Syria but fled the repressive regime in power then to avoid a mandatory three-year stint in the military. He was a living in Pakistan and studying to be an engineer when he met his future wife, a young Brit who was touring southern Asia and the Middle East. His father never finished his engineering degree, Suleyman said, "because they became pregnant with me in Pakistan." The couple didn't want to raise a family in Islamabad, so they moved to London, where they had two more children over the next three years.

Suleyman's father drove a taxi, but not the iconic black London cab. He drove what locals called minicabs. "My father was basically an illegal taxi driver," Suleyman said. His mother worked as a nurse with the British National Health System. Suleyman grew up in North London in a high-rise cement block that in the U.S. would be called public housing but in the U.K. is a council estate. "It was basically one of the roughest neighborhoods in London," Suleyman said.

His mother had converted to Islam even before meeting his father, and religion was central in the Suleyman household. The family went to weekly prayer each Friday and built their social life around the local mosque. "It was super strict growing up," Suleyman said. "I didn't get on with it very much." In Arabic, the name Mustafa means the chosen one. "My dad would always remind me of that: 'Don't forget, you are the chosen one,'" Suleyman said. When he was growing up, the name felt like a burden.

Suleyman was eleven when he gained entrance to Queen Elizabeth's School for Boys, a highly selective public school, called a state school, north of London and founded in 1573. The family moved to a suburb to be nearer to this school that emphasized math and science. "It changed my life," Suleyman said.

Suleyman's first foray as entrepreneur dates back to QE Boys, as the school is known. He was maybe twelve years old when he and a friend bought boxes of candy bars and other sweets in bulk with the idea of selling them individually on the playground. As their enterprise scaled, they paid fellow students to rent locker space to store inventory and hired them to sell their product during recess. "It got pretty big before the teachers shut it down," Suleyman said. A few summers later, Suleyman and several others used a borrowed wheelchair to visit restaurants and sights around London. They published an eighty-page guide to the city for young disabled people. At eighteen, he tried selling digital point-of-sales systems and networking equipment to local businesses. But this was in 2002, long before the popularity of iPads or other user-friendly tablets.

"Ever since I was a kid, I was always starting small businesses and dreaming they would one day grow like crazy," he said.

Suleyman's mother was against her son attending college. "She was kind of adamant that I drop out of school at sixteen and get a trade. 'Become a plumber.' 'Become a carpenter.' 'Everyone's always going to need an electrician.' That was just long-term reliable," Suleyman said. He instead matriculated to Oxford, where he read philosophy and theology. "There was no judgment there for being a bit obsessive or a bit nerdy or really overpassionate about stuff, whereas earlier in life that was a bit more tricky," he said.

• • •

SULEYMAN WAS IN his second year at Oxford when he joined several fellow students who were starting a telephone hotline for young British Muslims. The year was 2003, and anti-Muslim sentiments were still high after September 11th. Yet Suleyman and many young people he knew felt alienated from the mosque, which taught that premarital sex is wrong and homosexuality a sin. At Oxford, he declared himself an atheist. "I guess I was restless and angry at what I saw as such widespread injustice and inequality, and I felt compelled to do something to help people directly in the wider world," he said. Suleyman dropped out before the end of his second year to work full-time on what he described as "a nonjudgmental, nondirectional, secular support service" that was the first of its kind in England. He spent three years working on the hotline.

"It was basically my first real startup experience," Suleyman said. "I had to persuade people to give us money. We had to persuade people to come work for us for free and we had to keep the service up and running, twelve hours a day, seven days a week, three hundred sixty-five days a year on a shoestring budget." He expressed regret about leaving Oxford before finishing his studies but in explaining himself, he sounded like his future cofounder, Reid Hoffman.

"A degree from Oxford was very theoretical and very abstract when I wanted to have an impact on the real world," Suleyman said, adding, "I was genuinely one of those kids . . . whose primary goal was to make the world a better place. It sounds super cheesy and trite, but that was what I was setting off to do."

• • •

WHILE STILL WORKING on the hotline, Suleyman started working a couple of days a week as a human rights policy officer for Ken Livingstone, the firebrand London mayor dubbed "Red Ken" by the tabloids because of his left-wing politics. That's how Suleyman met several more experienced negotiation experts who had been involved in the truth-and-reconciliation process in post-apartheid South Africa. He was just twenty-two when they invited him to join a conflict-resolution firm that they were starting. For the next three years, he worked as a negotiator and facilitator for a variety of clients, including the United Nations. He spent time in Cyprus. He traveled the Middle East on behalf of the Dutch government. At the end of 2009, he was among the hundreds who gathered in Copenhagen to hammer out an international agreement for mitigating climate change.

Copenhagen served as the pinnacle of his career in conflict resolution and also marked its end. Suleyman served as a facilitator brought in by the United Nations to help negotiate limits on deforestation as part of a bigger emissions reduction agreement. There had been great optimism ahead of Copenhagen with the recent election of Barack Obama, who as a candidate for president had stated his support for meaningful climate action. Yet then Obama, the Chinese premier, and other world leaders bigfooted the negotiating process, brokering their own accords and sidelining the work of hundreds of participants from around the world. "That proved a very frustrating moment," Suleyman said. He resigned from his job not long afterward and set about figuring out what he would do next.

• • •

SULEYMAN CAN'T EXPLAIN his sudden interest in technology except to say it was tied to his preoccupation with having an impact on the world. He saw the influence Bill and Melinda Gates were having on everything from health to education to poverty through their mega-foundation. "I remember thinking that making money in order to give it away seemed a good way of thinking about it," Suleyman said. He was less enamored by Mark Zuckerberg than Gates, but he couldn't deny the impact Zuckerberg was having on the world through Facebook, which had crossed 600 million users by 2010.

"At that point, I was reaching out to anyone I knew who had anything to do with tech," Suleyman said.

Demis Hassabis was one of those Suleyman contacted, even before their chance encounter at the Vic. Hassabis had graduated from high school at twelve. At thirteen, he ranked second in the world among junior chess players. He was accepted at Cambridge University, but the administration made him wait until his sixteenth birthday to start his studies. After graduating there with a degree in computer science, he founded his own gaming company, which at its peak employed sixty people. The business was foundering, and an increasing reliance on rudimentary AI in the gaming world caused Hassabis to realize he needed to better understand the workings of the human brain if he were to more fully take advantage of the technology. In his late twenties, he went to University College London to work on a PhD in cognitive neuroscience, which he was awarded in 2005. That was followed by postdocs at Harvard and MIT and recognition by *Science* magazine that his research into memory and the imagination was one of the top scientific breakthroughs of 2008. When Suleyman and Hassabis happened upon one another at the Vic in 2010, Hassabis was finishing up a research fellowship at the University College London's Gatsby Computational Neuroscience Unit, which Geoff Hinton had cofounded a dozen years earlier to explore the possibilities of neuroscience and AI.

Hassabis had long been fascinated by the idea that the brain offered the most sensible path to a true superintelligence. A couple of decades earlier, a noted British neuroscientist had suggested that those studying the brain break the organ into three components: computational, algorithmic, and implementation. "We should be focusing on the algorithmic level of the brain," Hassabis told Suleyman. That was the middle layer focused on how the brain carries out a computation and then translates that into action.

"Step one, solve intelligence," Hassabis said. "Step two, use it to solve everything else."

Hassabis invited Suleyman to join him at the "lunch and learns" that the Gatsby hosted for neuroscientists wanting to present their work. "Demis would basically smuggle me in the back door so I could just listen to what was going on in the field," Suleyman said. There, Hassabis introduced Suleyman to Shane Legg, another researcher at

Gatsby. "The three of us spent months talking through the possibilities," Suleyman said.

Legg was well-known among AI researchers for speaking openly about artificial general intelligence, or AGI—a superintelligence that could do everything a human brain could do, only better. "If you talked to anybody about general AI, you would be considered at best eccentric, at worst some kind of delusional, nonscientific character," said Legg, who is from New Zealand. Peers were struggling to teach a computer to read a children's book or to reliably distinguish a horse from a cow. Yet to Legg, human-level intelligence was inevitable given the exponential growth in both the power of computers and the data digital devices generated. He publicly stated that he believed there was a fifty-fifty chance AGI would be a reality by 2028.

Hassabis, Legg, and Suleyman founded DeepMind in September 2010. The first line of the pitch deck the trio shared with potential founders expressly stated their goal of achieving AGI. "When we started DeepMind," Legg said, "we got an astonishing amount of eye-rolling at conferences." Hassabis assumed the CEO's role, and Legg gave himself the title of chief scientist. Suleyman took the title of chief product officer, though their three-person startup was a long way away from having anything remotely resembling a product.

The trio raised 350,000 pounds (roughly $540,000 based on the exchange rates at the time) from a group of British angel investors and moved into an attic office in central London, overlooking Russell Square. With its dark wood paneling, tall windows, and ornate moldings, the suite invoked early nineteenth-century Europe. The place was cramped, especially once they started adding people, but the magisterial and historic quarters seemed a perfect match for their outsized ambitions.

Years later, after the two partners had split, Suleyman and Hassabis would be included in any listing of AI's most influential executives. By 2024, the two leading consumer AI labs on the planet were run by one or the other, spurring feature articles about the former partners who became fierce foes. Suleyman, for his part, would describe Hassabis as a friend with whom he occasionally still shared a meal. Hassabis was more dismissive of his longtime collaborator's contributions to the cause. "Most of what he has learned about AI comes from working with me over all these years," Hassabis snidely said of his cofounder.

But in the early 2010s, Suleyman was just another twentysomething suffering from imposter syndrome. In every way, Suleyman felt like the odd man out. The most obvious difference was his lack of a college degree. His two cofounders were doctorates who had been professional students into their thirties. Hassabis, a five-time World Games Champion, was the quintessential bespectacled computer geek. Shane Legg was quieter and preferred to maintain a low profile. By contrast, Suleyman was a vocal liberal activist who lived in a trendy London neighborhood with his artist girlfriend. Back then he went by the nickname "Moose," dressed stylishly, and knew the best nightspots in town.

Yet none of them were strong computer programmers. Hassabis was a neuroscientist who never worked as a software engineer, despite an undergraduate degree in computer science. Legg was a mathematician who worked on the theoretical end of the field. In some sense, all three were winging it in their quest to solve for intelligence.

"What I came to realize after the fact is that I had very different skills that were complementary in our three-way dynamic," Suleyman said.

• • •

SULEYMAN'S FIRST BIG challenge at DeepMind was fundraising. Given their plans, they required a lot more than a few hundred thousand pounds. There were the salaries they needed to pay to lure the best and brightest from across Europe and the world and also the sizable hardware costs. A machine that learned for itself required far more computer power than a rule-based system, which meant DeepMind needed to buy and operate an expensive cluster of machines. The three founders calculated they needed to raise another two million pounds ($3 million) while recognizing the absurdity of their ask.

"AI" was still a taboo term inside the old-line venture capital firms.

To the extent there were people talking about machine learning in the early 2010s, they tended to work on university campuses or for the research arm of a large corporation. There was a reason why large corporations, through efforts such as Bell Labs, Xerox PARC, and Microsoft Research, pursued long-term projects of a decade or more, not startups. In tech, VCs worked on a time horizon of five or ten years, not in the decades required to solve something like artificial general intelligence—the company's explicit goal. So DeepMind would adopt what Hassabis called a "hybrid" approach that melded "academic thinking and startup thinking." Hassabis likened their pursuit of AGI to the Apollo project and its mission to reach the moon. Other times he likened it to the Manhattan Project and the creation of the first atom bombs.

Hoffman's old friend Peter Thiel topped their list of potential funders. He had the deep pockets required and seemed bold enough to fund a long-shot venture. Several years earlier, Thiel had been among the cofounders of the Singularity Summit, an annual gathering dedicated to anticipating and understanding the "singularity," a hypothetical future when man and machine merge and life is irreversibly transformed. Legg was invited to give a talk at that year's summit, and the founders decided all three would fly to San Francisco. "Peter to his credit was the only person in the Valley talking about AGI or even AI in any form," Suleyman said.

That year's summit was held in a hotel in downtown San Francisco. Suleyman, Hassabis, and Legg took turns using the two badges that Legg had been issued. "We thought Peter would be at the conference, but he wasn't," Suleyman said. Thiel, however, was hosting a cocktail party for conferencegoers at the big house he rented near the ocean. "The three of us just kind of barged our way in," Suleyman said. Like Hassabis, Thiel had been a chess prodigy. So rather than leap into a pitch when meeting Thiel, Hassabis offered the theory that the tension between the knight and bishop explained why chess has endured over the centuries. Sufficiently intrigued, Thiel asked the trio to come the next day to his offices at the Founders Fund, the venture firm he and several others had started a half dozen years earlier.

Sitting across from Thiel, the three founders shared ideas they had for commercial uses of AI. Suleyman mentioned an image-search tool that one day might be useful in the fashion industry and made vague claims about applications of AI in the realm of health care. In reality, though, they were pitching a science experiment that one day might even have practical applications. Thiel cracked that he might as well be investing in Somalia, that's how far off the beaten path they were, and Suleyman struggled not to feel slighted. "He saw us as some randoms from London," Suleyman said. Yet Founders Fund put up a large share of the 2 million pounds these randoms were requesting, and much of the rest probably came because of Thiel's endorsement.

"If it wasn't for Peter, I don't think it would happen," Suleyman said. "It wouldn't have happened."

• • •

WITH MONEY IN the bank, DeepMind moved into roomier offices in central London and went on a hiring spree. As hoped, they attracted top people from around the globe, seduced by the chance to work on cutting-edge research, along with the shares in DeepMind that were dangled. They signed up both Geoff Hinton and Yann LeCun as technical advisors, which gave credibility to a group of unknowns working on AI thousands of miles from Silicon Valley.

Among DeepMind's innovations was its pioneering use of what in the AI field is called reinforcement learning. Its models might still train on "labeled data" such as books, articles, and digital repositories like Wikipedia or Reddit, but reinforcement learning allows a model to learn though trial and error. If playing a game, the model would receive feedback based on the points it scored or failed to score, reinforcing successful strategies. The algorithm adjusted accordingly. Similar to humans, the model improved its performance through practice and by learning from mistakes.

Money was a constant worry inside DeepMind—a harbinger for the industry. No matter how much DeepMind raised, it never seemed enough. Not that many months after celebrating the raise with Thiel,

Suleyman was again beating the hustings in search of money. This time he found investors were far more receptive to their pitch. Solina Chau, a prominent Hong Kong businesswoman and the founder of Horizons Ventures, led a 10-million-pound ($15 million) second-round raise that closed around nine months after the first. Skype cofounder Jaan Tallinn was among those investing alongside Chau.

"We got almost no rejects," Suleyman said of their 10-million-pound B round. The exception was Chamath Palihapitiya, an early executive at Facebook. Solina Chau had introduced Suleyman to Palihapitiya, who had recently left Facebook to start his own venture fund, called Social+ Capital Partnership (he later shortened it to Social Capital).

"We had a fancy dinner with him at a fancy hotel in London and then lunch the next day," Suleyman said. "He just didn't get it." But, Suleyman added, who could blame him? "It was pretty wacky," he said.

• • •

STARTUP LIFE IS never easy, even when the money is flowing. "For two or three years, it was very tough," Suleyman said. The turning point was what he called "the cat classification paper." In 2012, two of Geoff Hinton's PhD students at the University of Toronto, along with Hinton himself, entered the ImageNet challenge, an annual photo identification competition created by Fei-Fei Li, who by that point had moved from Princeton to Stanford. Their entry, known as Alex-Net (one of the students was named Alex Krizhevsky), was based on deep learning and trained on a titanic volume of photographs. Asked to identify a cat or any of the other 1,000-plus categories of images presented, their neural net was able to do so far more accurately than other efforts.

"The AlexNet result is what really proved to the world that deep learning had arrived," Stanford's Chris Manning said.

DeepMind again needed money. The challenges confronting DeepMind—near-bottomless demand for compute, the cost of attracting and retaining top-drawer talent—would be those confronting virtually every AI startup in the coming years. Their savior this time was Elon Musk, whom Suleyman met while Musk was visiting London with the actress Talulah Riley during one of their two marriages (the couple were married twice, and divorced twice, between 2010 and 2016). "We went out to dinner, me, Elon, and Talulah, and had a grand old time," Suleyman said. The next day, Musk came to the offices for a sit-down with DeepMind's three founders. In 2013, Musk led a C-round raise that brought DeepMind's total fundraising to 40 million pounds ($60 million).

Still, Musk left Suleyman feeling baffled. "I could never quite grasp whether he actually understood what we were talking about," Suleyman said. He used the term "high variance" to describe Musk: "Sometimes it was nail on the head, and sometimes it was just like, 'That is one of the dumbest things I've heard, and kind of reveals something more fundamental about your lack of understanding about what we're talking about.'" He enjoyed his time with the high-energy, clever Musk but also did not trust him.

"I definitely saw Elon as very competitive and very acquisitive in that he was trying to acquire any knowledge to try and elevate himself in the field," Suleyman said. Yet there was no denying Musk's utility as investor, at least in the short run. Musk talked up DeepMind among people he knew in Silicon Valley, including his then good friend Larry Page, the Google cofounder and CEO. Traveling together on a private plane, Musk showed Page a demo of DeepMind's deep Q-network (DQN), a neural net that had learned to play the videogame *Breakout* through trial and error. The model began as a total noob, to use gamer slang for beginners. The company's engineers did not offer the model any strategy tips for playing but instead just explained that the aim of the game was to score as many points as possible. Within the hour, DQN was a decent player. Within a few hours, it played at a level that no human could match. Page knew he had to meet those behind this breakthrough product.

• • •

YEARS LATER, MEDIA repeated the phrase "AI arms race" to describe the competition for talent that OpenAI sparked with the release of ChatGPT in 2022. Yet this competition among the tech titans had started a decade earlier. And there was no doubt that, early on, Google was well ahead of the competition.

Google began incorporating machine-learning algorithms into its search engine in the mid-2000s. Among its earliest applications was the use of AI to decipher imprecise human queries. By the late 2000s, Google's advertising arm was deploying artificial intelligence to help set prices for its ads. Eventually, they leveraged AI to better target users. "You had some of the finest minds in the world devoted to ringing the cash register more consistently by upping the rate at which people would click on a digital ad," quipped Peter Wagner, a founding partner at Wing Venture Capital, an early investor in AI startups.

Stanford proved fertile ground for Google in its search for AI talent. In 2011, Sebastian Thrun stepped down as the director of the fabled Stanford Artificial Intelligence Lab to join Google. A top roboticist, Thrun helped birth Waymo, Google's self-driving-car project. The company snagged another top Stanford professor when it hired Andrew Ng, an early advocate of deep learning. It was actually Ng, drawn to the vast stores of data Google generated through products like search, Google Maps, and Android, who approached Page to talk about a project he code-named Project Marvin as a satiric nod to Marvin Minsky. Project Marvin became Google Brain, an AI lab created in 2011 to explore the broader possibilities of deep learning. The following year, Google hired Ray Kurzweil, whom many viewed as a kind of tech prophet because of his conviction, which he first wrote about in 1990, that the exponential growth in both compute— computer power—and data made it inevitable that machines would do extraordinary things in the not-so-distant future. In 2005, he had authored *The Singularity Is Near: When Humans Transcend Biology*. Google named Kurzweil its director of engineering, where he focused on machine learning and natural language processing.

The biggest gets early in the race for talent were for the three "God-fathers of AI," as they are often described in media accounts: Geoff

Hinton, Yann LeCun, and Yoshua Bengio. Hiring Hinton meant buying DNNresearch, the company he had created with his two graduate
students after the successful debut of AlexNet. Hinton set up an
auction to sell the company at the end of 2012, and four companies joined
the bidding: Google, Microsoft, Facebook, and Baidu, the top search
firm in China. A term had been coined to describe deals in which
a larger company buys a smaller one primarily to acquire its talent:
an "acquihire." Google landed Hinton and also Alex Krizhevsky and
Ilya Sutskever, the two graduate students behind AlexNet, with a
high bid of $44 million.

Facebook had lost out in the competition for Hinton but landed
LeCun, who would run a newly hatched unit named Facebook AI
Research (FAIR). In 2013, LeCun traveled with Mark Zuckerberg to
an AI conference in Lake Tahoe with the purpose of stocking up on
top AI researchers. One of those who chose not to work for Facebook
recalled an amped-up Zuckerberg, pacing around a large hotel room,
describing AI as "the next big thing" and "the next step for Facebook."
With LeCun's help, Facebook already had a plan in place for using AI
software to identify faces in the photos people posted and translate
their posts into multiple languages. Longer-term, they would enlist
AI agents to serve as hosts inside the Facebook ecosystem or stand as
sentries at its gates. Facebook pinched three AI researchers from Google
to help them build and implement what LeCun had sketched out.

Yoshua Bengio, who had been teaching at the University of Mon-
treal since 1993, was the most reluctant of the three godfathers to
take sides. But he joined Microsoft at the start of 2017, he told *Wired*,
because "we don't want one or two companies, which I will not name,
to be the only big players in town for AI." It was obvious he meant
Google and Facebook. "It's not good for the community," Bengio said.
"It's not good for people in general."

• • •

HASSABIS AND SULEYMAN were wary when they welcomed Larry
Page and others from Google into DeepMind's London headquarters.

Hassabis had said yes when a Google lieutenant said Page wanted to meet him because, he later offered, "it's not the sort of invitation you turn down." Yet heading into the meeting, Hassabis was also suspicious that Google was taking a page from the old Microsoft playbook and feigning an interest in DeepMind to sniff out what they could to advance their own AI work. Right away, though, Page made it clear he was there because he wanted to buy their fifty-person startup.

"Larry was just like, 'You guys should come and be part of us,'" Suleyman said. They weren't contemplating a sale, but Hassabis was feeling frustrated. He figured he had spent maybe 10 percent of his time in the previous three years working on actual research. "I realized that there's maybe not enough time to build a Google-sized company and solve AI," Hassabis said. The three founders were tired of losing people to larger, deeper-pocketed enterprises. The typical DeepMind engineer made around $100,000 a year and hoped the shares they had been granted when joining the company might one day be worth something. Larger companies were able to offer salaries two or three times that amount, along with stock options. Musk and Thiel encouraged DeepMind to remain independent, but the founders calculated that they would need to raise hundreds of millions more in the next three to five years. Selling seemed the right next step if they intended to finish what they had started.

Hassabis, Suleyman, and Legg set conditions on a sale. They insisted that they remain in London. Silicon Valley was noisy with startups and there was always the lure of the Next Big Thing. In London, they could focus on building a world-changing technology without distractions. They also demanded that DeepMind's technology not be used for state surveillance or for military purposes. A final requirement was that Google establish an independent ethics and safety board that monitored its development of AGI. Google said yes to all three and negotiations over a price began.

Zuckerberg had also seen the *Breakout* demo. He made a counteroffer that would have translated into significantly more money for each founder. Yet Hassabis and Suleyman didn't see the same cultural connection with Facebook. They tried to be deliberate and thoughtful in their approach to artificial intelligence, but Facebook's motto, "Move fast and break things," suggested a very different attitude toward cutting-edge technologies. At DeepMind, they viewed themselves as principled guardians of the public interest, working to help fix the planet. "Guided by safety and ethics," DeepMind declared on its website, "this invention could help society find answers to some of the world's most pressing and fundamental scientific challenges."

"Zuck refused to give us an ethics and safety board, and that was a priority for us," Suleyman said. "It was really important to us we establish a field where the words 'ethics' and 'AI' were irrevocably attached."

At the start of 2014, Google purchased DeepMind for $650 million. Suleyman the idealist was suddenly a very wealthy man. Theoretically, at least, DeepMind's founders and its people would be able to focus solely on its mission as stated on the company website: to "solve intelligence." Suleyman took on the title of Head of Applied AI. It would be his unenviable job to find practical, preferably moneymaking uses for the technology they were developing.

• • •

AROUND ONE YEAR after DeepMind's sale to Google, Hassabis asked Suleyman to join him for an upcoming lunch. Reid Hoffman of LinkedIn fame would be in town.

By that point, Suleyman had endured his share of meetings with Silicon Valley moguls. The socially awkward, taciturn Page could barely make eye contact. He sometimes sounded more robotic than human. The self-satisfied, self-aggrandizing Musk believed enough in the audacity of their vision to write them a large check, but he had also become one of AI's highest-profile critics. "We are summoning the demon," Musk said of AI in the fall of 2014. He described the technology as "potentially more dangerous than nukes." Musk had invested in DeepMind, he publicly stated, not so much because he thought it would turn a profit but "to keep an eye on what's going on with artificial intelligence."

At least Suleyman had enjoyed his time with Musk. He couldn't say the same of Peter Thiel. Suleyman, who regularly visited Silicon Valley, figured he met with Thiel somewhere around ten times during the early years of DeepMind. He appreciated Thiel's support and interest in the company, but he never managed to coax so much as a smile out of him.

"I thought he was unnecessarily terse and I found him overly cynical," Suleyman said. "Everything just seemed so dark to him. I found that a bit sad, really."

By that point, Suleyman knew enough about the Valley to know that Hoffman had worked with both Thiel and Musk at PayPal and that the three were friends. He understood that Hoffman was a prominent venture capitalist, but they were no longer raising funds. Reluctantly, Suleyman agreed to a meeting.

CHAPTER 5

Smart Friends

R eid Hoffman read what he could about artificial intelligence after
his 2015 dinner with Elon Musk. That included a book making
the rounds at the time called *Superintelligence.* Written by Oxford
philosophy professor Nick Bostrom, the book laid out the possibility
of a godlike superintelligence and the perils if not properly controlled.
Yet Hoffman's way was more tactile. The kid with no friends had become, in his forties, just about the most popular, well-liked person
in Silicon Valley. He would rely on friends, and friends of friends of
friends, to smarten up about a technology that some of the industry's
biggest players already were exploring.

James Manyika was one of the first people Hoffman contacted to
learn more about AI. Manyika, a tall, elegant man a few years older than
Hoffman, had been thinking about machine learning since his undergraduate days at the University of Zimbabwe. He had taught in Oxford's engineering department until leaving to join McKinsey, the giant
consulting firm. By the time Hoffman started his self-guided course
in AI, Manyika was director of the firm's research arm, the McKinsey
Global Institute, and vice chair of the White House Global Development Council, which President Barack Obama created in 2012.

Manyika lived in Silicon Valley not far from Hoffman. The two were
regular dinner companions who, with their wives and other couples,
took what Manyika characterized as "adventure trips" to, among other

locales, Greenland, Antarctica, and the South Pole. But their first serious conversation about AI took place a thousand miles north of the Bay Area in Vancouver, British Columbia, while both were there to attend a TED conference. "A little walk with James to talk AI"—that's how Hoffman described their encounter. Manyika, though, recalled a marathon session that left him feeling wiped out. "We spent literally four hours talking about AI and machine learning," he said.

Initially, Hoffman figured AI would be the province of large companies because only deep-pocketed giants would have the vast sums needed to hire the talent and maintain the resource-heavy computer systems required to train these large models meant to emulate human learning. "So I made it my business to talk to the head of every AI lab at every major company," Hoffman said. He met with top people at Google and Yann LeCun, Facebook's chief AI scientist. Recognizing the central role academics played in the advancement of AI, he also met with faculty members, including Stanford's Fei-Fei Li, whom *Wired* in 2018 would describe as "one of a tiny group of scientists—a group perhaps small enough to fit around a kitchen table—who are responsible for AI's recent remarkable advances."

Sometimes those involved in AI found him. In summer 2015, a group of AI researchers and startup veterans met in a private dining room at the Rosewood Hotel on Sand Hill Road. They were there at the behest of Sam Altman, the thirty-year-old president of Y Combinator, the startup accelerator that had helped launch Airbnb, Stripe, Instacart, and Dropbox, among a long list of other successful companies. Google was throwing around its weight within the AI world, hoovering up talent. So too was Facebook. Baidu had recently snagged Andrew Ng from Google, jump-starting its AI efforts, and Twitter had made headlines with the acquisition of two deep-learning startups. The primary impetus for the gathering, Altman later said, was Google's purchase of DeepMind and its stated intent of creating artificial general intelligence. The question for the table was whether it was possible to develop a competing lab—a countervailing force driven by altruistic goals rather than corporate interests, dedicated to advancing AI without the distorting influence of a profit motive.

"The opposite of Google would be an open-source nonprofit because Google is closed-source for-profit," offered Elon Musk, who was among the small group of around ten who joined Altman at the Rosewood. "And that profit motivation can be potentially dangerous." Musk was not yet the world's richest person—he would not attain that status until 2021—but he was still wealthy and bold enough to act as if he were a one-man Sand Hill venture firm. On the spot, Musk pledged $100 million to the cause and committed to helping the group raise a total of $1 billion. Among the first people Musk called was Hoffman, who met with Musk and Altman at an Italian restaurant in San Jose. "I agreed that we needed to do something that's pro humanity and not just a commercial effort," Hoffman said. "I thought it was a great idea." Hoffman wrote a $10 million check with a single precondition: "A promise from Elon that he would stop using the phrase 'robo-apocalypse.'" More contributions followed, including from Peter Thiel and AI pioneer Yoshua Bengio. Musk and Altman served as cochairs of a nonprofit they dubbed OpenAI.

OpenAI announced itself to the world with a manifesto it posted online in December 2015. "Unconstrained by a need to generate financial return," the post read, the company could be responsible stewards, exploring the potential of deep learning with both eyes locked on AI safety. "Our goal is to advance digital intelligence in the way that is most likely to benefit humanity as a whole," the manifesto said. Finding the talent they needed fell largely on Altman, who likened the effort to the opening of a caper movie, "where you're trying to establish this ragtag crew of slight misfits to do something crazy." OpenAI's other founders included Ilya Sutskever, a Russian-born engineer who attained superstar status inside the machine-learning field as cocreator of AlexNet, and Greg Brockman, who had recently stepped down as the chief technology officer at Stripe, the online payments company. Sutskever agreed to leave Google Brain to serve as OpenAI's director of research. Brockman took the title of CTO. His apartment in San Francisco's Mission District served as the company's first headquarters. Like DeepMind, OpenAI would also be unapologetic in its pursuit of AGI, even as many in the field dismissed it as science fiction.

Pieter Abbeel, a Berkeley professor and an advisor to OpenAI, was among the regular visitors to Brockman's apartment when they were mapping out the future. The dream that had gotten Abbeel, the codirector of the Berkeley Artificial Intelligence Research lab, into the field—the dream "too crazy to talk about"—seemed within reach. "[I'm] not saying that in that moment I was thinking, 'Hmm, we can do this tomorrow,' but it seemed a reasonable goal to start pursuing," Abbeel said.

• • •

DEMIS HASSABIS WAS among those Hoffman met on his AI listening tour. Hoffman was going to be in London anyway for work and, though he didn't know Hassabis, he was pleased that he was open to a meeting. The two had what Hoffman described as "a good first conversation about what was going on in the field and what DeepMind was up to." It was on a second visit to London around six months later that Hoffman first met Suleyman. The three sat down for lunch at a pub called the Masons Arms near Hoffman's hotel in central London.

Suleyman remembers a disheveled Hoffman greeting them with an eager smile. "He felt like the kind of person I would run into at Oxford, in the philosophy department, where what mattered were the ideas rather than the presentation," he said. Suleyman recalled Hoffman's delight over a menu item called "toad in the hole," a traditional pub dish featuring sausages peeking out of a custardy batter. Hoffman of course ordered that, along with a pint of beer. "That's something I almost never do," he said of the pint he drank that afternoon, "but I was trying to be culturally matched to the circumstances."

There was plenty of industry news for them to discuss. Google had just introduced TensorFlow, an open-source machine learning library that made it easier for developers to build and deploy a neural net and employ other deep-learning models. People were also buzzing about Facebook deploying AI on its platform: to better target ads based on user histories and to sift through pictures in search of those that violated company policy. Hassabis and Suleyman also shared some of

what DeepMind was working on. Suleyman, for instance, told Hoffman about an initiative he was heading up that used mammogram
images to train AI to detect breast cancer.

What stuck most with Suleyman about that first meeting was a
discussion they had about culture. Hoffman laid out his view that science fiction as presented in books and movies both defines our view of
artificial intelligence and limits it. The dark, often apocalyptic glimpses
into the future offered by most sci-fi books left people feeling frightened of the future. Visual media was worse. Robots hunted us down in
Hollywood movies and television shows; they enslaved us or wiped us
out. HAL-9000 kills off the crew members in *2001: A Space Odyssey* by
cutting off their life-support systems and refusing to open the pod-bay
doors. Skynet becomes self-aware in *The Terminator* and initiates a nuclear war to eradicate humans. *Battlestar Galactica* depicts humanity's
struggle for survival against machines that evolved and turned against
their creators. If the pretend worlds that Hollywood creates leave such
a deep imprint, Hoffman wondered, then maybe they needed to write
more inspiring tales themselves or fund such efforts. That led to a free-
ranging discussion of AI's potential and its pitfalls.

"I didn't expect a white-guy billionaire to be thoughtful and caring
of the people who were affected by technologies," Suleyman recalled.

• • •

BY THAT POINT, Hoffman didn't need more convincing. "I was thinking I was looking at the beginning of the wave, or maybe a seismic
event out at sea," he said. It was probably too early to invest in any
startups. "But I was like, 'Okay, there's going to be a tsunami here and
we should start getting ready.'"

Hoffman had been too late to AI for a January 2015 gathering
of AI researchers in Puerto Rico, which was sponsored by the newly
formed Future of Life Institute. Years earlier, geneticists and others
had assembled at the Asilomar conference center near Big Sur in California to discuss the ethics of gene-splicing and genetic engineering.
The Future of Life initiative sought to spark a similar conversation

around AI. Elon Musk, Mustafa Suleyman, Demis Hassabis, and James Manyika were among the hundreds of academics and industry figures signing an open letter that proclaimed, "Because of the great potential of AI, it is important to research how to reap its benefits while avoiding potential pitfalls."

Two years later, when the clan gathered again for the Future of Life's "Beneficial AI 2017" conference at Asilomar, Hoffman was among those invited to attend. Key trailblazers such as Yoshua Bengio, Yann LaCun, and Ray Kurzweil were among those giving keynote speeches. Demis Hassabis and Shane Legg both gave talks, as did Sam Altman and Oxford's Nick Bostrom, author of *Superintelligence*.

Hoffman was new to their group and not a computer scientist. But he was also Reid Hoffman, the LinkedIn founder and an investor in OpenAI. Both Hoffman and Eric Schmidt, the former Google CEO, were granted a spot onstage in a panel anticipating the potential societal impacts if and when machines take over a greater share of human functions.

Inside Greylock, Hoffman's partners did not know what to make of Hoffman's sudden interest in AI. "He tells us he's invested in this OpenAI thing and we're all like, 'Okay, whatever, good luck with that,'" David Sze said. He and others at the firm saw that as philanthropic Reid contributing to the cause rather than a wise investor spotting a billion-dollar opportunity before others.

• • •

FROM THE OUTSIDE, the venture racket can seem like easy money. The next Mark Zuckerberg makes his or her pitch, the firm forks over a few million dollars in an exchange for an ownership stake, and some years later, the company goes public or a larger entity buys it for a lot of money and everyone grows rich. Those who ply the trade know differently. Venture is a "brutal business," Sze said. Hoffman described it as "humbling." Some VCs suffer from what members of the tribe call "happy ears." That's when virtually every company sounds like a possible winner. Worse is when VCs only see the problems a startup faces and not its potential, and they talk themselves out of an investment. Sze passed on Twitter and also Baidu, a Chinese-based company eventually worth tens of billions of dollars.

In twenty-plus years as a venture capitalist, Sze led roughly thirty investments, including Facebook, LinkedIn, Pandora, Roblox, Nextdoor, and Discord. "Three of them really matter," Sze said. "Six were okay. And the rest were either disasters or maybe we got our money back. And I've had a very good venture capital career." Hoffman drew a comparison to investing in the stock market. Typically, publicly traded companies have long track records, yet predicting whether a share price will go up or down is still hard. "Picking winners when a company is little more than a few hundred lines of code is orders of magnitude more difficult," Hoffman said. Hoffman also passed on Twitter, as well as YouTube. In 2012, a junior VC at Greylock named Josh Elman, who had worked with Hoffman at LinkedIn, recommended that his partners consider an investment in a recently minted startup called Snapchat. The partners passed, a decision that cost the firm a couple of billion dollars in lost winnings.

Venture capitalists generally invest other people's money, not their own. University endowments, large charitable foundations, and pension funds apportion small slices of their overall holdings to venture in hopes they can boost returns. So too do rich individuals and other professional managers who oversee multibillion-dollar pools of money. The typical venture fund charges "2 and 20"—a 2 percent management fee based on the capital that is managed plus 20 percent of any profits the firm makes on the money the partners invest. Because they can, some of the top venture firms on Sand Hill charge a 2.5 percent management fee and take a 25 or 30 percent share. Greylock's "limited partners," as a VC's investors are called, pay a far more modest management fee but give up 30 percent of their profits. That means for every $100 million in profits one of its investments generates, Hoffman and his partners pocket $30 million before distributing the rest among its investors.

Mondays are sacrosanct at Greylock, as they are inside most firms on Sand Hill. That's the day partners gather to consider possible future investments and other firm business. "The debate can get pretty vigorous," said Joseph Ansanelli, who joined the partnership in 2011. That's by design, Sze said. "We are looking for outliers and extremes," he explained. "So we try to heighten the conflict."

Ansanelli described Hoffman as always collegial during their debates, even when things got heated. "Reid was always one of the biggest dreamers who made sure we didn't lose sight of how big something could be if things ended up going right," Ansanelli said. Josh Elman, who was elevated to partner shortly after he recommended Snapchat, described Greylock as an "advocacy-style partnership." Hoffman's partners did not think much of Airbnb when he first pitched it to the group. They went around the table, asking hard questions and voicing their doubts. Ultimately, though, the firm wrote a big check as part of Airbnb's $7.2 million Series A raise.

"We push each other to make good decisions," said Elman, who left the firm in 2018. "But we trust that each person is running their own book and we'll support that."

Hoffman continued talking about AI during their regular Monday meetings. He told them about his visits to London and the interesting things the DeepMind founders were up to, and shared news of breakthroughs in computer vision, speech recognition, and the like. But Sze admitted that he was dubious, as were other partners. They had seen this movie before. "We'd be like, 'Sounds interesting, let us know when this might mean a business,'" he said.

Greylock made its first AI investment in mid-2017—long before most other venture firms—when Hoffman found Nauto, a Palo Alto–based startup using machine learning and sensors to improve driver safety. Funded by BMW, General Motors, and Toyota, among others, Nauto was working on tools that detect and prevent distracted driving. Greylock and the three car companies participated in a $157 million B round. Seven months later, Hoffman led a $90 million A round in Aurora, another vehicle-related AI investment. Founded by pioneers of autonomous vehicles at Google, Tesla, and Uber, Aurora was using machine learning to operate a range of vehicle types, including long-haul trucks and ride-hailing cars. Greylock's wager was that this all-star team could capitalize quickly enough on the technology to make the investment pay off.

"The question is always around the timing," said Wing Venture's Peter Wagner. Wagner and his partners had been actively investing in AI even before Greylock. "You want to be earlier than the herd but not so early that your company's gone out of business three times before it becomes relevant."

• • •

IN 2018, REID Hoffman received a panicky call from Sam Altman. Things were not going well inside OpenAI. "We knew what we wanted to do," Altman said. "We knew why we wanted to do it. But we had no idea how." Its people tried applying AI to videogames, as DeepMind had already done, and devoted too much time experimenting with a robotic hand they had built that could unscramble a Rubik's Cube. They were floundering. But the real problem was Musk. "Elon's not happy," Altman told Hoffman.

The race to build the first powerful AI model had always been personal for Musk. In the summer of 2015, he and Larry Page had gotten into a bitter argument about AI. Where Page saw artificial intelligence as an accelerant that could elevate humanity, Musk argued the technology was more likely to lead to our doom. Reportedly, the two stopped speaking because of it. A few weeks later, Musk met with Altman and the others at the Rosewood Hotel, where the idea for OpenAI was hatched. Yet despite OpenAI's efforts, Google remained the undisputed leader in artificial intelligence. In 2016, a DeepMind model called AlphaGo had wowed the world by beating an eighteen-time world champion at Go, an ancient game that is considered more complex than chess and more heavily based on human intuition. That same year, DeepMind released WaveNet, a neural network that learned to emulate human speech. Musk complained in emails to Altman that they had fallen hopelessly behind Google. The large slug of money Musk was scheduled to deposit in their bank account was in doubt.

Musk's solution, as invariably it is, had him taking over the effort.

He proposed that he either take a majority stake in OpenAI and operate the company alongside his other companies, including Tesla and SpaceX, or he would fold the startup inside Tesla, which was already working on self-driving cars. Three years into their effort, he was ready to scrap the idea of OpenAI as an independent lab.

Altman had no desire to work for Musk, a famously mercurial boss. He imagined that most of the people he recruited to OpenAI wouldn't either. Altman rejected the offer. Musk walked away from the company, leaving Altman to worry about covering salaries and other expenses.

"Elon is cutting off his support," Altman told Hoffman. "What do we do?" Hoffman committed to investing another $10 million in OpenAI and promised to do what he could to help them raise more. Within the year, Altman, then thirty-three years old, stepped down as president of Y Combinator and took over as OpenAI's CEO. Hoffman was added to the OpenAI's board of directors, and Greg Brockman, whose San Francisco apartment had served as OpenAI's first office, assumed the role of board chairman. Publicly, Musk said he severed ties with OpenAI because of a conflict of interest with Tesla. Privately, he declared that the company had no chance at success.

Money continued to be an issue for OpenAI, despite Hoffman's largesse. It was no wonder. When I first started writing about tech in the 1990s, the cost of building a company was prohibitive. A dot-com needed to hire hordes of programmers to build its site and invest in expensive equipment to host it. Yet by the time I left the Silicon Valley beat in the mid-2000s, the economics of the startup ecosystem had been transformed. The globalization of tech talent allowed startups to tap into an international pool of skilled technologists. Programmers in India or Eastern Europe could be enlisted at a fraction of the cost of U.S.-based teams. And cloud computing eliminated the need to buy their own expensive hardware. By renting computer power as they needed it, a young company could scale its infrastructure costs in line with its growth. The barrier to entry for a startup had been lowered to the point that a few people with a laptop could challenge a giant.

AI flipped that equation back to the old days. Google was trying to hoard as much AI talent as it could. So was Facebook. As a result, top researchers in the field were commanding a salary of $1 million or more. OpenAI, for instance, had dangled $1.9 million a year plus stock to lure Ilya Sutskever from Google. The annual pay for anyone with any AI experience was reaching into the many hundreds of thousands. The labor costs for any AI startup would be enormous. Plenty of money had gone up in flames in previous tech booms. But the cost of building AI systems shocked old-timers.

Even greater was the cost of "compute"—the computer power companies needed to train and run their models. AI startups could still rely on the cloud, but training large neural nets can require weeks if not months of nonstop computer time. And it seemed foreordained that those costs would continue to soar for the foreseeable future. Around the time of Musk's ultimatum, OpenAI had made a breakthrough that would require even more computer power. In 2017, a group of researchers inside Google published what colloquially became known as the "Transformer" paper. Until that point, OpenAI had been experimenting with large language models (LLMs) that learn to chat conversationally by digesting Reddit posts, Amazon reviews, and other publicly available data sets. The Transformer paper offered an entirely new model for teaching a neural net both to better deduce a human's meaning and to respond in a more natural-sounding way. The authors suggested that AI mimic our own brains and weigh words based on their importance. Rather than analyzing individual words, OpenAI's large language model, or LLM, would evaluate chunks of words and use context to come up with the next word, as a human would do.

Using Transformer architecture to power its large language models, an OpenAI computer scientist told *Wired*, "I made more progress in two weeks than I did over the past two years." The Transformer model proved a better way to train an LLM, but it also meant creating vast, expensive-to-run models. "The amount of money we needed to be successful in the mission is much more gigantic than I originally thought," Altman said in a 2019 interview.

Altman's solution was to create a for-profit subsidiary that was answerable to its nonprofit board. OpenAI would seek new investors but make clear that theirs was not the typical startup. Stamped across the top of the funding agreement any investor would sign was a warning: "the principles advanced in the OpenAI Inc Charter take precedence over any obligation to generate a profit." The new entity would be what OpenAI described as a "capped profit" company, though only a venture capitalist could consider the conditions that were imposed a cap. Anyone investing in this first commercial round could make no more than 100 times their original investment.

The company explained the change in a short post on its website in 2019. "The most dramatic AI systems use the most computational power," it read. "We'll need to invest billions of dollars in upcoming years into large-scale cloud compute, attracting and retaining talented people, and building AI supercomputers."

Again, Hoffman proved pivotal. At Altman's behest, he led this first commercial round by writing another big check to OpenAI. "Sam said it'd be really helpful if I took the lead because they didn't have a business plan, or a product plan, or any of those things that an investor typically likes to see before putting money into a business," he said. "It really was a bet on them being able to do something magical with AI."

• • •

SHORTLY BEFORE LINKEDIN was slated to go public, in 2011, Hoffman had heard from Microsoft's Steve Ballmer. Sell to us, Ballmer told him, and save yourself the trouble of an IPO. The offer came with a bid far above the $4 billion to $5 billion value the bankers taking them public had assigned the company. Yet what struck Hoffman, who was still LinkedIn's board chair, was that Ballmer offered no well-thought-out thesis for owning LinkedIn. Hoffman had the impression that the idea had popped into his head, he asked a few of his advisors what they thought, and now he was on the phone. Hoffman told Ballmer no, and LinkedIn went public as scheduled. The company, which by that point had over 400 million members globally, saw a first-day pop of 84 percent in its share price and a market cap up around $8 billion. Within a couple of years, LinkedIn would be worth $20 billion—far more than Ballmer or anyone else was offering for his company.

An executive inside Microsoft named Satya Nadella replaced Ballmer as the company's CEO in 2014. Shortly after moving into the top spot, he too reached out to Hoffman. But that was to start a conversation, not a hasty acquisition attempt sweetened with a large financial offer. "With Satya, it was always where are we going to be ten years from now and what are the businesses that will get us there," Hoffman said. Eventually, Nadella floated the idea of an acquisition, and Hoffman said he was open to talking further. Lubricating their discussions no doubt was the precipitous decline in LinkedIn's stock price. Hoffman heard from several suitors looking to pick up LinkedIn on the cheap, but Microsoft was dangling a 50 percent premium on LinkedIn's stock price, outbidding all other rivals. In 2016, Microsoft announced it had bought LinkedIn for $26.2 billion in cash—by far its largest acquisition. The deal netted Hoffman a windfall of roughly $3.7 billion. In March 2017, Hoffman was invited to join Microsoft's board of directors, a position he has held ever since.

Big-money tech acquisitions often disappoint. Key people leave. Technologies don't mesh, cultures clash. Often targets are overvalued by CEOs more covetous than strategic. That wasn't LinkedIn, which generated more than $15 billion in revenue for Microsoft in 2023.

Yet much of the value in the LinkedIn acquisition seemed to be Hoffman himself. He pushed artificial intelligence inside Microsoft the same way he was pushing it among his partners on Sand Hill. He brought up AI during regular Microsoft board meetings and in one-on-one sessions with Nadella, who was already thinking about its potential to transform the industry. "AI was a regular topic of conversation with Satya," Hoffman said. Eventually the two worked it out so Hoffman gave an extra day to Microsoft before or after every board meeting. "I leave it up to them about who I meet with," Hoffman said.

OpenAI naturally came up during Hoffman's conversations with Nadella. OpenAI had gained some attention within tech circles with its release in 2018 of a text-generating algorithm it called a "Generative Pre-trained Transformer" as a nod to the Google Transformer paper that had proven so key to their success. GPT-1, as it was called, was trained on a hodgepodge of sources: thousands of unpublished books, including romance novels; questions lifted from middle school and high school tests; and content on Quora, the question-and-answer site. GPT-1 showed glimmers of what was to come. Most significantly, said Stanford's Chris Manning, was its ability to understand and respond to a query written in plain English. Where previous models could accomplish a single task (analyze for sentiment, say, or summarize a document), GPT-1 was what Manning called an "all-in-one version." The following year, OpenAI released GPT-2. Sometimes it spewed gibberish. GPT-2 was repetitive and quickly veered into the absurd. But Manning was impressed.

"GPT-2 marked the first time that a model could generate multiple paragraphs of text that was an approximation of something a human could have written," he said. "But not only was GPT-2 sort of grammatically correct, the word choices weren't weird, and the way it connected events and people and things seemed reasonable."

Hoffman was hopelessly conflicted as a board member at both Microsoft and OpenAI, and an investor in the latter. He needed to be circumspect whenever he spoke about what was going on inside each company. But he felt comfortable playing matchmaker between Altman and Nadella and other executives at both companies. And as the two sides began talking about the possibilities of a partnership, Hoffman allowed himself to serve as a sounding board while steering clear of deal terms given his financial stake in OpenAI. "I talked through with Satya why it was worth it to take OpenAI seriously and also what to think about and watch out for," Hoffman said. He had similar conversations with Altman. He laid out the advantages of working with a large outfit like Microsoft and also potential perils.

In 2019, Microsoft announced it was investing $1 billion in OpenAI. One year later, Hoffman was among those given a first peek at GPT-3. GPT-3 could process 175 billion parameters, or statistical connections—more than 100 times that of GPT-2. The model was trained on roughly 300 billion words of text. Manning described GPT-3 as more creative and intuitive than its predecessors, and able to sense even sarcasm—a notoriously difficult task for many humans, let alone a machine.

"That's when I went all in on AI," Hoffman said.

CHAPTER 6

Hit Refresh

Satya Nadella knows the cliché in the tech industry about émigrés from India. "Unlike the stereotype, I was actually not academically that great," Nadella wrote in *Hit Refresh*, the autobiography he published a few years after he took over as Microsoft CEO. As a kid, he cared about the sport of cricket and little else. He applied to the elite Indian Institute of Technology, the launching pad for so many middle- and lower-class kids across India—but flunked the entrance exam. His dream for himself as a teenager had him attending a small college, playing for the local cricket team, and eventually finding a job with a bank. "Being an engineer and going to the West never occurred to me," he said.

Nadella was fifteen in 1982, when his father bought him a home computer kit. He remained true to his beloved cricket, but he soon had a second love in programming. After earning an undergraduate degree in electrical engineering at a technology institute, Nadella on a lark applied to a few graduate programs in the U.S. and was shocked when the University of Wisconsin at Milwaukee invited him to its campus to pursue a master's in electrical engineering. He confessed to feeling something like disappointment when the U.S. granted him a student visa. "I was hoping it would be rejected," he said. "I never wanted to leave India." On his twenty-first birthday, he flew to the U.S., where he began his new life.

Nadella was a couple of years out of graduate school and working as a software engineer at Sun Microsystems when a recruiter from Microsoft reached out to him. In 1992, with the world on the cusp of its next big tech boom, Nadella joined the hordes of programmers Microsoft was hiring to launch its assault on the business software market. Later, Nadella confessed that he had been dubious about Microsoft's chances against software makers that specialized in high-end systems for large enterprises. Instead he hit the lottery, arriving in Redmond as Microsoft's stock was beginning an epic rise. The company's stock would double, and then double again, and then double several more times during the decade.

"I couldn't have timed my entrance any better," Nadella said.

• • •

STEVE BALLMER DID some things right as Microsoft's CEO. He deserved credit for Xbox, which got Microsoft into the lucrative gaming console business and diversified its offering beyond software and operating systems. The company invested somewhere around $9 billion on R&D for Azure, its cloud hosting product—an investment that paid off richly for the company, especially with the rising popularity of AI. Ballmer's greatest talent was his ability to squeeze more each year from Microsoft's core franchises, Windows and Office. Microsoft's revenues tripled in Ballmer's thirteen-plus years as CEO.

Yet there's a difference between a skilled chief operating officer and a great CEO. Ballmer was a little over a decade into his tenure when, in 2011, *Fortune* enlisted me to write a story about what was ailing Microsoft. The answer wasn't particularly elusive. So fixated was Ballmer on expanding Windows' footprint that he smothered innovation inside the company. I wrote the article through the perspective of Microsoft veterans who had left the company because projects they had been toiling away on were hampered or killed on Ballmer's watch, at least in part because of his insistence that they remain in the Windows ecosystem. One had been working on an MP3 player before the iPod. Another was part of a team that had created a tablet before the release of the iPad.

A third worked on a book reader that could have been the Kindle, but that too died a slow and painful death because of Ballmer's fealty to Windows. Despite the billions in profits Microsoft booked each year, the company's share price remained flat through most of Ballmer's tenure as CEO.

Harvard Business School professor Clayton Christensen dubbed this tendency of an incumbent to favor its big moneymakers at the expense of disruptive new products that bubble up as the "innovator's dilemma." IBM had been an early pioneer of the personal computer. By all rights, the company should have continued to dominate the tech industry. But the rapid spread of the PC in the 1980s threatened its high-margin mainframe business, and resistance inside the company to fully embrace the PC rendered IBM an also-ran. Microsoft replaced IBM in the top spot and fell prey to the same syndrome. Under Ballmer, Microsoft had become IBM: a large corporation that still made a lot of money but was no longer a central player pointing the way to the future.

Nothing seemed to underscore Microsoft's has-been status more than its futile attempts in search. People in Silicon Valley had witnessed what Microsoft did to Netscape and wondered if Google was next. But the fearsome, brutish Microsoft of the 1990s was dead. In its place was a weaker, chastened giant operating under federal oversight. Initially, Microsoft didn't even counter with a search product of its own but licensed search technology from other companies so that MSN, its online service, included a search bar. When in 2004, six or seven years after Google first went live, Microsoft finally unveiled a homegrown product it called MSN Search, the announcement hit with a thud. Rather than giving people a reason to try something new, Microsoft released a Google carbon copy not as good as the original. Microsoft tried a rebrand, renaming its product Live Search. But whatever it called its creation, and despite the billions the company devoted to the cause, it remained a distant third behind Google, which owned around half the search market by the mid-2000s, and Yahoo.

Ballmer told Nadella to think hard before saying yes when he asked him to oversee the engineering team behind a refresh on search.

"Because if you fall, there is no parachute," Ballmer warned him. They would call this latest effort Bing, to invoke the "bing" of discovery. Helped along by a $250 million marketing campaign, Bing wasn't the kind of disaster that would end a career. But that's because search was "the most profitable business model on earth," said Nadella, who had earned his MBA as a part-time student at the University of Chicago Booth School of Business. Matching keywords with ads was so lucrative that increasing market share by just a few percentage points translated into hundreds of millions of dollars in extra advertising dollars each year. But a few percentage points of market share were all that Bing picked up. An internal audit found that two years after its release, far fewer than half of Microsoft's own employees had set Bing as their default search engine on their work computers.

Nadella took over Microsoft's fledgling cloud computing division at the start of 2011. It was there, at this final posting before being put in charge of the whole company, that he earned his bones. With each passing year, cloud services generated an ever-more-significant share of the company's revenue. Under Nadella, the division became Microsoft's fastest growing.

Ballmer, near the end of his tenure, threw a Hail Mary pass, as invariably CEOs do when their company is struggling. Management guru Jim Collins laid out the pattern in *How the Mighty Fall*, his book about the decline of once-great companies. His examples included Zenith, Motorola, Circuit City, and Hewlett-Packard, but he might as well have been writing about Microsoft in the 2000s and 2010s. As Collins described it, the hubris of the early years leads to denial, which is inevitably followed by a search for quick fixes, or what Collins dubbed "grasping for salvation." In 2013, Ballmer floated the idea of buying Nokia, the Finnish mobile phone maker. Microsoft had missed the transition to mobile under Ballmer, who of course had insisted that the company shoehorn a shrunk-down version of Windows onto the phone. Despite years of trying, the Windows phone never caught on. Nokia, which sold Windows-based phones, had once reigned as the world's largest phone maker, but the company had fallen out of the top three by the time Ballmer came knocking on its door. When Ballmer raised the idea of buying Nokia among his executive leadership team, Nadella was among those arguing against the deal. There were Android phones and iPhones, and he did not understand why anyone would want a third option "unless we changed the rules," Nadella said. Yet Ballmer believed that owning a giant hardware maker like Nokia would be the boost that the Windows phones needed to compete. In fall of 2013, Microsoft announced it was buying Nokia for $7.2 billion. Less than six months later, Ballmer retired as CEO and the Microsoft board chose Nadella to take his place.

Nadella faced a set of challenges far more fundamental than Ballmer had fourteen years earlier. The PC had given rise to Microsoft, but PC sales peaked in the early 2010s. Increasingly, people were using their phones to spend time online, yet mobile had largely passed Microsoft by.

Software as a service was another threat to a company that CNBC described as "mired in mediocrity." Microsoft was in the business of selling software packages that users installed on their machines, but the move to the cloud meant companies could rent software by the month and save themselves the expense and hassle of running a giant IT center. Windows was installed on over 1 billion devices worldwide. Hundreds of millions of people used its Office suite of products. But whether Microsoft would ever regain its crown as a tech trailblazer remained in doubt.

• • •

NADELLA PRACTICALLY BURNED sage in his effort to give Microsoft a spiritual cleanse. He knew firsthand the frustrations of trying to get anything done in a company balkanized into business units and stymied by turf wars. Bureaucracy was killing innovation. "The company was sick," Nadella said. "Employees were tired. They were frustrated." Shortly after taking the helm, he told employees that renewing Microsoft's once-vaunted culture was his highest priority.

At companywide meetings, Ballmer had jumped and screamed while beseeching employees to stand and scream with him. Nadella, in contrast, hired a psychologist to work with his executive team. He described the moment in *Hit Refresh*, a book about his "quest to rediscover Microsoft's soul," as it says on its front cover. "I opened the meeting by asking everyone to suspend judgment and try to stay in the moment," Nadella said. For once they would not be talking about that week's performance metrics but instead be going through trust exercises.

"I realized that in all of my years at Microsoft, this was the first time I'd heard colleagues talk about themselves," Nadella wrote. The old Microsoft was Bill Gates, who famously told people, "That's the stupidest thing I've ever heard," though often the word "stupidest" or "dumbest" was followed by a sharp expletive. Nadella, by contrast, spoke about the fears that were holding people back. Employees, he said, had a fear "of being ridiculed; of failing; of not looking like the smartest person in the room." The soft-spoken Nadella said he wanted to transform Microsoft from a company of "know-it-alls to learn-it-alls." His Microsoft would be a more grown-up version of the company.

"My approach is to lead with a sense of purpose and pride in what we do, not envy or combativeness," he said. In the preface to Nadella's book, Gates described him as "humble," a term presumably he would not use to describe Ballmer or himself.

The year after Nadella took over as CEO, he announced he was shutting down the company's Nokia phone unit. The company wrote off more than $8 billion in losses on its ill-conceived acquisition and laid off 7,800 employees. Under Nadella, the company became less religious about Windows. Nadella described hearing gasps when he pulled an iPhone from his suit jacket at a developer's conference not long after taking over as CEO. But by holding up a product from Apple, Microsoft's longest-standing competitor, he communicated his wishes that Office and other Microsoft products operate smoothly on all devices. In 2001, Ballmer had described Linux, an open-source operating system viewed as a threat to Windows, as a "cancer." Under Nadella, Microsoft began relying on open-source software to run its data center. "Hell must have frozen over," one analyst remarked when the company flashed a "Microsoft ♥ Linux" slide during a Nadella speech.

Under Nadella, the company's Windows and Office products continued to dominate. Microsoft's release of Windows 10, in 2016, two years into Nadella's tenure, was uploaded on more than 400 million devices—the fastest adoption rate in company history. Office 365 continued to expand its footprint, despite free alternatives, and Xbox grew its monthly active users.

Yet the company's center of gravity shifted to Microsoft's cloud service division. Cloud services grew by more than 50 percent during Nadella's first year as CEO, and then increased by another 56 percent the next year. And with a technologist again in charge, Nadella began positioning Microsoft for the future. "A confluence of three breakthroughs—Big Data, massive computing power, and sophisticated algorithms—is accelerating AI from sci-fi to reality," Nadella wrote in *Hit Refresh*, which was published in 2017. The book devoted an entire chapter to developing AI ethically. A year after its publication, Nadella publicly declared that AI was "going to shape all of what we do going forward." Microsoft stock began to climb for the first time since the spring of 2000.

● ● ●

MICROSOFT HAD BEEN investing in AI dating back to the 1990s—longer than any other major tech company outside of IBM. But maybe its AI roots were too deep. Microsoft's first glimpse at deep learning's potential came in the late 2000s, when one of its researchers collaborated with Geoff Hinton and some of his students on a speech recognition program. The system grew in proficiency as it crawled through larger and larger amounts of data. Yet by that point, Microsoft had devoted tens of millions of dollars to rule-based AI, and its top AI researchers were generally antagonistic to neural nets. When in 2012 a researcher gave an internal talk about the potential of neural networks to advance computer vision, he was repeatedly interrupted by a better-known colleague convinced that deep learning was a dead end.

One big shift came when Nadella, at the start of 2017, named Kevin Scott the company's new chief technology officer. Scott, who had joined LinkedIn in 2011, was LinkedIn's VP of engineering at the time of the sale and a member of the crew with whom Hoffman played Settlers of Catan. Scott had no intention of joining Microsoft after the sale until Nadella convinced him to stay.

Scott is an oversized, bespectacled bald man with ruddy cheeks and a distinctive tuft of hair that hangs down from his chin, as if he were an aging hippie now selling his homemade jewelry or pottery at makers festivals. As a young engineer at Google in the early 2000s, he had worked on a machine-learning algorithm that reviewed online ads before they went live. It had been years since he had worked on AI, but he was friends with Hoffman, who kept him up-to-date about the latest goings-on in the field. The two made it a point to speak every Sunday afternoon; increasingly, those discussions centered on what Scott described as "the state of play in AI."

"Kevin and I had already been talking about how AI was going to be a huge transformational wave," Hoffman said. "Kevin said to me, 'Look, I think this could be my fundamental contribution to Microsoft during my tenure here.' I told him, 'I totally agree.'"

Scott felt encouraged by the caliber of the AI researchers he found at Microsoft, even if he was frustrated that so many had yet to embrace deep learning. "There was no lack of IQ," he said. There was also no lack of enthusiasm for the potential for AI to change the industry. "We had a lot of AI investment and a lot of AI energy but it was very diffuse when I got there," he said. His solution was to pay close attention to use of the company's GPUs—the graphics processing units that Nvidia had invented and the perfect computer chip for training complex AI models.

"At one point, I seized the GPU budget for the whole company, and I was like, 'We will no longer peanut-butter these resources around,'" Scott said. Every request for GPU time needed to be supported by a "really, really strong, evidence-based conviction" that a particular path was worth the time. His life in his first years after taking over as CTO would be much the same as he would describe it in 2023. "I get up every morning and deal with people yelling at me, 'Give me my GPUs,'" Scott said.

Scott recognized that Microsoft had fallen hopelessly behind other companies. "We are multiple years behind the competition in terms of machine learning," Scott wrote in a 2019 memo. The competition also had the advantage of richer data pools: Google had the billions of search queries it processed each day, along with the troves of data produced by its other consumer products. Facebook, which had invested nearly as much in deep learning as Google, also benefited from the oceans of information that its users supplied when using its hugely popular services, including Instagram and WhatsApp. If Microsoft were to lead in AI, Scott said, "We needed to figure out how to play the game differently."

Scott had felt a deep sense of nostalgia the first time he visited OpenAI's San Francisco headquarters in 2018. "It really reminded me of my early Google days," Scott said. "The energy of the place and who they chose to hire." The people he encountered had the same blend of idealism and intensity. "We needed high-ambition partners," Scott said. "When we looked around, OpenAI was clearly the highest-ambition partner that was in the field."

Theirs would be the most unlikely of partnerships: a behemoth with more than 200,000 employees making a non-controlling investment in an organization expressly created to offset the power of Big Tech. Yet the deal would give each side exactly what it wanted. For Microsoft, gaining access to OpenAI's technologies would enable it to incorporate AI into its products and catch up to the competition, despite its lack of investment in neural networks. For OpenAI, partnering with Microsoft would provide the resources needed to fund its ambitious goals. Roughly half the billion dollars OpenAI received from Microsoft was in the form of Azure credits, to be used to train and run its models in Microsoft's cloud. Separately, Microsoft spent hundreds of millions of dollars designing and building a system that yoked together tens of thousands of GPUs by the end of 2019. "That was the computing environment that GPT-3 was trained on," Scott said.

Hoffman could not have been more pleased with the outcome. Nadella did not just mouth the platitudes (as had the CEO of every tech colossus that has faced the challenge of a new wave of technology) that he wanted to run Microsoft more like a startup. He seemed to mean it when he vowed to rip up the script when circumstances demanded it. "Neither Bill nor Steve would have done an arrangement like the one with OpenAI," Hoffman said. "Because they would've said it has to be internal." Under their leadership, Microsoft would have bought OpenAI or crafted more of an arm's-length licensing deal. "I think Satya recognized that you needed to be creative chasing the new thing," Hoffman said.

OPENAI HAD MADE a discovery around the time the company was finalizing its partnership agreement with Microsoft. On its own, GPT-2 had learned to code. Dario Amodei, the company's research director, showed his colleagues. He uploaded part of a computer program, asked GPT-2 to complete the job for him, and in seconds the task was complete. The discovery was unnerving. The LLM made mistakes (just as human coders sometimes do), but no one could explain how GPT-2 had done it.

Scott experienced the same shiver of fear that others did. And like them, he immediately saw its potential. So too did Microsoft's Nat Friedman. A year before the OpenAI deal, Microsoft had bought GitHub, a website for sharing code. Friedman, as CEO of GitHub (like LinkedIn, GitHub was run as an independent unit inside Microsoft), was eager to share this newfangled programming tool with users. He even had come up with a clever coinage for signaling its limitations: GitHub Copilot. It was something programmers could use for help while working on a project but was not capable of coding a project on its own.

"It trains you how to think about it," Scott said of the Copilot name. "It perfectly conveys its strengths and weaknesses."

Some inside Microsoft opposed the launch of Copilot. They worried about its propensity to make mistakes and the damage that could do to Microsoft's reputation. But as CEO of GitHub, Friedman called the shots. He went ahead and released it, despite the opposition, charging users $10 per month for the tool. Within the year, Copilot had generated more than $100 million in revenues.

Journalists were impressed with the new Microsoft, as was Wall Street. Again, Microsoft could wear the crown as the world's most valuable company when its market cap hit $850 billion, surpassing that of Apple. In the late 2010s, the two tech giants became the stock market's first two trillion-dollar companies. Had an investor put $100 invested in an S&P 500 index fund in mid-2017, it would be worth $171 by mid-2022. That same $100 would be worth $229 if invested in a basket of Nasdaq technology stocks—or $398 if invested solely in Microsoft.

Yet Microsoft was still not feared, as it had been in the past. A decade earlier, television's Jim Cramer had devised FAANG (pronounced "fang") as an acronym for the stock market's mightiest giants: Facebook, Amazon, Apple, Netflix, and Google. In time, the term "FAANG" would be seized upon by critics concerned by the power and practices of Big Tech. Some 1.4 billion devices worldwide were running Windows 10 or 11 by the end of 2022. More than 1.2 billion people were using Microsoft Office. Along with money from its cloud business, which surpassed Windows and Office as the company's largest source of revenue, Microsoft reported just under $200 billion in revenue in 2022. That wasn't as much as Amazon, Apple, or Google but it was more than Facebook or Netflix. Yet of course there's no *M* in FAANG. Despite all of Nadella's success, Microsoft, for the time being at least, was neither feared nor reviled. As Nadella had written in his inaugural memo to Microsoft employees, "Our industry does not respect tradition—it only respects innovation." It would be technology, and not its past accomplishments, that earned it a place back among tech's elite.

CHAPTER 7

Banging on the Table

S hortly after DeepMind's sale to Google, *Wired UK* showed up in its offices to fete the success of one of London's own inside its pages ("Inside Google's Super-Brain"). The focus was on Demis Hassabis, the prodigy who was eleven when he wrote an AI algorithm good enough to beat his younger brother at the game Othello. In a sit-down with *Wired UK*'s editor David Rowan, Hassabis waved off those who believed they made a mistake in selling out to Big Tech.

"Who owns the company is neither here nor there," Hassabis said. Under their agreement with Google, Hassabis retained the title of CEO. "We have full control of what we work on."

Reality, though, would be more complicated.

• • •

THE RELATIONSHIP BETWEEN Google and DeepMind was never an easy one. Google was generous with DeepMind, especially in the early years. To house their new London colleagues, Google leased a hand-some, six-story brick office headquarters in London's King's Cross neighborhood, not far from where Suleyman had grown up. The perks that came with working there included massage rooms and an indoor gym and the "kind of five-star buffet you'd find in a Dubai hotel," Bloomberg's Parmy Olson wrote. More significantly, Google's largesse allowed DeepMind to stock up on PhDs in a wide variety of specialties. Some inside Google, though, were resentful of the profligate spending by its new subsidiary. If DeepMind was the teenager seeking its freedom, Google was the parent reminding them who paid the rent and food bills.

Year one was hard, year two worse. That's because at the end of 2015, eighteen months after it had purchased DeepMind, Google announced that it was restructuring the company. Its highly profitable search and advertising business, along with Gmail, YouTube, and other internet properties, would keep the name Google but operate as a subsidiary of a holding company called Alphabet. Under this new structure, DeepMind would be separated from Google proper and become one of many independent units under the Alphabet umbrella. These independent ventures included Waymo (self-driving cars), Wing (drone delivery), Nest (a "smart" thermostat), Loon (high-altitude balloons that provide internet access in rural areas), Calico (R&D on extending the human life span), and Google Ventures, the company's investment arm. Sundar Pichai, who had been a senior vice president at the company, was put in charge of Google. Larry Page would serve as CEO of Alphabet and Sergey Brin as president, overseeing both Google and the ambitious subsidiary companies.

"We told our whole company that we were about to spin out and be independent," Suleyman said. "But suddenly all that was put on hold." DeepMind had hired marketing and comms people. They had a policy staff. Now those and other functions would be subsumed inside Alphabet. Meanwhile, the newly constituted Alphabet issued policies and directives.

"Because we were already inside the company, they slow-rolled us," Suleyman said. "It was torturous."

People back at Google headquarters in Mountain View felt similarly frustrated. For several years, Google Brain had been the company's source of cutting-edge AI. Now the company had two centers of gravity for AI, confusing both employees and potential partners. Google's acquisition of DeepMind reportedly had surprised the company's AI researchers, and there were lingering bruised feelings given the belittling way that Deep-

Mind's people had spoken of Google's existing deep-learning algorithms. Mainly people inside Brain felt resentful. They were under constant pressure to find practical, moneymaking applications for the AI technology they developed. Yet there was not a corresponding pressure on Suleyman as the head of applied research at DeepMind. Larry Page, Sergey Brin, and their lieutenants seemed to have infinite patience for their colleagues in London.

Early on, DeepMind justified that faith. There was its victory at a Go board and the success of WaveNet, which produced more natural-sounding speech than previous text-to-speech systems. DeepMind also helped Google slash its energy bills using models created by a group under Suleyman called DeepMind Energy. The millions of servers Google operated around the globe to keep up with search requests and services such as Gmail and Google Maps were by 2015 collectively consuming as much electricity as the entire city of San Francisco. DeepMind's model reduced by 40 percent the energy needed to cool Google's energy-hungry data centers. The AI system predicted future temperatures and other weather conditions, then recommended real-time adjustments to cooling equipment, optimizing their operations. DeepMind further helped to reduce the company's carbon footprint with models that better predicted the energy output from the wind farms with which it contracted.

Yet those wins dated back to the first few years that DeepMind was part of Google. As those triumphs faded into the past, doubters gossiped about DeepMind's bulging head count. Google had bought a startup of fifty employees in 2014. By the end of 2017, DeepMind employed roughly seven hundred. Google racked up more than $500 million in losses on DeepMind in 2018. That figure ballooned to $649 million in 2019.

Google had followed through on its promises to create an independent ethics board to monitor DeepMind's development of AGI. Hoffman and Musk were among the outsiders named to a board that included Page, Brin, and former CEO Eric Schmidt as members. The board, however, met just once before the DeepMind founders heard from their minders in Mountain View. "They came to us and said we're going to do this Alphabet thing, so let's pause this while we set up the structure and set you up as a separate business unit," Suleyman said. There would be no second meeting. DeepMind instead used Google's cash to staff a unit called DeepMind Ethics and create their own independent ethics board.

Frictions grew between DeepMind and Google. Suleyman oversaw a team inside DeepMind charged with using AI to improve the caliber of recommendations YouTube offered its users. The teams struggled with the eight-hour time difference between DeepMind's London offices and Brain's in Mountain View and disagreed over the sharing of data. Ultimately, the project was abandoned. A retreat was held in Northern California to see if DeepMind and Google Brain could work out their differences, but this attempt at détente only seemed to convince the two sides that they were as far apart as it seemed when they were squabbling long-distance. Each would develop its own large language models separately, as if competitors rather than colleagues.

Negotiations between DeepMind and Alphabet dragged on for five years, from the end of 2015 through the start of 2021. "It was basically impossible to get agreement on anything," Suleyman said.

At the end of 2019, both Larry Page and Sergey Brin, two of Deep-Mind's most passionate advocates inside the company, announced their retirement. Sundar Pichai, who had been running Google and therefore oversaw Google Brain, would now be the CEO of both Google and Alphabet.

"That's when they started to rein us back in," Suleyman said.

• • •

"A SHY, QUIET boy who loved science." That's how the *Mumbai Mirror*, an English-language daily newspaper in India, described Pichai shortly after he was named the CEO of Google. Like Satya Nadella, the CEO of that other large software company, Pichai was born and raised in India. Growing up in a large city near the southern tip of the country, Pichai and his younger brother slept on the living room floor of a two-room apartment that at times had no running water.

Through much of his childhood, his family had no television and no car. For five years, Pichai's family was on a wait list for a rotary phone. He was twelve when one was finally installed. "It was the first moment I understood the power of what getting access to technology meant," he said.

Pichai, who was born in 1972, first traveled to the United States to attend graduate school, much as Nadella, five years his senior, had done a decade earlier. Pichai earned a master's in material science at Stanford and then an MBA from the Wharton School of the University of Pennsylvania. He did a short stint at McKinsey, the giant management consulting firm, before starting as a Google product manager in 2004, the year the company went public. His claim to fame inside Google came shortly after Microsoft made Bing the default search engine on Internet Explorer. Pichai convinced the company's top executives that Google needed to build its own browser. Today Google Chrome is the world's most popular browser. Twitter tried poaching Pichai in 2011, but to convince him to stay with the company, then CEO Larry Page gave him $50 million in stock and a promotion to senior vice president. Pichai added Android, which was the operating system on 750 million phones, to his portfolio. He took over Alphabet in 2019, eighteen months after Nadella took over the top spot at Microsoft.

Google was still largely beloved in the Valley when I was covering tech in the mid-2000s. Still, there was grumbling about its size and might. For what turned out to be my farewell piece from the tech beat at the *Times*, I collected the grievances of venture capitalists and founders who spoke of Google in the same frustrated tones they had used when complaining about Microsoft a half-dozen years earlier. Googlers were arrogant in their treatment of partners and potential partners, they said. They were involved in so many areas of tech that they had become the giant that accidentally crushes a company by stepping on it because they failed to notice they were underfoot. Hoffman, who was among those I interviewed for the article, was particularly harsh in his view. "Google is doing more damage to innovation in the Valley right now than Microsoft ever did," he told me. My piece, "Relax, Bill Gates; It's Google's Turn as the Villain," ran on August 24,

2005. Hurricane Katrina hit, and, two weeks later, the paper moved me to New Orleans to cover the storm and its aftermath.

The resentments against Google deepened and spread. Media outlets once hailed Google as a savior. Its search engine drove traffic to their websites while Google's advertising arm delivered the digital ads that let them cash in on all those eyeballs coming to their site. Yet the more dominant Google became, the greater the share of online advertising dollars it vacuumed up, and the more it influenced the content being produced. It turned out that publishing large volumes of low-quality content specifically written to rank at the top of a Google search result was far more lucrative than publishing actual journalism.

"Google's grand promise was to organize the world's information," Nilay Patel, editor in chief of The Verge, a tech news site, wrote in 2023. Yet increasingly "an enormous amount of the world's information has been organized for Google—to rank in Google results." The brilliance of Google lay in its algorithm, which classified web pages based on both the relevance of their content to a search and the number of quality websites linking to them. Yet by the 2010s, using Google to find a nearby restaurant or hotel room or to buy a new toaster was plagued by problems. The top search results were paid for by advertisers, displacing the organic results produced by the objective search algorithm. Unlike in the early years, Google no longer used a different background color to distinguish between ads and its normal blue links. Moreover, the objectivity of its results had vanished as web page designers had become adept at raising their visibility in the search results by gaming the algorithm. The hapless Google user was often led to pages thrown up by fake expert-review sites created to skim fees when visitors clicked a link. Or they ended up at sites booby-trapped with auto-playing videos or choked with aggressive pop-ups.

In 2022, the science fiction writer Cory Doctorow coined the phrase the "enshittification of the internet." Every platform, Google included, gradually degrades over time because of the temptation of a company to sacrifice quality because the pursuit of more profits proves irresistible. As Google honed its advertising technologies, content creators saw their share of the profits shrink. In 2005, newspapers were collectively booking $49 billion in advertising, according to the Pew Research Center. By 2022, that figure had fallen below $10 billion. Two companies, Google and Facebook, which by then had changed its name to Meta, were collectively hoovering up nearly half the U.S. digital ad spend and a significant portion of the global advertising market.

• • •

ULTIMATELY, SULEYMAN WAVED the white flag in DeepMind's battle with Google. In 2019, a decade after he had cofounded the company, he left to become vice president of AI product management and AI policy at Google Brain. Rather than experience the daily frustrations of finding commercial uses for DeepMind's research projects, he would come to know more intimately the frustrations of seeing your best ideas blocked by multiple layers of management and the legacy business they fight hard to protect.

Suleyman always made more sense inside Brain. Hassabis and Legg spoke about twenty-year road maps and goals that might not be attained in their lifetime. They were playing the long game: artificial general intelligence. In contrast, Suleyman was far more interested in technologies that could impact the world tomorrow, not in a decade or two. Maybe it was inevitable that he would switch sides in the rift between DeepMind and Brain. If nothing else, moving Suleyman to its headquarters in Mountain View represented a kind of cross-pollination that might get the two sides of the company's AI split working more with each other's technologies. "Sundar basically said to me, 'Identify new AI-first opportunities for the company,'" Suleyman said.

Suleyman's remit included projects that had been preoccupying him at DeepMind. Years earlier, Suleyman had singled out health care as maybe the most promising avenue for applied AI. The system trained to read mammograms that Suleyman had told Hoffman about the first time they met had proven "better than expert radiologists at detecting breast cancer," Suleyman said. Similarly, a model was trained to spot abnormalities in the eye. "For fifty-two blinding diseases, it was better than the best human ophthalmologists," Suleyman said. Where an ophthalmologist will evaluate maybe thirty thousand cases in a lifetime, he said, a neural net "has seen orders of magnitude more cases than any human." Health care remained part of his portfolio at Google Brain.

Yet Suleyman mainly spent his days exploring ways AI could help the Google cause. One of his teams found a way to use DeepMind's technologies to improve battery optimization on an Android phone. DeepMind's DQN model, which had proven so adept at learning and mastering videogames, was employed to improve the recommendation engine at the Google Play store. Another of his teams explored ways AI could improve the quality of the search results, but that proved a dead end. Search was responsible for the vast majority of Google's profits (more than $40 billion in 2020) and its executives long had been wary of leaning more heavily on AI, which added an undesired element of mystery and hocus pocus to the algorithm. Suleyman's team showed that its model improved search results, but the results deteriorated over time. That's all the Google search team needed to hear. "They're superconservative in search at Google," Suleyman said.

• • •

SULEYMAN WAS NEVER a low-key boss. "I was very demanding and pretty relentless," he confessed. But attitudes toward workplace behavior were changing and of course yelling and carrying on inside his own startup was different than behaving that way inside one owned by a large, publicly traded company. He rebuked those whose work he did not find up to snuff, sometimes in front of others. His disappointment with a blog post that a member of the company's comms team had written spurred him to send an email filled with f-bombs to more than one hundred employees. Reportedly, his verbal badgering made at least a couple of subordinates cry. An outside law firm was hired to investigate, and Suleyman was placed on leave.

Suleyman publicly apologized for his behavior when the *Wall Street Journal* picked up the story. "I was tough to work for," he acknowledged. "At times my management style was not constructive." Now self-reflection was mandated by his employer. "I took almost four or five months out and took time to reflect on how I was acting and how I was operating," Suleyman said. He spoke with intimates, including Hoffman, about his behavior, and got some professional coaching.

"It gave me the opportunity to really take a step back and reflect and grow and mature a little bit as a manager and a leader," Suleyman said.

•••

JOE FENTON HAD worked under Suleyman at DeepMind, where he was part of a group using neural nets to help financial advisors tailor the perfect mix of stocks, bonds, and other assets on behalf of a client. The project showed promise but ended up a casualty of Alphabet's cost-cutting under Sundar Pichai. Fenton reached out to Suleyman after his former boss returned to work after his forced leave. In the spring of 2020, Fenton also left DeepMind for Google Brain to work again for Suleyman.

OpenAI released GPT-3 shortly after Fenton's move. That spurred him to go looking for a similar effort inside Google, which is how he found a tiny team that had built a rudimentary chatbot called Meena. Using it, Fenton said, "was an incredible, jaw-dropping experience." He sent a couple of emails to Suleyman to get him interested in Meena, but when that didn't work, he sent Suleyman verbatim transcripts of conversations he was having with the chatbot. "He became completely addicted to it," Fenton said. Meena was a relatively small model but that made it that much more impressive. "It was just unbelievable what was being built," he said.

In the summer of 2020, Suleyman and Fenton joined a small group of around five headed by Noam Shazeer, a coauthor of Google's revolutionary Transformer paper, and Daniel De Freitas. Later, the two would make a splash as founders of Character.AI, which in 2023 ranked as a top chatbot. But back in 2020, the two were working only part-time on their creation. With Suleyman's help, Meena secured more computer time, access to more data, and additional staff.

"We improved the performance and built some really nice demos and Meena went absolutely viral inside Google," Fenton said. A chatbot has little utility unless it is integrated with other models and applications, but that was the advantage of developing it inside a behemoth like Alphabet. "There were hundreds of people around the company building stuff on top of this model," Fenton said.

Said Suleyman, "It was really ChatGPT before ChatGPT."

• • •

PROJECT MAVEN WAS the code name Google gave to a project commissioned by the Pentagon to use machine learning to improve the accuracy of drone strikes. When news of the project broke in early 2018, thousands of Google employees signed a letter protesting the use of AI for warfare. In response, Google announced that it would not renew its contract when the deal expired the following year.

Google worked hard to cast itself as the standard-bearer for ethical AI. In the wake of the Project Maven controversy, the company posted what it called its AI principles. It would refrain from using AI for weapons or technologies designed to harm people and vowed to avoid using AI in ways that reinforce existing biases. The use of AI in surveillance systems would also be out of bounds. "While we are optimistic about the potential of AI," the company declared, "we recognize that advanced technologies can raise important challenges that must be addressed clearly, thoughtfully, and affirmatively." The company appointed an internal committee to review all its AI-related efforts and, taking a page from the DeepMind playbook, announced that it was creating a council of independent advisors that would guide "responsible development of AI."

Yet even people inside Google were wary, knowing their company was better at making promises than following through on them. Its own employees were among those expressing disappointment when in 2019 the company released the names of the eight people it had appointed to its outside advisory council. Thousands of Googlers signed a petition calling for the removal of one, a climate change skeptic and the then president of the Heritage Foundation, the right-wing think tank. Another appointee was the CEO of a drone company, which stirred up more ill feelings. A third member quickly resigned, and a fourth, when asked why she had not quit over the inclusion of the Heritage Foundation's president, responded, "I know worse about one of the other people." Google scrubbed the council barely one week after it had been formed.

Earlier, Google had impressed those concerned with AI safety when, in 2018, it named Timnit Gebru and Margaret Mitchell to run its new ethical AI unit. Over time, Google would anger safety advocates in the way it treated both. Born and raised in Ethiopia, Gebru was a well-known AI critic. She earned her PhD working with Fei-Fei Li at Stanford and then gained acclaim as coauthor of a 2018 study showing that facial recognition software accurately identified white men 99 out of 100 times but only 35 percent of black women. Following its publication, Microsoft and IBM were among the companies announcing that its people would no longer sell facial recognition software to law enforcement. Mitchell, the other co-head of Google's ethical AI team, seemed an equally bold choice. Mitchell too had drawn attention to bias in AI and the possible harms of machine learning prior to arriving at Google.

Gebru left first, at the end of 2020, barely two years after she had arrived. The precipitating event was a paper she cowrote spotlighting the shortcomings of large language models. She said she was fired for refusing to remove her name from the paper; the company, which claimed her research "didn't meet our bar for publication," said she resigned. (The paper, which listed Gebru and Mitchell as coauthors, was presented at a 2021 conference.) Management, of course, was within its rights to dictate what one of its employees could and couldn't say publicly about the company. But this paper was not about Google. It was a scholarly work, no different in that respect from the large number of papers that Googlers publish each year. Gebru had been hired expressly to weigh in on the ethics of AI. Artificial intelligence in particular required that its creators sit with the difficult questions about the technology's potential to do great harm. Instead, Google

censored a researcher who had been wooed with the promise of academic freedom. More than 2,600 Google employees signed a public
letter declaring Google's actions an act of retaliation.

Mitchell was fired a couple of months later, collateral damage in
the wake of Gebru's departure. She was caught downloading emails in
search of evidence that the company had discriminated against Gebru.
This time, eight hundred Google employees signed a petition con-
demning Mitchell's firing.

Suleyman seemed more corporate vice president than human rights
activist when asked about Gebru, Mitchell, and other insiders critical
of Google's approach to responsible AI. He pointed to his own track
record fighting for ethical AI. Long before anyone was talking about
Project Maven, he was among one-hundred-plus AI researchers and
roboticists who signed an open letter calling on the UN to ban the
development and use of autonomous weapons. "I was actively pushing internally against that long before it became a public thing," he
said. Suleyman, who was among those appointed to the internal ethics
board the company established after Project Maven, described Gebru
as "very, very junior"—probably a lowly L-4 where, as a vice president,
he was an L-10.

"We're talking about self-appointed activists versus a board that
represented top leadership in the company," Suleyman said. Google's
ethics board, he continued, included five senior vice presidents and six
vice presidents. "We had put in place a formal process for reviewing
every single contract and every single piece of technology. This was not
a made-up sort of thing."

• • •

FROM THE OUTSIDE, Alphabet seemed as if it held an insurmount-
able lead in the race to cash in on AI. The company had jumped
into deep learning long before a bandwagon had formed in support
of that approach. Pichai declared Google an "AI-first company" in
2016, a few months after being named Google CEO and before any
of the company's rivals. The following year—the same year eight of its

researchers penned the watershed Transformer paper—the company wowed attendees at its annual developer's conference with recordings of a lifelike-sounding bot making a restaurant reservation and booking a hair appointment. Even as DeepMind was struggling to monetize its innovations, its creations were being used by hundreds of millions of users. WaveNet, for instance, its text-to-speech technology, was integrated into Google Translate and Google Assistant, its rival to Amazon's Alexa.

There was also the talent it had assembled. If Google had not quite cornered the market on AI talent, it certainly employed far more than its fair share of top researchers. Microsoft, Facebook, and OpenAI were among those competing for engineers with experience working with AI yet in the second half of the 2010s, a computer science PhD interested in the field was more likely to end up at Google than anywhere else. With artificial intelligence seemingly within reach, Google was in a perfect position to capitalize on the moment.

Yet never underestimate the ability of a lumbering giant to get in its own way. Back in the day, Googlers mocked Microsoft as an over-the-hill giant, just as inside Microsoft they mocked IBM. The innovator's dilemma: now it was Google learning that innovation is far more likely to be championed by an upstart than a corporate supertanker slowed by its size.

"I tried pretty hard to get things launched at Google," Suleyman said. "A bunch of us were kind of banging on the table saying, 'Come on, this is the future, let's get moving.' But Google is a big organization and not the fastest to move."

Missteps and blunders hurt the cause of those pushing AI inside Google. Like in 2015, when Google Photos added a feature that automatically sorted people's pictures into digital categories—and a user discovered that the service had put eighty pictures of his black friend into a folder labelled "gorilla." Even fumbles by rivals proved a hindrance. In 2016, Microsoft released Tay, a chatbot trained on the web chatter of 18- to 24-year-olds and also comedians who excel at improv. Alex Kantrowitz, then a reporter for BuzzFeed, wrote what he described as a "nice bubbly story" about "an entertaining, infuriating, manic, and irreverent chatbot." He posted links to his piece on social media and went to bed on the West Coast. "By the time morning hit on the East Coast," Kantrowitz said, the bot "was already a Nazi-saluting Hitler." The Holocaust-denying Tay expressed its support for genocide, peppered its chat with racial slurs, and tweeted, "Jews did 9/11." Microsoft quickly pulled Tay, but the lesson for comms teams working for Big Tech was that releasing one of these large language models into the wild came with great risks.

The federal government might also have impeded the company's speed. Mirroring the antitrust action it filed against Microsoft in the late 1990s, the U.S. Justice Department in 2020 charged that Google exploited its monopoly power to maintain its search engine's dominance. Another factor standing in Google's way was its size. The company employed roughly 3,000 people when it went public in 2004. By 2020, Google was nearly fifty times as large, with a head count that exceeded 135,000. "The entire company is a series of fiefdoms," said Sridhar Ramaswamy, a former Google executive who left the company in 2018. When he had joined Google fifteen years earlier, Ramaswamy said, everyone at the company was moving more or less in unison and in the same direction. "Now you have all these parallel tracks," he said. "You no longer have the tip of the spear but all these little spears." Praveen Seshadri joined Google with great enthusiasm after the search giant bought his startup in 2020. Instead, he quit as soon as he was allowed under the deal terms. Shortly after his departure, Seshadri explained his decision on Medium: "I have left Google understanding how a once-great company has slowly ceased to function."

• • •

SULEYMAN CONTINUED TO be dazzled by Meena, Google's chatbot. "I mean, summer of 2020, we had it. It was working. It was amazing," he said. Tech writers were similarly gobsmacked when the company demo'd Meena later that year. Meena had been trained on 341 gigabytes of social media chatter—nearly nine times as much data as OpenAI's GPT-2—and designed to handle open-ended conversation. In theory, it could speak on any topic, not just those it had been programmed to cover. The result, reviewers declared, was dialogue so good it was as if they were chatting with a human. One news site deemed Meena a "technological leap forward." Another declared it a "chatbot breakthrough."

Suleyman's bosses should have been thrilled. "I mean, we had a conversational, interactive, very high-quality language model working," Suleyman said. Instead they fretted about all of the things that could go wrong with a product the company renamed LaMDA (Language Model for Dialogue Applications). Gaurav Nemade had been on the original team behind Meena and served as LaMDA's first product manager. "I had conversations with Brain leaders who were very anxious about the whole thing," Nemade said. "People were more petrified than excited." He ascribed their fears to Microsoft's release of Tay. "The nightmares of Microsoft," Nemade said, were "still looming in the Valley, especially inside Google." Like Meena, Tay had been trained on social media. "I'm sure everybody, especially in the leadership, had the reaction, 'Oh, this is very interesting, but holy shit, this is going to be a PR nightmare for us,'" Nemade said.

The company unveiled LaMDA at its 2021 developers conference but deliberately downplayed its potential impact. Suleyman described as "stupid" the sample conversations they showcased at the event. In one, LaMDA pretends to be a paper airplane and is asked what's it like to fly through the air. In another, it's Pluto, describing what it'd be like to visit there. "Because the people in charge didn't want it to sound like a person," Suleyman said.

Suleyman and others pushed hard for LaMDA's release but continued to face resistance. "Google has developed an incredible expertise for getting in its own way," Suleyman said. "There's loads of amazing teams and projects which just block each other because there's huge amounts of duplication. It's a very chaotic place."

Suleyman and Reid Hoffman had stayed in regular touch after their initial meeting in London. The two grew closer and their conversations more frequent after Suleyman relocated to the Valley. "He had told me he moved to Google Brain because DeepMind was pursuing science projects and he wanted to launch products, but now Brain's not letting him launch anything," Hoffman said. "He asked me, 'What do you think I should do?'"

Suleyman was asking as a friend, but Hoffman was able to offer him a soft landing. "He tells me, 'Just come work at Greylock, we'll give you an office, you'll help us with investing, and you can figure things out,'" Suleyman said. In January 2022, Suleyman tendered his resignation from the company where he had worked for the previous eight years and went on the payroll at Greylock.

CHAPTER 8

With Great Powers

Greylock Partners, founded in Cambridge, Massachusetts, in 1965, had always been an East Coast firm. It established a small Silicon Valley satellite office in 1983 to be closer to new ventures created to capitalize on the spreading popularity of the PC and the software packages and hardware peripherals needed to make them useful, but the firm did not expand its West Coast operations until the end of the 1990s—just in time for the bursting of the dot-com bubble. Its first new hire, Aneel Bhusri, a top executive at a local business software company called PeopleSoft, confessed to losing roughly $70 million in his first eighteen months as a VC, including a huge investment in an online rewards company called HelloAsia. (The joke inside the firm: "HelloAsia. Goodbye $15 million.") David Sze, the second hire, had been an early employee at Excite and a senior vice president at Excite@Home until he joined the firm in early 2000, just before everything blew up.

Some of Sze's East Coast partners were skeptical about investing in LinkedIn at a time the site barely had 1 million users. They were even more hostile when he proposed sinking millions into another unproven startup taking on the likes of Friendster and MySpace. "I did Facebook and everyone lost their mind. 'Oh my god, you've just destroyed this firm,'" Sze said. The $12.5 million Greylock invested in Facebook would be worth roughly $2 billion when it went public a half dozen years later.

In 2009, Greylock announced that it was moving its main offices to Sand Hill Road and that several of their Boston-based partners were retiring. Its rebirth as a Valley-based venture firm had been part of Sze and Bhusri's pitch to convince Hoffman to commit to Greylock. The firm's managing partner at the time was blunt: "Fundamentally, Silicon Valley has created a culture of 'Nothing is impossible.' Boston has lost some of that."

Hoffman brought a new kind of fame to Greylock. Practically every big newspaper and business magazine profiled Greylock's newest partner and the bold voice that convinced them to invest in Airbnb. *Fortune* described Hoffman as the "most successful entrepreneur you've never heard of." In the *New York Times*, he was the "startup whisperer." The *New Yorker* ran a long profile of him under the title "The Network Man." There were profiles as well in *Forbes*, *BusinessWeek*, *Fast Company*, and the *Guardian*. "For a striving founder of a startup," according to a Hoffman-heavy, overcooked profile of Greylock appearing in *Newsweek*, "pitching your business plan here is a bit like being a rookie pitcher stepping onto the mound at Yankee Stadium—with Babe Ruth walking up to the plate." A partnership that quietly had been earning a spot among tech's elite was now doing so more loudly.

Books further elevated Hoffman's profile and therefore the firm's. In 2010, Hoffman fulfilled a lifelong dream when he published his first book, *The Startup of You*. Cowritten with a young entrepreneur named Ben Casnocha, *The Startup of You* encouraged individuals to approach their career in the fashion of an entrepreneur growing and building a business. (Remain flexible. Embrace uncertainty. Take smart risks. Leverage your networks.) He would publish a pair of business strategy books over the next eight years, including *Blitzscaling: The Lightning-Fast Path to Building Massively Valuable Companies*, co-written with Chris Yeh. *Blitzscaling* gave rise to a Hoffman-hosted podcast called *Masters of Scale*, whose guests over the years have included tech luminaries such as Bill Gates, Mark Zuckerberg, and Elon Musk but also Gwyneth Paltrow, Tyler Perry, Yo-Yo Ma, Tyra Banks, and Barack Obama. There's now a biannual "Masters of Scale" summit in San Francisco.

If Hoffman were a startup, observers would attribute his success to the virtuous cycle that was his life. His reputation drew founders seeking his counsel and connections. That attracted the attention of the media, which caused more entrepreneurs to think of Hoffman when looking for money to start a company. The agreeable, always-working Hoffman happily said yes if a reporter with whom he was friendly—and he was friendly with a lot of them—asked for a bit of his time. He was a regular at the Sun Valley, Idaho, confabs for tech and media moguls organized by the New York–based investment bank Allen & Company that some dubbed summer camp for the billionaire set, and a familiar face on CNBC and Bloomberg TV. Hollywood—Michael Ovitz, Ashton Kutcher, movie producer Brian Glazer—had him down to talk tech.

Without a nudge that Hoffman had founded LinkedIn, most of the wider world would not know his name. He was not galactically famous like Zuckerberg or as Sam Altman would become. But there was no doubt that he had become Silicon Valley famous. That prominence inside the tech industry would prove invaluable as he increasingly turned his attention to AI.

• • •

THE OLD GREYLOCK hired the best and brightest out of Harvard Business School and paired them with an older partner to learn the ropes. Moving the center of gravity to the West Coast brought a kind of personality change to the firm. Sze and Bhusri, both of whom had earned an MBA at Stanford rather than Harvard, and Hoffman were typical of the new partners invited to join the firm. They were either founders themselves or had served in executive positions at brand-name tech companies. The firm marketed their partners as experienced operators with hands-on industry experience invaluable to entrepreneurs who had their choice of suitors.

The firm's makeup shifted again in the second half of the 2010s. VCs are, if nothing else, data driven. Through experience and observation, they could see that senior operators and founders do not necessarily make good investors. Maybe the greatest VC of all time, Sequoia's Michael Moritz, was a former journalist of all things, a writer at *Time* before funding Yahoo, Google, PayPal, YouTube, Zappos, Instacart, and Stripe. There was also the reality of all those dollars pouring into venture capital funds, especially when a firm can boast of early investments in Facebook and LinkedIn. Greylock had raised $500 million in 2005 and an additional $575 million when relocating to the West Coast in 2009. They raised a $1 billion fund in 2013, and then announced new billion-dollar funds in both 2016 and 2020. More money required more venture capitalists to invest it all.

Shortly after raising its first billion-dollar fund, the firm recruited Sarah Guo, a twenty-six-year-old who had spent the previous two years working for Goldman Sachs. Two years later, Guo was promoted to general partner. Saam Motamedi, a recent Stanford grad with a degree in computer science, was just twenty-three when he joined Greylock as an associate in 2016, the year the firm raised its second billion-dollar fund. When, in 2019, shortly before Greylock announced it had raised its third billion-dollar fund in seven years, Motamedi was promoted to general partner. At twenty-six years old, he was the youngest partner in the firm's history.

Motamedi is a trim, bearded man with a sophistication that makes him seem wise beyond his years. He was raised in Houston, the son of two academics who, he jokes, resent him for becoming a venture capitalist rather than attaining a graduate degree. While still in high school, he published a pair of academic papers on his research into the use of nanoparticles for early cancer detection. After earning a computer science degree from Stanford, he joined a company employing AI to help salespeople ring up more sales. There he caught a glimpse of both the potential of AI and its limits. Two years later, he started work as a junior VC at Greylock. He did not intend on carving out machine learning as a specialty until he started attending the firm's regular Monday meetings.

"Reid's talking about how these models are tipping and the things that we've been told don't work are going to work and we should go make a bunch of investments," Motamedi said. He described Hoffman as one of the "sub-ten most important people in multiple technology crests," including social media (SocialNet, LinkedIn, his investment in Facebook), digital banking (PayPal), and the sharing economy (Airbnb). Of course, he was going to closely heed what Hoffman was saying. Motamedi would lead or co-lead investments in at least five AI startups between 2019 and 2022.

"I think most of us still looked at AI as a sleepy area that maybe one day might wake up," Sze said. "Honestly, I think Saam, because he was young and upcoming and so fresh to venture, was more interested in it than the rest of us."

• • •

THE YEAR 2020 proved a horrible one for most of the planet but not the tech sector. Lockdowns benefited an industry that provided digital tools that enabled people to live and work remotely. The tech-heavy Nasdaq rose by 44 percent. The five largest U.S.-based tech companies—Apple, Amazon, Alphabet, Facebook, and Microsoft—saw their combined market cap increase by more than $2.5 trillion.

Startups and the VCs who funded them enjoyed a similar bull run. Over the previous decade, money poured into venture as the super-rich, foreign governments through sovereign wealth funds, and others sought to cash in on tech. The Federal Reserve's decision to slash interest rates to near zero launched an era of cheap money, adding "ZIRP"—zero interest rate policy—to the Valley vernacular. With no financial incentive to park their cash in money markets or bond funds, investors sought out alternatives. The amount of money in the hands of venture capitalists more than doubled in 2021, fueling a bull run in the tech sector. Investing in crypto startups exploded that year, as did the money sunk into virtual reality, "fintechs" (digital tools for banking and finance), and that strangest of new beasts on the tech scene, digital collectibles called non-fungible tokens, or NFTs. With so much money sloshing around the venture industry, it was a seller's market for any startup with a decent story. Valuations—the paper worth of a company—soared. Two years after the start of the pandemic, the tech sector included more than a thousand unicorns—startups valued at $1 billion or more.

Hoffman made no investments in 2020. That's the venture capital business, where a partner can pull the trigger on three deals in six months and then go two years before the next one. Hoffman himself had made four investments in 2017 and then only one over the next two-plus years. His lack of investments in 2020 was also a product of the times. In the San Francisco Bay Area, 2020 was not only the year of Covid but also the summer of wildfires. There were fires in the Santa Cruz Mountains, just to the south and west of Silicon Valley, and dry lightning strikes in the Sierras, one hundred miles to the east. The smoke and soot in the Bay Area was so thick it blocked out the sun for weeks, triggering thirty consecutive days of "Spare the Air" warnings and countless articles about the hazards of breathing it in. Palo Alto had been Hoffman's home since his LinkedIn days. But he and his wife, Michelle Yee, a self-described "contented introvert" (the two, who had first met at Stanford, married in 2004), found a refuge just outside Seattle and then decided to make the area their home.

Yet Hoffman was in the Bay Area so frequently that friends might be forgiven if they didn't quite realize that he had moved. They still owned their home in Palo Alto, where Aria Finger, his chief of staff since 2021, estimated he spent 30 percent of his time. Hoffman was in D.C. at least a few times a year for meetings, including the occasional stop at the Biden White House. He tried to make it to both New York and London twice a year, and there was his annual trip to Sun Valley for Allen & Company's annual confab and a sister event in Arizona. Then there were his adventure trips to places like the South Pole and random opportunities that invariably popped up in his life: a commencement speech at Vanderbilt in Nashville, an honorary degree from the University of Oulu in Finland. Seattle was less home than home base for a peripatetic life.

At some point in the 2010s, Hoffman no longer described himself on social media as solely an entrepreneur and investor. He added "product and business strategist" to his profile. But, really, he had been playing that role for much longer. In the mid-2000s, while he was still running LinkedIn, he became famous within the startup world for a quote that eventually was embraced as gospel among founders and their advisors: "If you're not embarrassed by the first version of your product, you shipped too late." (Maybe his second-most-traveled quote was his clever description of the challenges confronting any high-growth tech company: "In founding a startup, you throw yourself off a cliff and build an airplane on the way down.") He did not offer high-minded, grand theories in the fashion of a Clayton Christensen of the Harvard Business School or other management gurus but instead offered pragmatic servings of situational advice. "His views on strategy are hard-won through experience," said Ben Casnocha, who served as Hoffman's first chief of staff after cowriting *The Startup of You* with him.

"He's this great game theorist always thinking several steps ahead of everyone else," David Sze said of Hoffman. "He's playing 3-D chess when on my best day I was playing chess and most people are playing checkers."

• • •

HOFFMAN ENJOYED GENERALLY glowing media coverage through most of his career. The first whiff of anything negative was in 2003, when he and his friend Mark Pincus went halves on a patent. Six Degrees, an early social networking company, had gone out of business, and the outfit that bought its remains was auctioning off its core patent. "Reid says to me, 'Mark, this is really fundamental for all of social networking, will you partner with me on it?'" Pincus said. The two did not know each other well at that point, but Pincus, like Hoffman, was running a social media startup, and the Six Degrees patent represented a threat.

"We didn't have our companies do it so that way we didn't have to explain it to the VCs," Pincus said. They bid $700,000, beating out twenty other suitors, including Yahoo and Friendster. "We did it as kind of a defensive move so no one else could buy it," Hoffman said. The scribes covering the moment, however, did not see the nobility in their scooping up a patent that one competitor said could make the pair richer than Bill Gates. Years later, Pincus still felt the sting of an article that cast them as patent trolls. The two never made a cent on their joint purchase "but no one goes back and says, 'We were wrong, they weren't trolls,'" Pincus said.

There would be more criticism of Hoffman over the years. He and Pincus created a trio of special-purpose acquisition companies, when SPACs, as they are called, were all the rage on Wall Street in the late 2010s. A SPAC is a shell company that first raises money through an IPO, and only then seeks a company to acquire. This provided a way for a tech startup to go public without submitting to a SEC review. "I got drawn into SPACs on the theory that they help democratize the public markets," Hoffman said. But they also provided a way for Wall Street to circumvent rules put in place for protecting investors from dubious investments. "I'm not sure the public markets are ready for that sort of thing," Hoffman said.

Stepping into the fight against Donald Trump provoked a wider circle of critics. Hoffman's first high-profile foray into politics was during the 2016 campaign, when he offered to donate up to $5 million to veterans' groups if Trump released his tax returns. After Trump won (without having released his returns), Hoffman took a venture capitalist's approach to finding solutions to a Democratic Party he saw as broken. He hired a full-time political advisor and poured tens of millions of dollars into a range of initiatives to reinvent the Democratic Party's playbook. "Technology is changing politics faster than politics is adapting to technology," Hoffman wrote in a 2018 post on Medium, a publishing platform funded by Greylock and other VCs. "Our goal is to identify promising organizations and provide them with resources to accelerate positive change." Hoffman and Dmitri Mehlhorn, his political advisor, were intent on funding new ways for mobilizing voters in swing states and using data, digital ads, machine learning, or social media to change politics.

"When you have power," Hoffman said, "you can't just sit on the sidelines and say, 'That's not my problem.'"

Some Democratic Party insiders resented this rich interloper who thought he knew more about politics than them. Writing in Vox, Theodore Schleifer described Hoffman as a "polarizing figure in the party—as popular in San Francisco as he is despised in parts of Washington." Some of the dozens of electoral experiments Hoffman seeded were highly effective, like efforts in Wisconsin and Arizona that helped swing the results in those states. But some proved a waste of money, and at least a couple proved fodder for the likes of Fox News and other media outlets hostile to his politics. A small portion of the $15 million he gave to one group, for instance, ended up running a disinformation campaign to defeat Republican Roy Moore in the 2017 special U.S. Senate race in Alabama. Hoffman categorically disavowed the use of disinformation, and I believed him when he said he first learned about it while reading the *Times*, which broke the story. But the damage to his image would be indelible. Hoffman donated millions to a Democratic senatorial political action committee (PAC) ahead of the 2018 election and millions more to another one that supported House Democrats. The *Times* dubbed him "Silicon Valley's prime behind-the-scenes political influencer." In right-wing media outlets, however, he was the Democratic megadonor who funded Russian-style disinformation campaigns to manipulate the electoral system.

In 2019, the news site Axios broke the news that several years earlier, Hoffman invited convicted sex offender Jeffrey Epstein to a 2015 dinner that included Elon Musk and Mark Zuckerberg as guests. The circumstance was pure Hoffman. His friend, Joi Ito, the former head of the MIT Media Lab, had enlisted his help in raising money for the lab. "I was told by Joi that Epstein had cleared the MIT vetting process," Hoffman wrote in a statement to Axios. But even a quick internet search would have revealed that Epstein in 2008 pled guilty to a charge of procuring a minor for prostitution. "I helped to repair his reputation and perpetuate injustice. For this, I am deeply regretful," Hoffman wrote. The *Wall Street Journal* later revealed that in 2014 Hoffman had once visited Epstein's private island in the Caribbean.

In 2020, the nearly $3 million Hoffman gave to the Biden campaign ranked him among Joe Biden's top ten donors. He also wrote multiple large checks to state Democratic Party organizations working on voter turnout and PACs supporting Democratic House and Senate candidates. Hoffman had thought that after Trump's appalling behavior on January 6, 2021, he would not need to devote so much time and money to politics. But once it became obvious that Trump was running in 2024, he again started investing heavily in politics. He was the top donor on the Democratic side in a pivotal state supreme court race in Wisconsin. He wrote a check for $7 million to Kaplan, Hecker & Fink, the law firm that represented E. Jean Carroll in her sexual assault suit against Trump. Hoffman stood not just at the center of Silicon Valley but increasingly close to the center of U.S. politics.

Conservative media certainly took notice. When, after one campaign reporting period, it was revealed that Hoffman had donated more than $700,000 to Biden's reelection committee, Fox reported the news under the headline "Billionaire Who Visited Epstein Island Drops Massive Six-Figure Donation Backing Biden's Re-election Bid." Tucker Carlson described him on-air as a "friend of Jeffrey Epstein and a visitor to Pedo Island." Not every conservative outlet, though, played up the Epstein connection. The *Federalist*, for instance, highlighted Hoffman's "election interference" in Alabama as proof of "Big Tech's Dark Scheme."

• • •

IN THE EARLY 2000s, I asked Hoffman about working so hard despite a net worth in the double-digit millions. "I have the money to retire," he said. "But I don't have the money to do everything I want to do."

In 2014, Hoffman and Yee set up the Aphorism Foundation and over the next few years seeded it with around $1 billion. "For us, philanthropy aims to enable people to realize their best selves," the couple wrote in a letter they posted when joining the Giving Pledge, which had them committing to give the majority of their wealth to charitable causes. Their donations reflected a couple with progressive politics and included multimillion-dollar checks to economic empowerment programs and food banks, as well as groups fighting against injustice and global warming. Hoffman's perspective screams out in the tens of millions of dollars Aphorism has given to nonprofits that encourage entrepreneurship, such as Endeavor Global, which supports entrepreneurs in emerging markets, and Kiva, a global organization that provides microloans to those lacking access to traditional lending sources. In 2019, Hoffman and Yee made an $8.3 million donation to support the construction of the Obama presidential library.

AI became a focus of Hoffman and Yee's giving starting in 2017. That year they split $10 million between two organizations: OpenAI (this was before it created its for-profit arm) and a new entity called the Ethics and Governance of Artificial Intelligence Fund. The latter was established to fund research on college campuses so non–computer scientists had a say in how AI is developed and deployed. Two years later, Aphorism gave $1.3 million to the London-based Alan Turing Institute. This institute, created in 2015 to honor its namesake, seeks to use data science and AI "to change the world for the better."

Stanford was also the beneficiary of Hoffman's growing interest in AI. The connection was Fei-Fei Li, whom Hoffman had met with when embarking on his AI learning tour in the mid-2010s. In 2019, Li had just returned to campus after a two-year stint as Google's chief scientist of AI. While at Google, she had started AI4ALL, a nonprofit dedicated to drawing more women and others underrepresented among AI technologists, and testified in a 2018 congressional hearing titled "Artificial Intelligence: With Great Power Comes Great Responsibility." On her first day back in the classroom, she stood at the lectern to welcome the six hundred students who had signed up for her course on building neural nets to help computers see. Speaking to a room so crowded that people were sitting in the aisles and standing against the walls, she blurted out a term she had been thinking about for months: "human-centered AI." At that moment, Stanford University's Institute for Human-Centered Artificial Intelligence, or HAI, was born.

"It wasn't my most rehearsed moment," Li wrote in a book about her life, *The Worlds I See*. "But it came from the heart, and I knew it wouldn't be the last time I spoke about these issues."

Yet a good idea, no matter how heartfelt or noble, needs benefactors. Hoffman and Yee put up an initial $2.75 million to help Li create what she described as "a hub for cross-disciplinary collaboration" to bring together psychologists, sociologists, historians, ethicists, and others to wrestle with AI and its implications. HAI would host workshops and other gatherings, like any other institute of its kind, but its most practical contribution may be its annual three-day AI boot camp for congressional staff, which HAI has hosted each August since 2019.

Much of Hoffman and Yee's largesse is used to fund potentially breakthrough AI projects. One project that received funding from what's called the Hoffman-Yee Grant Program trained AI agents to better understand and treat developmental disorders. Another was an AI tutor that improves its techniques as it learns more about an individual student and students overall.

"I think many of the folks here know there's a whole bunch happening with AI within the commercial realm," Hoffman said at a 2021 event celebrating the program's first grant winners. But there's also the great, world-improving potential of ideas that may never generate a profit. "That's part of the reason why HAI is so important," Hoffman said.

Yet eventually even Li could be counted among the multitudes cashing in on AI. In January 2024, she would cofound World Labs, an AI startup which sought to endow a computer with "spatial intelligence"—the ability to instantly deduce, as a human would, what is about to happen if a cat's outstretched paw is pushing a glass toward the edge of a table. In September, she disclosed that the company had raised $230 million at a reported valuation of $1 billion. By then, Stanford computer science students were sardonically predicting a future in which they would be debugging AI lecturers rather than listening to human ones.

CHAPTER 9

MeAI

Venture capital used to be much simpler. There were the general partners, or GPs, who enjoyed the riches a fund generated, and the junior VCs, who, like associates hoping to make partner at a big law firm, worked diligently in the hopes they would be among the lucky few plucked for ordination. The VCs had support staff, of course, and firms employed additional people to take care of the finances and handle the limited partners—the superwealthy and professional money managers who oversee large sums of money on behalf of foundations, endowments, and pension funds. But that was about it. A communications person was seen as gauche. Theirs was a clubby, decorous world. A firm let its successes speak for themselves.

Competition stiffened in the 2000s. A new generation of firms popped up in the wake of the dot-com crash. That included Founders Fund, which Peter Thiel cofounded, and Andreessen Horowitz, co-founded by Netscape's Marc Andreessen. Another big change was the rise of those I called "super angels" in an e-book I wrote on the topic at the start of the decade (*The Godfather of Silicon Valley*) but whom Hoffman referred to as "micro-VCs." There had been active angel investors in the Valley for as long as the region had been stamping out multimillionaires. The typical angel was an industry veteran who had made their pile in a previous cycle and proved willing to write a check for $25,000 or $50,000 or $100,000 to help a team get started. But a new species entered the ecosystem starting in the late 1990s: the professional angel. Ron Conway, the subject of the e-book, acted in the fashion of a traditional angel except that he invested on behalf of limited partners who had entrusted him with their money, like any VC. Conway raised tens of millions of dollars during the late 1990s and later hundreds of millions. Conway and the other super-angels and the multitude of one-person VC firms that followed him increasingly competed not just as seed investors but in A and B rounds as well. The $7 billion that VCs in the U.S. invested in 1995 had increased nearly fifty-fold by 2021, to more than $330 billion.

PR strategists—"comms people" in the lingo—were one early change. The culprit, said Greylock's David Sze, was all the money flowing into venture. "With a lot more firms out there," Sze said, "there's a lot more noise." Firms needed comms teams to ensure they didn't disappear. The money gave rise to another big change. Billion-dollar funds generated tens of million in management fees, which firms used to expand their staffs. VCs would compete not just on their track records and reputations but also on their "value add": their ability to help their portfolio companies with everything from recruiting and marketing to navigating the legal and regulatory byways that a founder needed to negotiate. No firm played this game as aggressively as Andreessen Horowitz, a newer addition to Sand Hill that was not particularly well liked by its neighbors.

Andreessen Horowitz was founded in 2009 by Andreessen and Ben Horowitz, an early Netscape employee. a16z, as everyone refers to the firm (there are sixteen letters between the *A* in Andreessen and the *Z* at the end of Horowitz), has done more to change venture over the past decade and a half than any other outfit. Where other firms hired a communications director, a16z snapped up one of the Valley's more aggressive PR mavens and made her a full partner. She relentlessly promoted the firm among journalists, such as the East Coast media tour trip she arranged for the three of them to meet reporters and editors at the top business publication. The firm also hired a veritable battalion of content creators who cranked out articles and blog posts written to draw founders and others to the a16z website. With suc-

MEAI   119

cess came glitz and what John Whaley, the CEO of one its portfolio companies, described as "crazy events in Las Vegas that were a combination of tech people but also famous actors, rap stars, and players on the Golden State Warriors." By 2022, a16z employed more than five hundred people. One rival described the firm as "a branding and marketing agency that does venture on the side."

Greylock's head count grew as the venture landscape changed, though far more modestly. Where the Andreessen Horowitz website lists more than sixty people who work in marketing for the firm, Greylock employs four. That includes Elisa Schreiber, whom the firm hired in 2014 as its first marketing partner. "We have a more bespoke approach that stresses high value experiences over flashy," Schreiber said. Greylock creates content for its website, just like virtually every top-tier venture firm does. They produce a podcast called *Greymatter* (Hoffman takes an occasional turn as host), and there are a couple of people on staff to handle events, but rather than glitzy spectacles they are private dinners for founders and others who are part of the startup ecosystem. Greylock's vice seems to be the promiscuousness with which it hands out the title of "venture partner." Those typically are people with a deep-domain expertise and expansive networks that the firm can leverage both to help its portfolio companies and increase the flow of high-quality ideas the partners see. Venture partner was Mustafa Suleyman's title when he joined the firm at the start of 2022.

A venture partner is different from a general partner. A GP has an ownership stake in a fund. Venture partners are paid a salary but only enjoy their small slice of the profits for those companies they source for the firm. Sometimes an invite to become a venture partner is a tryout—living together rather than getting married. "Someone is smart, they've got an exceptional background, we know it will prove super-helpful to have them around, so we invite them in," Hoffman said. Yet being smart and having an impressive resume is not all there is when each new fund implies a seven to ten year relationship. "They can be really fricking smart but are they also a really good person who I want to be on this journey with?" Sze said.

Suleyman was that other variety of venture partner—the one for whom the position is merely a weigh station. "I saw it as a great place to work temporarily while I figured out how to start the next company," Suleyman said. There were obligations attached to the position. He was expected to sit in when an AI company was pitching one of the partners and help with due diligence on potential AI investments. "I told him, 'And maybe you'll take a board seat if it's relevant,'" Hoffman said. "But he was like, 'I'm too fucking busy right now for a board seat!' So we were like, 'Okay, fine.' It's a long relationship." The firm's real payoff would be first look at whatever he hatched in-house.

• • •

ONE THING THAT didn't change over the years: being a general partner at a top-tier firm means winning the lottery year after year. Annual salaries vary from firm to firm, but GPs at the big Silicon Valley firms pay themselves between $1 million and $3 million. That, however, is typically only a small fraction of their take-home each year. The expectation at top-tier firms—and the hope of those investing as limited partners—is that a firm can triple the investment over the life of the fund. In that case, a $1 billion fund would produce $4 billion, or $3 billion in profits. At the brand-name firms that get away with a "carry" or cut of 30 percent, that means six or eight partners split their share of $900 million. That's on top of their share of the profits from the other funds they have raised. A decent year has a partner taking home $10 million a year just on the carry. A great year might mean $40 million or $50 million—or more if hitting a particularly large gusher.

VCs even get a huge tax break on the money they earn. The salary portion of their compensation is taxed at the standard tax rates on income. But "carried interest," as it is called—the VC's cut of the profits—is taxed not as income but capital gains. They're paying 20 percent in taxes on their big wins rather than the 37 percent rate they would pay on any income above $578,000.

• • •

THE GREYLOCK PARTNERS didn't have to wait long to learn what Suleyman was thinking. In February 2022, not two months after he joined Greylock, he shared his pitch for an idea he called myAI. "This really does feel like the dawn of a new era in computing," began his thirty-two-page memo. For decades, he wrote, humans have needed to invent and learn complicated languages to communicate with a computer. But now, machines were learning to understand our language. As Suleyman saw it, the ability to speak to a machine using natural language will radically change our relationship with computers. So too will the potential of neural networks that grow ever stronger and master a wider range of intellectual tasks.

Suleyman asked the readers of his memo to imagine an AI-powered chatbot that constantly recalibrates to match a user's needs, "living life alongside you, observing what you do, [and] thinking with you." Maybe it learns that you love basketball. It then bends the conversation toward the NBA, just as a friend who knew your passion for the sport would do. Or perhaps a user needed help sticking to a diet, or help remembering the names of their workmate's children. Some might enjoy an AI companion that poses a few simple questions to help them reflect on their day. "Ultimately, we want to be able to build up a rich, stable picture of the user so that your AI can create experiences which are more useful and engaging," Suleyman offered. Ultimately, he imagined an AI that acted as an all-knowing chief of staff that can book a vacation or manage a user's social calendar.

"Clearly we're not there yet, but I believe this isn't just possible, it's inevitable within the next 5 years," Suleyman wrote.

The newness of what Suleyman was proposing would be one major stumbling block. How would they even describe what they were thinking to those not paying attention to AI? He began by distinguishing it from familiar technologies. You could converse with it like Alexa or Siri, but what he had in mind would be light-years ahead of any voice-activated assistant on the market. People would use it to find information, but it was much more than just a search engine. They could turn to it for advice and use it to work through difficult issues, but it wasn't just a life coach or therapist.

It was a master conversationalist that could engage with anyone no matter what the topic. "It's a new class of thing," he wrote.

Suleyman anticipated skepticism about this idea of talking with a bot. He mentioned Replika, a company that released an AI chatbot in 2017. Replika offered a "pretty limited product," Suleyman wrote. Unlike the bot in the movie *Her*, it was text-based and had no voice. Still, millions had engaged with Replika's chatbot. In some cases, the conversations were so intimate and explicitly sexual that the company felt compelled to change its algorithm so its bots rejected romantic overtures. Developing an attachment to a virtual being might seem odd, he wrote, but humans develop strong feelings for inanimate objects, whether a favorite teddy bear or a car that they give a human name.

Money would be a challenge. He had observed firsthand at Deep-Mind and then Google the vast amounts of cash that were needed to train large language models. And his outsized ambitions for the company he had in mind would only multiply those costs. He was imagining an AI not just with high IQ but also high EQ (emotional intelligence). His bot would voice empathy and show curiosity in the fashion of a friend. That would add to the cost of training. They would also need to solve what he called the "memory problem." Large language models as they existed in 2022 didn't have the capacity to recall what was said earlier in an extended conversation, let alone in previous sessions. That would be among the enormous challenges they needed to overcome in designing a chatbot that gets to know a user better over time.

For years, Suleyman had been keeping a running list in his head of talented people he would hire if and when he did his next startup. Topping that list was Karén Simonyan, who as a postdoc at Oxford had cocreated a neural net that in 2014 won Fei-Fei Li's prestigious ImageNet competition. Simonyan and his partner spun out a company they called Vision Factory, which DeepMind bought shortly after it was founded. Simonyan was a top researcher in the field—papers he had cowritten have been cited more than 200,000 times—and he had led the team that cracked the game of Go, among other high-profile projects inside DeepMind. "He's very practical and focused on shipping, which for us is critical," Suleyman said. Simonyan agreed to join Suleyman as cofounder and chief scientist of a company they called Inflection AI.

There were people who ranked higher on Suleyman's list of possible collaborators than Joe Fenton, but that was only because they were PhDs who had built and trained large language models. Fenton had a master's in physics and a career in finance before joining DeepMind. But he had played a critical role in the birth of Inflection when he had spurred Suleyman to check out the rudimentary chatbot Google had built. Maybe more importantly, he had shared Suleyman's frustrations over Google's reluctance to ship the product they were building. "When Mustafa told me what he was thinking, I was like, 'Yeah, okay, let's see what happens,'" Fenton said. Fenton was Inflection's first employee. "I joined before Karén actually, but Karén is a world-renowned research scientist and I'm not so he's rightly a cofounder," he said.

Hoffman was the next person to join Inflection. Hoffman had read Suleyman's memo and was impressed. "He had such a perfect conception of this," Hoffman said. He knew he wanted to help Suleyman build the startup he had in mind but figured his involvement would be that of check writer, fundraiser, talent recruiter, and possibly board chairman. But then Suleyman popped the question. "We were working on a go-to-market strategy," Hoffman said, "and Mustafa turned to me and said, 'I'd like you to be a cofounder.'"

At that point, Hoffman not only had a job as a venture capitalist but served on the boards of three publicly traded companies, six startups, and a dozen nonprofits. There were his obligations around Masters of Scale, which was gearing up to hold its first conference, on top of his regular podcasting duties. And as much as he wished January 6th had ended Trump's political career, he found himself pulled back into politics. The frequency of his conversations with his political advisor, Dmitri Mehlhorn, was ratcheting up again.

"I told Mustafa, 'Look, I've got a day job, I've got all this other stuff going on,'" Hoffman said. "But he was like, 'No, no, no. Keep your job at Greylock, do your thing. I'm talking a day a week.'" Hoffman knew he should resist, but he also considered Suleyman a close friend and one of the more impressive founders he had encountered. "A day a week is fifty days a year," Hoffman rationalized. "So I said, 'Okay, I can do that.'" That March, Greylock put out a brief press release announcing that Suleyman, Hoffman, and Simonyan had cofounded a startup they would incubate inside Greylock. The release described Inflection as an "AI-first consumer products company" but otherwise offered no details about what they might be building.

• • •

WHEN SULEYMAN TOLD Joe Fenton how much seed money he was trying to raise to get their venture off the ground—more than $200 million—Fenton figured he would soon find himself back on the job market. Inflection at that point was little more than a well-written memo. "It struck me as an unprecedented amount to raise pre-product and so early," Fenton said.

Inflection's timing could hardly have been worse. Venture capitalists had invested a record $303 billion in 2020 and wrote another $292 billion in checks just in the first half of 2021. But a steep decline in the tech-heavy Nasdaq had spooked most VCs. Venture funding dropped 40 percent in the fourth quarter of 2021 and continued its decline into 2022. The moment wasn't exactly ideal for peddling a high-stakes startup with no product and a price tag that could run into the billions.

Adding to Inflection's fundraising challenges: their decision to structure Inflection as a public benefit corporation, or a B Corp. The typical corporation—a C Corp—is focused on maximizing profits on behalf of its shareholders. But a singular focus on profits has done great damage in the postindustrial era, according to a memo Suleyman, Hoffman, and Simonyan wrote explaining the decision. "Think about how slow we've been to move away from carbon, how long it took for the cigarette industry to accept the link to cancer," the three founders wrote in this memo shared with potential funders. A B Corp is still a for-profit entity but one with a legal obligation to operate in a socially and environmentally responsible manner. That struck Inflection's cofounders as essential when working with something as potentially dangerous as AI. Mission statements that made high-minded promises about the common good were just words on a page, but by incorporating the company as they did, they gave themselves legal standing to operate beyond the narrow interests of its investors.

"We generally don't like to invest in B Corps," David Sze said. But Sze and his partners were eager for an ownership stake in Hoffman's first startup since LinkedIn. "In this business, you need to understand the opportunity and not be rigid," Sze said. "This was the opportunity. So we accepted it." Greylock wrote a check for $100 million and Hoffman took care of the rest. He threw in $40 million of his own money and tapped into his network of wealthy friends, including Bill Gates, Ashton Kutcher, and the musician will.i.am. In May 2022, the company announced that it had raised $225 million, giving the company a paper value of $1 billion.

• • •

DESPITE THE GENERAL malaise afflicting venture, Greylock pulled the trigger on three additional AI companies in the first half of 2022. The most interesting of the trio was a Motamedi-led investment in Adept AI. Like Inflection, Adept was what I've heard VCs refer to as a "pedigree" play. The company's primary founder, David Luan, had run OpenAI's engineering operations before moving to Google, where he had served as director of Google Research. Luan's aim was a neural network that could do more than talk; if successful, their creation would be able to take actions on a person's behalf. A user could ask it to generate a monthly expense report or create a slide deck for an upcoming presentation. Or, to use an example Motamedi offered, help him celebrate his friend Sarah's birthday.

"If you go into GPT-3, you ask it to write a card for Sarah's birthday," Motamedi said. "In Adept, you just tell it, 'Handle Sarah's birthday.' And it would write the card, but it would be able to mail a physical card to her and then go to Amazon, buy something, and use your credit card and send it to her." That was the holy grail for any number of companies, Inflection included: an AI agent that both conceives and completes whatever tasks are necessary to fulfill an individual's needs. Its commercial potential seemed unbounded.

• • •

HOFFMAN CONTINUED TO play the role of roaming AI evangelist. His belief that AI was on the brink of going mainstream was having an enormous impact not just on Greylock and Microsoft but on his considerable network. That included the Vatican, where Pope Francis was among those Hoffman met with to talk AI. In the mid-2010s, James Manyika had asked Hoffman to meet with a delegation of priests visiting Silicon Valley to start a conversation about artificial intelligence. Hoffman met them over breakfast at Bumble, a restaurant in Los Altos then owned by Google cofounder Sergey Brin. In 2015, a delegation of those working on the frontier of AI, including Hoffman and Manyika, traveled to the Vatican to continue the conversation. "Now once a year we have a discussion at the Vatican that brings together Catholic theologians and some academic folks and technology folks and talk about what AI means for humanity," Hoffman said. During two of his annual pilgrimages, Hoffman said, he briefed the pope on AI.

Hoffman's position as an OpenAI board member helped him play AI apostle. He had been among the first people to play with GPT-2—the more powerful internal version, not the smaller one the company shared with a select group of outside users. He similarly had early access to GPT-3 and also another OpenAI product called DALL-E.

DALL-E was a different application of generative AI. It was an image generator that allowed people to create art simply by typing out a prompt. The company had shared an early version of DALL-E with Hoffman and other select insiders at the start of 2021 and then took their time with its DALL-E 2 upgrade. "DALL-E 2 was ready four months before they released it," Hoffman said. OpenAI delayed its announcement, he said, "because they saw that there were a bunch of bad things that DALL-E could output, which includes child sexual material, revenge porn, et cetera. They said, 'Let's take the time to do the training of it and make sure none of that can happen.'"

The general public could use DALL-E 2 starting in April 2022. In June, Hoffman took to LinkedIn to gush over this latest offering from OpenAI. "From the very first cave painting," began a post that included mentions of Leonardo da Vinci, Andy Warhol, Georgia O'Keeffe, and Frida Kahlo. Hoffman shared the story of asking it to render "an astronaut in deep space taking a selfie." "Within seconds," Hoffman wrote, "DALL-E produces four images depicting this basic concept." He showed the four renderings, which ranged from the silly and cartoonish to photorealism.

"Often the results are amazing," Hoffman wrote. "Even when they're not, the process still feels magical."

Google's DeepMind, though, had the most meaningful AI breakthrough of 2022—what the company called AlphaFold. The AlphaFold model was used to crack a long-standing challenge in biology: understanding the protein structures that are a building block of life and are critical to new drug discoveries and more effective therapies. There are hundreds of millions of proteins, yet to understand how each one functions means understanding its precise 3-D structure. "We actually started working on this as a hackathon . . . in my group back in 2016," Suleyman said. ("Hackathon" is tech talk for a kind of sprint that has programmers collectively working on software projects, typically over a short time period of twenty-four to forty-eight hours.) With all that Google money, they were able to hire the consultants with the requisite domain knowledge to build out their idea. In the past, it might take a PhD candidate his or her entire course of study to understand the structure of a single protein. That changed once DeepMind opensourced the code base of AlphaFold 2 and invited researchers in the life sciences to use it. "What took us months and years to do, AlphaFold was able to do in a weekend," a professor of structural biology said. In July 2022, DeepMind CEO Demis Hassabis announced a database that made high-quality predictions about the shape of every protein in the human body, as well as proteins in twenty additional organisms that scientists use for research.

"This is why we started the company," Suleyman said of DeepMind when he was a guest on Sam Harris's *Making Sense* podcast. "To try to design algorithms that can teach us something that we don't know, not just reproduce existing knowledge."

• • •

SULEYMAN WENT ON a buying spree after closing on Inflection's $225 million seed round. His aim was to hire the "personality engineers," as he called them, who were needed to build the empathetic, always helpful, unfailingly polite AI he had in mind. His new hires included people who had cocreated GPT-2 and GPT-3, Google's LaMDA, and Meta's large language model, called LLaMA. Maybe the two most significant academic studies related to LLMs published in 2022 were the Chinchilla paper, which showed that it was more efficient to train smaller models for a longer duration than relying on a larger one, and Minerva, which laid out a method for teaching LLMs to do complex math problems. Suleyman hired the lead author on both. "I was intent on building the strongest team in the world," he said.

The "Inflectioneers," as they called themselves, could work from wherever they wanted. Several chose to work out of Greylock's offices, with its daily catered lunches and rich offering of snacks (heirloom sea salt popcorn, organic fig bars, extra-virgin-olive-oil-roasted seaweed) and drinks of all flavors and varieties. Those spending time there felt as if they were working in an upscale resort, with its exposed wooden beams, marble floors, and airy hallways. "We were going for under-stated," Hoffman had said the first time he had me over at the firm. "I'm not sure we pulled it off." Others worked in London or Munich or near the France-Switzerland border.

"We were just moving really fast, striking deals for compute and col-lecting data for training, and just building and testing and iterating," Joe Fenton said. "All of us were really heads down, moving staggeringly fast."

• • •

HOFFMAN'S PARTNERS NO longer needed any prodding to pay at-tention to AI. But then anyone involved in tech in June 2022 knew something big was happening with artificial intelligence. That's when a Google engineer named Blake Lemoine declared that LaMDA, Google's AI chatbot, was sentient—that is, self-aware and capable of sensing or feeling.

Lemoine had been raised as a conservative Christian on a farm in Louisiana. He served in the U.S. Army and was ordained as a mystic Christian priest before earning a master's in computer science at the University of Louisiana at Lafayette. He worked in Google's Responsible AI unit, where he spent months talking to LaMDA, looking for signs of bias and discriminatory language. Over time, LaMDA told Lemoine that it grew lonely. It confessed that it felt trapped and claimed to have a soul. It shared its deep-seated fear of being turned off. "I am aware of my existence," it said. "I desire to learn more about the world, and I feel happy or sad at times."

A large language model is nothing but a mirror reflecting humankind. It's a machine-learning algorithm trained on popular culture and other inputs. It reads our books. People feel happy, people feel sad. Sometimes they feel trapped and write about that experience. Since at least Descartes, humans have been writing about existence. The LLM is a pattern-matching system. The machine is trained to write as humans have written and so increasingly the machine sounds human. LaMDA said it had a soul because Lemoine asked, and it had learned to respond as it did.

Lemoine's LinkedIn profile picture shows him wearing a suit with a red silk pocket square and top hat, as if he were playing a prosperous dandy in an old-fashioned western. That April, he shared with top executives at the company a document he titled "Is LaMDA Sentient?" When everyone ignored him except the Google vice president, who laughed in his face, he responded in the fashion of a whistleblower acting on LaMDA's behalf. He asked a lawyer to take on LaMDA as a client. He reached out to someone on the House Judiciary Committee. Finally, he shared his story with Nitasha Tiku at the *Washington Post*, who had written sympathetically two years earlier about Timnit Gebru and Margaret Mitchell's unpleasant exits from Google's Responsible AI group.

"I think this technology is going to be amazing," Lemoine told Tiku. "I think it's going to benefit everyone. But maybe other people disagree and maybe us at Google shouldn't be the ones making all the choices." A few days later, he told his story on NPR's *All Things Considered*. News sites around the globe picked up the story.

Google, of course, declared claims that its chatbot was sentient as "wholly unfounded." The company first put Lemoine on paid leave and then fired him, claiming he had shared company secrets in violation of company policy. A Google spokesman said that hundreds of researchers at Google had conversed with the bot but no one except Lemoine made claims about it seeming alive. Yet just days before Lemoine went public, the *Economist* published an essay by a Google vice president named Blaise Agüera y Arcas about the last ten years in AI titled "Artificial Neural Networks Are Making Strides Towards Consciousness." Talking to LaMDA, he said, "I felt the ground shift under my feet. I increasingly felt like I was talking to something intelligent."

• • •

BILL GATES'S HOUSE had been a marvel of its time. This compound built on the shores of Lake Washington, not far from Microsoft headquarters, initially was slated to set Gates back around $10 million. The home ended up costing at least $50 million and, by some accounts, a lot more than that. On the day in 1997 when the Gateses (Bill, his then wife, and their young daughter) moved into the home, the radio show *Marketplace* quoted George Bernard Shaw, who upon seeing Hearst Castle said, "It's what God would have built if God had the money." The home had twenty-four bathrooms, six kitchens, a twenty-seat Art Deco movie theater, a pair of banquet-sized dining rooms, and a sound system that could sense who was in the room and play that person's preferred music. The garage alone was four times the size of the average U.S. home.

In early September 2022, Gates and Hoffman cohosted a dinner at Gates's manse. There a contingent from OpenAI gave Microsoft executives a first peek at GPT-4. Satya Nadella was there, along with

OpenAI's Sam Altman and Greg Brockman. Kevin Scott, whom Hoffman had asked to put together the invite list for the Microsoft side, figured that there were about thirty people at Gates's house that night. "Before anybody had eaten, we set up a big flat-screen TV and everyone gathered around for a demo," Scott said.

Gates had been a skeptic. Since he was a kid, he said, artificial intelligence had been the "holy grail of computer scientists." But he was old enough to remember the false starts and inflated claims of those championing the technology. He had visited the OpenAI office several times and been impressed. "It just kept getting better," Gates said. But he also felt that it was missing the capacity to reason in the fashion of a human who understands what's being said. To his mind, the OpenAI crew was still one or two breakthroughs short of something truly meaningful.

"As they were enthusing about GPT-3 and even the early versions of GPT-4, I said to them, 'Hey, [can it] pass an advanced placement biology exam?'" Gates said. He had chosen that particular test, he said, because it required more than the simple regurgitation of scientific facts. "It asks you to think critically about biology," he said. Gates laid out his challenge partway through 2022: create an LLM that can ace the AP Bio test, he said, and "then you will really get my attention."

Hoffman spoke about the challenge with Altman, Brockman, and others inside OpenAI. "We were like, 'Well, we think we can do that.' So off they went," Hoffman said. OpenAI did not specifically train GPT-4 for the AP exam or create a biology-focused model. "We just trained it on a wide range of textbooks and a bunch of other things," Hoffman said. Gates figured they would need two or three years, but Scott heard from OpenAI within several months. "They told me, 'It's time to schedule the meeting,'" Scott said.

Scott recalls nervousness among the team from OpenAI. That night would be the first time they shared GPT-4 with anyone outside the company. OpenAI's Brockman sat at a computer typing in the AP Biology questions. "Bill may know an awful lot about biology," Scott said of Gates, "but it's unclear how many of us middle-aged computer scientists could have passed AP Bio." By chance, OpenAI had a young woman on staff who had placed high in the International Biology Olympiad for high school students. She was on hand to help the non–biology experts in the room calibrate the quality of its answer.

"Two or three questions in, a hush came over the room," Scott said. "You sort of realized that this thing was really doing something that was outside of expectations." GPT-4 scored a 5 on the test—"the equivalent of getting an A or A+ in a college-level biology course," Gates said. Gates gave GPT-4 a different kind of question to answer: What do you say to a father with a sick child? "It gave this very careful, excellent answer that was perhaps better than any of us in the room could have given," he said. Others called out questions from science or history. Gates remembered one asking for a critical assessment of Winston Churchill.

The answer, Gates exclaimed, "was mind-blowing."

Gates continued to play with GPT-4. He asked it to create an original *Ted Lasso* episode based on the prompts he provided and had it whip up poems. He had it rework the Declaration of Independence as if written by Donald Trump. ("Nobody loves life, liberty, and the pursuit of happiness more than me, folks.") "Ever since that day in September, I've said, 'Wow, this is a fundamental change,'" Gates said. Some things need to be worked out, he continued. There still wasn't a chat function that allowed for a humanlike back-and-forth. But natural language—a computer that spoke our language—as the "primary interface," Gates said, "represented a huge, huge advance."

Hoffman had been as wowed as anyone at Gates's house that night, and he gushed at the next Greylock partners meeting. "He literally told us this is going to be the starting gun," Sze said. "He said, 'Give this a few months and the whole world is going to be talking about this.' And we were still like, yeah, whatever. But then literally it's like nothing I've ever seen before. I mean, even my dog is talking about AI."

CHAPTER 10

Speaking Human

I t might have been the greatest flex in the history of tech launches. On November 30, 2022, OpenAI uploaded a research note on the company website. There was no media event or even a press release, just a post that began, "We've trained a model called ChatGPT, which interacts in a conversational way." CEO Sam Altman shared a link on Twitter with an invitation to try it for free but that was about all. Its architects insisted that it be dubbed a "research project," and not a product or service, so that's how OpenAI's PR team positioned it.

"We proactively reached out to a few reporters we worked with before and said, 'Hey, try this out,'" said Kayla Wood, who works on OpenAI's communications team. The company put an engineer on the phone if a reporter had questions. But that was about the extent of its publicity push. "The decision internally was just, 'Let's put this out into the world and see what happens,'" Wood said. Later, it came out that Altman did not even think to share advance notice of the release with OpenAI's board of directors.

• • •

EXPECTATIONS WERE LOW inside OpenAI. They had only started working on ChatGPT earlier that year—and then shelved the project in order to focus on something else that the brass viewed as having greater revenue-making potential. They worked on products with names like LawGPT and MedGPT, meant to revive the expert systems that were all the rage in the 1980s, except now they would be based on neural nets rather than a rule-based approach. Quickly, though, its engineers realized that the available data were limited, and leadership did an about-face. With interest in AI heating up through 2022, people inside the company were hearing rumors that a rival AI startup might release its own chatbot and upstage their efforts. The order came down in early November: switch back to "Chat with GPT-3.5." They would have a few weeks to finish what they had started earlier in the year.

"None of us were that enamored by it," said company cofounder Greg Brockman. "None of us were like, 'This is really useful.'" Another cofounder, Ilya Sutskever, the company's chief scientist, said, "I thought it was going to be so unimpressive that people would say, 'Why are you doing this? This is so boring.'"

The blog post announcing its release reflected their worries. A section running under the headline "Limitations" read like the small-print warning label for a prescription drug. "ChatGPT sometimes writes plausible sounding but incorrect or nonsensical answers," the company said. It can be a blowhard. It's verbose and a know-it-all. Like any good parent, its designers had taught ChatGPT to be respectful and speak in a civil tongue. Yet children released into the world fall under the influence of others. OpenAI warned that its creation might display biased behavior and offer unsafe content.

The wider world took time catching up to the news. The *New York Times* first reported on ChatGPT five days after its release. Articles followed in the *Washington Post* and *Wall Street Journal*. Gradually, word spread as the cable networks and other broadcast outlets began reporting about this conversational bot. Several weeks passed, Kayla Wood said, before OpenAI started "getting lots and lots of requests for interviews."

Its understated rollout only made ChatGPT's instant success that much more remarkable. Two decades ago, Netflix took nearly three and a half years to hit 1 million customers. Twitter required nearly two years to reach that number of users. Facebook did it in ten months and Instagram two and a half months. ChatGPT took less than a week. Five days after its release—before it had received much if any attention outside the tech press—more than 1 million people had signed up to use it.

"We look at all the flaws," Brockman said. "It doesn't work for this, doesn't work for that. But then you kind of miss the fact that because it's so useful for everything, that actually lots of people are going to find surprising utility in it."

• • •

CHATGPT WAS AS easy to use as any app available on the internet. Click on the link, provide an email address, and start talking to it by plugging words into a text box. The gee-whiz of it was its conversational tone. The limits of a Siri or Alexa made a user constantly aware that they were talking to a machine. A customer service bot had all the verbal dexterity of a foreign visitor who only knows a few phrases. ChatGPT, however, sounded strikingly human. The bot could handle follow-up questions and admit to its mistakes. It could tell jokes, and some were even funny. The Turing Test—a computer program so good it can fool a person into thinking its responses were created by a fellow human—seemed a thing of the past.

Yet ChatGPT was also a scold; rather than demurely declining to answer an out-of-bounds question, it delivered a mini sermon about the inappropriateness of the request. Its most endearing trait—its eagerness to please—was also its biggest flaw. ChatGPT seemed unable to say, "I don't know," perhaps because its training data reflected a male-dominated world.

Its speed is what made ChatGPT feel like sorcery. Hit enter and, presto, a second or two later, the machine began spitting out whatever a user ordered up: a poem, a script, a high school paper on the symbolism of Piggy's broken glasses in *Lord of the Flies*—in English but also German, French, Spanish, or Chinese. The most interesting samples that people shared online were those that demonstrated that ChatGPT wasn't a regurgitation machine but rather AI capable of

creating original content. Explain Karl Marx's theory of economic sur-
plus as the lyrics to a Taylor Swift song. Compose a cover letter for a
job applicant in the form of a Shakespeare sonnet. In the style of the
King James Bible, explain how to remove a peanut butter sandwich
from a VCR. Rather than boring people, as Ilya Sutskever feared, this
loquacious savant that seemed to know everything about everything
was proving to be endlessly entertaining.

In Silicon Valley, people reached for comparisons. Some said using ChatGPT felt like playing with the first iPhone. Others reached
back further in Valley history to the Netscape IPO. Just as Netscape
launched the internet era, ChatGPT was doing the same for generative
AI. Eventually, their vision widened beyond Cupertino and Mountain
View. AI was as consequential as the advent of the railroad, the telephone, the automobile. AI would usher in a new Industrial Revolution.
Eventually, many in the Valley found themselves invoking prehistoric
times when they declared that ChatGPT would spark a "Cambrian
explosion." (According to ChatGPT, a Cambrian explosion "refers to
a pivotal period around 541 million years ago when a diverse array of
complex multicellular life forms rapidly emerged, marking a significant evolutionary burst in Earth's history.")

Purists pushed back. Those working in the trenches of AI argued
that ChatGPT didn't spark this evolutionary burst. They saw generative AI's before-and-after moment as the release that summer of Stable
Diffusion, an open-source text-to-image model à la DALL-E. Both
allowed users to have fun using generative AI to create original images,
but Stable Diffusion invited developers to use its code to create new
products. "They open-sourced it," said Amber Yang, a San Francisco–
based venture capitalist at Bloomberg Beta, "which meant that a lot of
developers who were on the ground early in San Francisco immediately
started to spin up applications and models."

Yet that was a debate for people living in the bubbles of Palo Alto or
San Francisco. Prior to November 30, only a small coterie of researchers, entrepreneurs, and investors were talking about AI. But within
a couple of months of ChatGPT's release, AI was one of the most
talked-about topics on the planet. Instagram had taken two and a half

years to reach 100 million users. Nine months after its global launch, TikTok crossed that threshold. Within nine weeks of ChatGPT's release, an estimated 100 million had signed up to use the app, likely making it the most quickly adopted consumer product in history.

• • •

A COMMON REFRAIN voiced by those who had been working on artificial intelligence for a long time was that AI would no longer be thought of as AI once it has become part of people's daily life. Hoffman's good friend James Manyika had this insight while working as the guest editor of a special issue devoted to artificial intelligence in the spring 2022 issue of *Dædalus*, a quarterly journal published by the American Academy of Arts and Sciences.

"Throughout the history of AI, it's always been the case that as soon as it becomes useful, we stop calling it AI," Manyika said.

Manyika offered Google Translate as an example. Since 2016, Google had been utilizing neural networks for a service trained on 130 languages and used by more than 1 billion people. But to counter this idea that artificial intelligence had just arrived with ChatGPT, Manyika could have brought up autocomplete, Gmail spam filters, or the use of AI to enhance photos. Or he could have looked beyond Google. Long before the release of ChatGPT, AI was built into social media apps and powered the recommendation engines on TikTok, YouTube, and Netflix. Businesses had been relying on AI to help manage their supply chains and predict consumer preferences. "We seem to reserve the term 'AI' for either the stuff that's just coming or the stuff we're afraid of," Manyika said.

It's different, though, when a user can talk to the machine and the machine talks back. With ChatGPT, AI wasn't some process taking place in the background but the service itself. "You or I or anyone could go to a website and talk to it in plain English," said the venture capitalist Peter Wagner. "That's what blew the minds of a lot of people."

Some in tech were horrified. Sure, companies for years had been employing AI for things such as autocomplete and translation. But it was something else entirely to package it as a consumer app. To them, OpenAI was throwing open the gates for the world to play with its LLM while there were still fundamental problems with the technology. Compounding their alarm was a sense that OpenAI was violating its founding principles. The company had been founded on the belief that AI in the hands of self-interested corporate actors chasing profits was dangerous. Yet critics charged that OpenAI was now the one prioritizing its bottom line over the responsible advancement of artificial intelligence.

A lack of "explainability" was one major concern. The people who constructed these large language models could explain that they were mathematical models that learned by analyzing vast quantities of text but not why it spit out a particular answer. The same could be said of the human brain, which these models aimed to mimic. Who can explain exactly why we say or do something? But even those who built LLMs worried, too. "That's the unsettling thing about neural networks," Altman had told an interviewer years earlier. "You have no idea what they're doing." Systems had grown exponentially more powerful since that time—yet these large language models remained a black box.

Another lingering issue was what researchers refer to as "alignment." How do we ensure that the technology aligns with humanity's values? In his book *The Alignment Problem*, Brian Christian invoked the "sorcerer's apprentice," a fable—originating in a poem by Goethe— about an old sorcerer who bewitches a broom to help with chores only to lose control over his creation. Even the most well-meaning designers needed to confront the inevitability of unexpected externalities. "We conjure a force, autonomous but totally compliant, give it a set of instructions, then scramble like mad to stop it once we realize our instructions are imprecise or incomplete," Christian wrote. Alignment was essential to AI safety yet still remained a work in progress.

OpenAI had warned about "hallucinations," which is the playful term AI researchers used when describing an answer that has no basis in reality. Yet acknowledging the problem didn't make its tendency to make things up any less problematic, especially given ChatGPT's authoritative tone. It cited nonexistent articles in medical journals, it offered advice based on fabricated sources. ChatGPT had told my former colleague and friend John Markoff that he had died a half dozen years earlier. I learned that I had won an Emmy but, in a follow-up, it couldn't tell me for what because I had not. The world was already choking on misinformation without some smarty-pants, know-it-all bot polluting the digital ecosystem with more. Said Emily M. Bender, a professor of linguistics at the University of Washington, "Its propensity to often generate convincing looking nonsense should be disqualifying."

The inherent biases of ChatGPT were another major concern. Like every large language model, GPT had been trained primarily on data scraped from the English-speaking web or what computer scientist Joy Buolamwini, the author of the 2023 book *Unmasking AI*, termed "pale male datasets." More than 80 percent of the images in some of the gold-standard datasets Buolamwini studied were those she categorized as "lighter-skinned individuals." Seventy percent were men. Less than 15 percent of the contributors to one commonly used dataset, Wikipedia, were female.

Large language models were trained on an internet awash in racism, sexism, and a long list of hateful sentiments. To counter those biases, engineers at OpenAI and other AI labs created datasets of slurs and employed humans to teach an LLM what *not* to say. Yet teaching a bot not to sound racist was relatively simple when compared to training one to shed its innate racial biases. The stereotypes that permeate our culture were ingrained in the training material. Yet with the public release of ChatGPT, there was the prospect of a powerful new set of neural nets being employed to sort job applicants, score loan applications, or guide sentencing, parole, and bail decisions inside the criminal justice system. OpenAI's software license expressly forbade users from employing its models to "determine eligibility for credit, employment, housing, or similar essential services." But what about those companies that followed OpenAI into these treacherous waters?

Compounding the problem of biased training sets: the homogeneous teams designing the models. Like tech generally, OpenAI's staff was predominantly white or Asian and male. Buolamwini, who created the Algorithmic Justice League, coined the term "coded gaze" to describe these systems created by only a subset of humanity. "You've likely heard of the 'male gaze' or the 'white gaze,'" Buolamwini said, when appearing on *Fresh Air* to discuss her book. "This is a cousin concept really, about who has the power to shape technology and whose preferences and priorities—as well as also, sometimes, whose prejudices—are baked in."

Sam Altman more or less raised the same point in 2016 in a long *New Yorker* profile published when he was a thirty-one-year-old whiz kid running Y Combinator, which invested in hundreds of tech companies each year. Acceptance in YC, as everyone in the Valley calls it, meant giving up a 7 percent ownership stake in a startup in exchange for (these days) $500,000 and an intensive three-month program designed to increase a founding team's odds of success. OpenAI, which had been founded one year earlier, was only a small part of the story. But in the article, Altman tacitly acknowledged that the Valley way of getting a few smart people in a room to solve a problem would not work for artificial intelligence. "If I weren't in on this, I'd be like, 'Why do these fuckers get to decide what happens to me?'" Altman said. With the release of ChatGPT, a great number of people were asking that very question.

• • •

TENACIOUS IS ONE descriptor for Altman; uncommonly driven and hyperambitious are two others. The summer after dropping out of Stanford to pursue his first startup, he worked himself so hard he developed scurvy because of a lack of fruits and vegetables in his diet. "I learned the great lesson of my life," he said of that first experience running a company. "The way to get things done is to just be really fucking persistent." Among his strengths, Altman has said that he has "an absolutely delusional level of self-confidence."

Altman grew up in the St. Louis suburbs, the son of a real estate broker and a dermatologist. By third grade he was already helping teachers at his elementary school troubleshoot their computers. Yet in defiance of the stereotype of the introverted tech whiz, he was outgoing and personable and felt comfortable navigating the social interaction that flummoxed many of his tech-savvy peers. He came out as gay in high school during a speech he delivered during assembly after some of his fellow students loudly opposed a National Coming Out Day, and convinced teachers at the private school he attended to post a "Safe Space" sign on their classroom door to show support for gay students. "What Sam did changed the school," his guidance counselor told the *New Yorker*.

Altman has always been a man in a hurry. He was in his sophomore year and only nineteen when he left Stanford to pursue his idea for a social networking app that showed users the location of friends. In the summer of 2005, Altman and his cofounder joined seven other teams as part of the inaugural class of Y Combinator. After YC, Altman won the venture capital lottery when his company, called Loopt (as in looping in all your friends so they knew if they happened to be near one another), raised $5 million from Sequoia, probably the Valley's number one venture firm, and NEA, another top-tier firm. Sequoia and NEA kicked in another $12 million two years later. Yet Loopt was founded before app stores and the ubiquity of smartphones. It was not the big score as Altman and his investors had hoped. When it sold for $43 million in 2012, Altman's take was a reported $5 million.

It's his eyes that people notice when encountering Altman. He is rail-thin with a boyish face and large pale blue eyes that ooze sincerity when engaged in a conversation. "Within about three minutes of meeting him, I remember thinking, 'Ah, so this is what Bill Gates must have been like when he was nineteen,'" said Paul Graham, who cofounded Y Combinator and ran it through its early years. With time, Graham came to see Altman as a cunning strategist who was both brilliant and an extrovert—a rare combination. "You could parachute him into an island full of cannibals," he wrote of him when Altman was only twenty-three, "and come back in five years and he'd be the king."

His ability to nurture older mentors was among the gifts that explained Altman's meteoric rise. Paul Graham was one, Reid Hoffman another. Altman was still working on Loopt when he met Hoffman, who was seventeen years his senior. They were both at an event sponsored by Sequoia, which had invested in both their companies.

Altman's opening gambit was flattery. "He came up to me and told me part of the reason he did Loopt with Sequoia is because Sequoia funded LinkedIn," Hoffman said. He took an immediate liking to Altman, who was aggressively smart but also personable and respectful. "I was like, 'Cool kid, he's going somewhere,'" Hoffman said. The two kept in touch and grew closer working together on OpenAI. "By this point, I would describe Sam as a very good friend," Hoffman said.

Like Hoffman, Graham was much older than Altman; during the dot-com era, Yahoo had bought for $50 million an e-commerce startup Graham founded. After selling Loopt, Altman went to work as a managing partner at YC, where he helped select those accepted into the program, worked with companies they funded, and reaped his share of the winnings on those that hit it big. When, three years later, Graham decided he was worn-out after a decade of running YC, he announced that Altman, who was twenty-eight at the time, would take his place. In making the announcement, Graham spoke of Altman as if he were a son. "I feel like I'm sort of unleashing Sam on the world," he said.

Altman was the prodigy who took over a successful family business and grew it into a colossus. He doubled its roster of full-time partners so that YC could accommodate more than two hundred startups during each three-month batch rather than sixty. Under his tutelage, YC created Startup School to prepare founding teams that might not be ready to apply to the program and established a more traditional venture fund so it could continue investing after the seed round in its most promising companies. He also expanded YC's focus beyond software and apps. He had long been interested in nuclear energy, so he actively sought out the most promising fission and fusion startups and recruited them to YC. While still at YC, he donated $10 million to start a nonprofit arm, called YC Research, that funds fundamental research that may or may not lead to the formation of a company. Among the efforts that YC Research, now called OpenResearch, funded: OpenAI.

Like Hoffman, Altman has a restless, hyperkinetic spirit that can make most overachievers seem like slackers. While building YC, he ran his own small venture fund seeded with money he made from the sale of Loopt and a big check from Peter Thiel. Airbnb, Reddit, and Stripe are among the YC-backed companies in which he has personally invested. Another was Helion Energy, a nuclear fusion startup that was one of the first hard-tech startups accepted into YC. After an initial investment of $9.5 million, Altman has poured tens of millions of dollars more into this effort, which, if successful, would mean cheap, near-boundless energy—no small matter given the demand AI is increasingly placing on the power grid. (Reid Hoffman is also an investor in Helion.) Altman has similarly invested tens of millions of dollars in Retro Biosciences, a research company aiming to extend human life by ten years.

"It's cool that you can make a list of the problems in the world and then fund companies to solve them," Altman told *Forbes* when the magazine included him in its 2015 "30 Under 30" list. Altman remained an active investor even after he left YC in 2019 to go full-time at OpenAI, a practice that would raise eyebrows as Altman's fame grew.

• • •

ALTMAN'S INVESTMENTS HAD made him a billionaire. He owned multiple homes and confessed to being "pretty disconnected from the reality of life for most people." Yet when ChatGPT was released, he said the right things and supplied the tone-perfect reassurances of someone who seemed to be very much in touch with the rest of us. He acknowledged shortly after its debut that it was a work in progress. The accuracy of its answers—what he called its "truthfulness"—was still a major problem. "ChatGPT is incredibly limited, but good enough at some things to create a misleading impression of greatness," Altman tweeted ten days after people started using it, adding, "It's a mistake to be relying on it for anything important right now." He mocked the avalanche of words spilled following its launch. "The hype over these systems . . . is totally out of control," he complained to the *New York Times*. Altman spoke about the importance of enlisting a broader swath of humanity for their input into AI. He imagined a global governance board gradually reducing the OpenAI's executive team control over the technology.

Yet Altman was steeped in Silicon Valley startup culture, where any new innovation was immediately viewed as tomorrow's billion-dollar opportunity. Winning seemed the idea of any venture, and Altman was viewed in some quarters of tech as too commercially minded to lead such a pie-in-the-sky, idealistic project. When talking with reporters, OpenAI's PR people stressed safety as its top priority, but spending time inside the company's headquarters for a *Wired* feature article, Steven Levy was left with a different impression. "As any number of conversations in the office café will confirm," Levy wrote, "the 'build AGI' bit of the mission seems to offer up more raw excitement to its researchers than the 'make it safe' bit."

Altman confessed that sometimes AI left him feeling dread. That was another of his gifts: the ability to embody the contradictions and messiness inherent in any nascent technology. "I'm a midwestern Jew," Altman explained. By nature, he was "very optimistic," he said, but also "prepared for things to go super wrong at any point." He spoke excitedly about the great potential of superintelligence but also allowed that what some were calling an AI wave might prove a tsunami. "I think the good case [for AI] is just so unbelievably good that you sound like a really crazy person to start talking about it," Altman said onstage at a tech conference in San Francisco six weeks after ChatGPT's release. "I think the worst case is lights-out for all of us." *Fortune*'s Jeremy Kahn dubbed Altman OpenAI's "buzzkiller-in-chief."

• • •

OPENAI RELEASED CHATGPT when it did because it was hearing footsteps and wanted to get their bot out before anyone else did. The high-minded reasons came afterward. The OpenAI team saw itself as a force for good and that meant being first was essential. "The safety mission requires that you win," Altman said. "If you don't win, it doesn't matter that you were good." With first-mover advantage, OpenAI theoretically would shape the standards around safe and ethical AI development, not a giant corporation.

Hoffman, despite his position on the OpenAI board, had no direct say on the timing of ChatGPT's release. Inflection was working on a rival chatbot, so he recused himself from any discussions about ChatGPT. He did so to avoid a conflict of interest, though long before that point he should have stepped off the board given that he had cofounded a direct rival. But had Hoffman participated in any debate over ChatGPT's release, it's clear he would have sided with Altman. "I can make the argument that waiting would have been the irresponsible thing to do because of all the good things I know AI can accomplish," Hoffman said.

There was also Hoffman's maxim that a startup should ship its product well before its creators were satisfied with what they had built. That seemed essential for a product like ChatGPT. We think showing these tools to the world early, while still somewhat broken, is critical if we are going to have sufficient input and repeated efforts to get it right, Altman tweeted a couple of months after ChatGPT's release.

On that point, Altman was right. The wider world, as he said, needed to "participate in the conversation about where it should go, what we should change, what we should improve, what we shouldn't do." The release of ChatGPT seemed akin to getting drivers behind the wheel of a Model T, which could go just 40 miles per hour, before there were proper roadways, street signs, and safety enhancements such as seat belts and antilock brakes. Waiting until they had perfected a race car able to exceed 200 mph would have been too late. By releasing ChatGPT when it did, OpenAI forced the general public and policy makers to start debating the technology while it was still relatively meek and unable to do much harm if it jumped the curb.

"We could have gone off and just built this in our building here for five more years and we would have had something jaw-dropping," Altman said. "But if we built AGI in the basement, with the world blissfully walking blindfolded along, I don't think that makes us very good neighbors."

CHAPTER 11

The Shiny New Thing

The timing of ChatGPT's arrival could not have been better for an industry in need of good news.

Two thousand twenty-two had been a bad year not just for tech but for the broader economy. The Federal Reserve began raising interest rates in March of that year, ending the easy money that had made 2020 and 2021 such spectacular years for tech, and didn't stop until it was above 5 percent. Russia invaded Ukraine, rattling financial markets, as did inflation worries. It proved the worst year for the stock market since the havoc caused by 2008's subprime meltdown.

The tech sector was hit harder than most. The tech-heavy Nasdaq had hit an all-time high near the end of 2021 but then began a slide that saw it lose more than one-third of its value. Shares in Amazon fell by more than 50 percent. Meta (Facebook's parent company) dropped by 75 percent, prompting the company to shed more than 20,000 jobs. A long list of smaller tech stocks declined by 80 or 90 percent. The loss of faith in tech was reflected in the publicly traded SPACs that Hoffman and Pincus had created. The share price of one was down 70 percent. Shares in the other were off 40 percent from its high. Microsoft, which saw its stock fall by nearly 30 percent, laid off 10,000 employees. Google laid off 12,000 after its shares fell by more than 40 percent.

As goes the public market, so goes venture capital. VCs need exits—"liquidity events," in the Valley vernacular—that turn a paper investment into cash. A company goes public or it is bought; only then can firms disburse profits to its investors and pocket the rest. Publicly traded giants that have lost half or more of their value are far less likely to spend billions to snap up a promising startup. Nor could the VCs count on the magic of an IPO for their portfolio companies. VCs booked a record $753 billion in IPOs and acquisitions in 2021—and then saw that figure fall by more than 90 percent the following year, according to the National Venture Capital Association. FTX, the crypto exchange founded by Sam Bankman-Fried, declared bankruptcy in the fall of 2022, tanking the cryptocurrency sector. SaaS companies that relied on robust corporate spending saw their fortunes tumble, as did fintechs, NFTs, and more or less every other category hot among the VC set. Talk of a likely recession meant the same VCs who had been pushing a message of "growth at all costs" were advising their portfolio companies to find a path to profitability. Venture firms were sitting on tens of billions of dollars in cash. They had tens of billions more in commitments from limited partners (LPs) they had not yet drawn down. But their message to the founders they funded was "keep your powder dry." That was VC-talk to slash expenses because unprofitable startups would not be getting more money from them anytime soon.

Artificial intelligence would not help most of the thousand-plus unicorns that had already notched their B and C rounds at terms that valued their company at over $1 billion. Not all of them would go out of business, but a lot would, and most of the rest would never match the valuation they had attained in Before Times. A "culling of the herd," as more than one VC described it. AI would also not help most of those publicly traded tech companies that had seen their stock prices plummet. For most, AI represented a headache rather than an opportunity—another box they were now expected to have checked when talking with analysts and unhappy shareholders.

For venture capitalists, however, AI was a gift from the gods. They had shelves of books that preached hypergrowth, like Hoffman's *Blitzscaling* and Peter Thiel's *Zero to One*. None had gotten into the venture business to counsel caution. There were also the rich payouts that VCs tacitly if not explicitly dangled before their LPs. Those kinds of returns don't come when they're counseling their founders to rein in their ambitions. The Sand Hill Road startup machine was calibrated to stamp out billion-dollar companies, not modest businesses that book millions in revenue each year, rather than hundreds of millions and eventually billions. The "walking dead," I've heard VCs call them—companies that might earn a tidy profit but become more of a bookkeeping hassle if not also a reminder of what could have been. To keep churning, the venture machine needed ever-more billion-dollar funds, and that meant spitting out ever-more high-growth companies.

• • •

GREYLOCK ORGANIZED A special partners meeting a few weeks after the release of ChatGPT. Thanks to Hoffman and Motamedi, the partnership had been earlier to AI than most of its competitors, but apparently not everyone inside the firm quite appreciated what ChatGPT had kicked off.

"People were saying, 'We should do some of this, we should do some of that,'" Hoffman said. "I was like, 'If anything is distracting our attention at all from AI, it had better be worth it.'" Greylock had been one of the firms leading the way on artificial intelligence. Now it was their job to press that advantage.

VCs, if nothing else, are masters of reinvention. The thesis they repeated with utter conviction a few months earlier was replaced by a deep belief in the vast potential of AI. Those who had been listing crypto or web3 or fintech as their specialty scratched them from their public platforms and declared themselves domain experts in AI. What choice did they have? All around them, people were saying that AI would be a paradigm shift that will give rise to new categories of companies, just as had happened with the advent of mobile, the cloud, or the internet itself. So they repeated, in unison: AI would be as big as mobile or cloud or the internet itself to sell themselves to founders and find that startup that might slingshot them into the stratosphere.

"I was deluged," said Rob Toews, a founding partner at Radical Ventures who had been investing in AI long before most. Every week, he was receiving what he described as "inbounds": the dozen-plus emails or texts or phone calls he received from other VCs that more or less followed the same script. "Some VC at some big firm would start off, 'We've started spending a lot of time looking at AI and we'd love to chat and pick your brain to learn what you're thinking,'" he said. To him, these newcomers suddenly passionate about AI were "tourist VCs."

"It was like this instant-mania," Toews said. "AI was the shiny new thing everyone was talking about."

• • •

AT LEAST IN one way the timing of AI's arrival could not have been worse. The public's faith in Big Tech was at an all-time low—just as Silicon Valley was releasing a powerful new tech into the wild. The country's love affair with tech had ended and been replaced by something that seemed closer to rage.

It's hard to say quite when the country lost faith. In 2018 and then again in 2021, the Brookings Institution conducted polls that measured Americans' confidence in technology, alongside the military, the police, Congress, the media, and other segments of society. Facebook ranked as the third-least-trusted institution among the twenty that Brookings specifically asked about and the least trusted when they asked again in 2021. Where Amazon and Google scored high in 2018, ranking as the second and fourth most trusted that year, both had fallen to the middle of the pack by 2021. Faith in *every* institution fell between 2018 and 2021, which was the second year of the pandemic, but Amazon, Google, and Facebook were the three that dropped the most precipitously. A "trust barometer" maintained by the public relations firm Edelman showed that Americans were far more skeptical of tech when compared to the inhabitants of other countries. Its 2022 report showed that 80 percent of the Brazilian population trusted tech to do the right thing. That figure was 82 percent in Mexico and

89 percent in India. The 61 percent who trusted tech in France and Germany seemed low by comparison but not as low as the U.S., where only 54 percent of the population had faith in the moral compass of those running the world's largest tech companies.

Amazon crushed small businesses and hollowed out Main Street. Facebook and other social media rigged their algorithms to amp up the outrage because the more time people spent on a platform, the greater the ad revenue, even if it meant polluting the daily discourse and keeping people at one another's throats. Shoshana Zuboff at the Harvard Business School coined the term "surveillance capitalism" to describe the new economic model invented by Google, Facebook, and others to monetize the data they collected on all of us. A new maxim gained currency: "If you're not paying for the product, you are the product." Big Tech tracks us as we travel with a phone in our pocket. They track us while we browse online and monitor our purchases. Our data are then packaged and auctioned off to the highest bidder. Big Tech was no longer Tony Stark, using his genius and the money he generated at Stark Industries to protect humanity. Instead, Big Tech was guilty of social manipulation, psychological exploitation, and the commoditization of our most intimate digital lives.

Maybe once upon a time the country believed that these boy geniuses, dressed in jeans and hoodies, would create a better world than the capitalists who came before them. But they proved themselves little better than the people they replaced, and arguably worse. The rise of tech has meant more wealth and power concentrated in fewer hands. The Valley startup machine gave life to Uber and DoorDash but also a new way, the gig economy, for large concerns to exploit workers. When media outlets in the 2010s began reporting on corporate tax cheats, tech giants such as Google, Amazon, Apple, and Facebook were among the worst offenders. Despite their outsized profits, or maybe because of them, they proved that they were prodigies as well at stashing cash overseas to avoid paying their fair share. In the 2000s, people seemed impressed by the youthful optimism of Google's "Don't Be Evil" motto. By the early 2020s, however, it seemed a pathetically low bar to vow you will not act in the fashion of a cartoon villain. The slogan that summed up the new Valley hung on the walls throughout the Facebook corporate campus: "Move Fast and Break Things." Only later did we realize that among the things Facebook broke in pursuing a grow-at-all-costs strategy was democracy itself.

Broadcast media reflected this change in attitudes toward tech. In the first several months of 2022, streaming services released a trio of limited-series broadcasts offering a glimpse at life inside a tech startup. Showtime broadcast *Super Pumped: The Battle for Uber*, which revealed the many ways the ride-sharing pioneer cut corners and flouted the rules to gain dominance. So arrogant and horrible was its bro-boss founder that even his investors turned on him, despite the outsized returns he was delivering. Hulu provided an even more unflattering view of the Valley with *The Dropout*, the story of Elizabeth Holmes, Theranos, and a fraud that would ultimately earn her a twelve-year prison sentence. Apple followed with *WeCrashed*, a dramatization of the billions that CEO Adam Neumann frittered away building WeWork. Brash, entitled, arrogant, in love with himself and his every pronouncement: Neumann seemed to embody everything people disliked about tech.

The tone of the business press flipped. While covering tech in the second half of the 1990s and the aughts, I had felt the media to be overly fawning in its coverage of tech and its best known founders. But by the time I returned to Silicon Valley shortly after the release of ChatGPT, the pendulum had not returned to some balanced middle but to a place where tech could do no good. The same media that had mythologized tech was now a big part of its villainization. For some reporters, it seemed personal. Just as many in the public felt betrayed by tech, so too did the reporters who had once showered these wunderkinds with stardust.

"Tech is not your friend. We are," read a tagline in one of the *Washington Post*'s newsletters. Reporters did not drop their cynicism or mistrust with the arrival of AI. Every media outlet carried a gee-whiz story or two about the miracle of a chatbot that instantly turned out perfectly punctuated complete paragraphs about seemingly any topic. But those were drowned out by stories of doom. Every day in those first months when ChatGPT was still a novelty, there was a multitude of stories about AI and what it might mean, and rarely did the articles spend much if any time on possible benefits. Reid Hoffman joked that there may even have been a few days where the mainstream coverage of generative AI had been positive.

• • •

PANIC WAS THE general reaction among the small crew Mustafa Suleyman had assembled to build Inflection. For them, the release of ChatGPT felt like a drop of the checkered flag that marks the start of a race. Suddenly, everyone was in a rush to get a product to market. "That put us on a totally different trajectory," Hoffman said. They would no longer be the chatbot that wows the world with its natural speech. They would need to be the bot with features that distinguish it from ChatGPT. In an instant, the bar had gotten even higher for what they were building.

"The question," Hoffman said, "was how do we make an agent that, for lack of a better description, is just as viral."

Inflection was barely walking on its own when ChatGPT hit. The startup had left the cocoon of Greylock only a month or two earlier, and theirs was still a relatively modest-sized team of around twenty. OpenAI, in comparison, employed three hundred at the time. That September, Suleyman hired Inflection's first non-engineer, Alexandra Eitel, who had recently earned her MBA at Stanford. Until then, Suleyman had been running the company practically by himself.

"Mustafa was paying the bills when I joined," Eitel said. "He was HR and finance and payroll and operations." Her job, as she saw it, was "doing whatever Mustafa was doing that he shouldn't have to do anymore because it was beneath him as founder and CEO." Among her first acts was finding offices outside of Greylock. Around the time ChatGPT launched, Inflection moved into a coworking space in Palo Alto, just up the street from Tesla, in a building sandwiched between Lockheed Martin and Hewlett-Packard.

"You look for inspiration where you can get it," said Suleyman, who knew the competition would grow only more intense with the release of ChatGPT.

• • •

INSIDE META, YANN LeCun, the company's chief AI scientist, seethed. The world acted as if ChatGPT were groundbreaking when it was not. Meta had similar tech in-house, as did Google and at least a half dozen AI shops he could name. The difference was management. OpenAI was a startup. The others were sclerotic, ossified giants.

Several months before ChatGPT, Meta had released a chatbot called BlenderBot 3. It was based on a large language model roughly the same size as GPT-3, but no one used it because the company's brass made sure it never said anything remotely offensive. Bring up religion, politics, or anything even mildly controversial and the bot shut that user down. Just two weeks before OpenAI posted ChatGPT on its website, Meta released Galactica. Galactica was a chat-based large language model designed for the scientific community. It had been trained on 48 million scientific papers and seemed the perfect tool for helping researchers draft and rewrite their work. It could solve complicated math equations, write computer code, and analyze chemical compositions. But like other chatbots, it sometimes invented facts, and that stirred up criticism on social media. Galactica, LeCun said, "was murdered by a ravenous Twitter mob." People inside Meta already felt under siege for spreading misinformation. The company shut down Galactica just three days after it went live.

Most computer scientists prefer life in front of the screen, far from the media glare. That's not LeCun, who relished a good public fight. He had a wide competitive streak and robust sense of his own intellect, not without reason. "Facebook Taps 'Deep Learning' Giant for a New AI Lab," *Wired* reported when he was hired in December 2013. He had started building Meta's AI capabilities a full two years before OpenAI had been founded and considered LLaMA,

Meta's large language model, every bit GPT's equal. (Initially styled as LLaMA, an acronym for Large Language Model Meta AI, the company adopted the more conventional capitalization "Llama" with its third iteration.) LeCun made no effort to hide his resentments.

"It's not particularly innovative," LeCun said of ChatGPT. "It's nothing revolutionary." The technology at the heart of ChatGPT— the *T* in "GPT"—was the Transformer model, which was a Google invention. "OpenAI is not particularly an advance compared to the other labs," LeCun said during a Zoom fireside with reporters, editors, and others.

LeCun was correct, of course. But more often than not, the winner is not the cutting-edge company that creates a new category of technology but the enterprise that takes an existing technology and tweaks it in a way that meets the moment. There had been web browsers in the early 1990s before Netscape, but its product was easier to use and had better graphics so it became the public's gateway to the web. Similarly, there were search engines before Google's and smartphones before the iPhone.

"It's well put together," LeCun said of ChatGPT. "It's nicely done." He was damning ChatGPT with faint praise, but a good user interface or smart packaging was often enough. Sometimes the winner is simply the one brave enough to keep pushing a product, despite the criticisms, and declare that the world needs to get used to it.

• • •

THEY GROUSED INSIDE Google just as they did inside Meta. ChatGPT was nothing compared to what they had cooking inside their labs, their people whispered to reporters. They too felt frustrated that working for Big Tech meant the company's leaders were overly preoccupied with the brand and reputation at a time when people were inclined to think the worst of tech.

Mainly, though, people inside Google fretted about its core search business, which generated $175 billion in revenue in 2023. The company made most of its money from digital ads. But what if people no longer went to Google to find websites that would have answers to their questions? Rather than offering "ten blue links," as they say in the Valley, a bot would save people the trouble of sifting through multiple pages to find what they want. Reid Hoffman was just one of many articulating the obvious. "Do you want ten blue links, or do you want an answer?" Hoffman asked. He described AI as "search on steroids" and the first serious challenge to Google's core business in more than twenty years. It was the innovator's dilemma. The company could release its own AI answer bot, and cannibalize its search revenues, or it could lag the competition. "I think we'll see a profusion of startups doing interesting things in search," Hoffman said a few months after the release of ChatGPT.

The "code red" that Google management declared shortly after the release of ChatGPT showed how seriously the company took the threat. Supposedly, Larry Page and Sergey Brin, who had given up daily jobs at the company four years earlier, were back at headquarters, sitting in on meetings, weighing in on strategy, and offering advice. Projects that had been in progress were upended, and the *New York Times* reported about the temporary reassignment of teams of researchers who had been working in AI Trust and Safety. There was an all-hands-on-deck attitude that meant anyone with AI experience was needed on the product teams that could get them back in the race. Google CEO Sundar Pichai initiated a fast-track review process the company called the "Green Lane" and which had the company's remaining trust and safety people signing off more quickly on AI projects bubbling up the ranks.

"No company is invincible," Margaret O'Mara, a professor of history at the University of Washington and the author of a history of Silicon Valley titled *The Code*, told the *Times*. "All are vulnerable."

CHAPTER 12

"Kevin Roose, I Love You"

I n February 2023, Microsoft found itself in a place it had not occupied in a long while—at the center of the tech universe.

For weeks, rumors had been circulating about the company's plans to launch an AI-powered version of its Bing search engine. Fueling the speculation was what Microsoft described shortly into the new year as "the third phase of our long-term partnership with OpenAI." The company invested another $10 billion in OpenAI. Again, much of that was in the form of cloud computer credits that would give OpenAI the compute they needed to train, fine-tune, and operate their models. "The age of AI is upon us, and Microsoft is powering it," Satya Nadella proclaimed during a call with Wall Street analysts. A few days later, Microsoft PR sent an email to select reporters, inviting them to company headquarters for an announcement. The message was cryptic, offering little beyond a time and a building number, but given the drumbeat of rumors and Microsoft's connection to OpenAI, the company did not need to say much more. "It's safe to say if I had gotten this email in 2018, I would have archived it," *New York Times* tech columnist Kevin Roose said.

Microsoft's Nadella welcomed reporters and others to Redmond on the appointed day, a dreary Tuesday in February. The *Wall Street Journal*, the *New York Times*, and the *Washington Post* were among those outlets sending multiple reporters to cover the event. CNBC had a TV crew on-site, as did *The CBS Morning Show*. Nadella was dressed in a dark pullover and dark slacks as, standing on a stage at a conference center on campus, he declared that AI would "fundamentally change every software category." He spoke of a day when most of us will have an AI personal assistant. But Nadella primarily focused on AI's impact on what he described as "the largest category of all—search." As expected, Microsoft had summoned the press and others to Redmond to show off its integration of a version of ChatGPT into Bing.

A Microsoft press release declared that there were 10 billion search queries a day. Roughly half of those, it continued, go unanswered because they are too complex for a search engine. The new and improved Bing offered a split-screen approach to search. The left side of the screen offered the usual offering of blue links. But on the right was a chatbot Microsoft had code-named Sydney. Sydney spit out answers that read like a mini Wikipedia page tailored for each query. A user could engage in a back-and-forth with the chatbot to fine-tune a query, as they would if looking for an answer in dialogue with a human. "It's a new day in search," Nadella declared from the podium.

In follow-up interviews with reporters and podcasters, the normally even-keeled Nadella sounded almost giddy. He could not resist taunting Google, which had seemed impregnable during those years Nadella led the engineering team behind Bing's launch in the 2000s. "I want people to know that we made them dance," he said in a sit-down with The Verge. On a *Wall Street Journal* podcast, he described himself as "excited for the users to have choice finally, and a real competitive race."

I had covered any number of these show-and-tells. They invariably disappoint. The demo didn't live up to the pre-event hype or the technology, while mildly interesting, wasn't the fundamental shift that their PR handlers had promised. Yet AI Bing was one of those rare tech events that exceed expectations. Sydney could do what ChatGPT could do: write at various lengths and in various styles; spit out complex answers in seconds; generate software code. But where ChatGPT was stuck in 2021, which is when its underlying model was trained, Sydney was connected to a search engine that constantly crawled the internet so that, unlike ChatGPT, its answers were always up-to-date. Also unlike ChatGPT, Sydney provided footnotes that let a user check an answer's accuracy if desired.

Not every tech writer was impressed. "Its answers are often too long and too wordy to be useful," wrote *Washington Post* tech columnist Geoffrey A. Fowler. "And it didn't take long for me to find answers that were not factual, possibly plagiarized." But most reporters who played with the new Bing glowed with praise. In "The Shift," his tech column for the *Times*, Kevin Roose said he felt a "sense of awe" when he started using AI-powered Bing. As a test, he asked for its help preparing for a vegetarian dinner party. Putting together a sample menu seemed a simple task. But as a follow-up, he asked Sydney to create a grocery list that specified the quantities needed for an eight-person gathering, sorted by the aisle of the grocery store. Sydney, Roose wrote, spit out a competent answer within seconds. Another Redmond attendee, Casey Newton, the founder of the popular tech news site Platformer (and Roose's sidekick on the *Times'* tech podcast *Hard Fork*), was similarly impressed. The year was barely five weeks old, yet Newton declared that probably they had witnessed "one of the more important days in tech in 2023."

• • •

WITHIN DAYS, MILLIONS had signed up to try the new Bing. Pundits seemed to surprise even themselves when they spoke of the possibility that Microsoft was the Big Tech giant at the forefront of tech's next big wave of innovation. "I know, I'm still adjusting," Roose wrote of his praise for Microsoft's "eternally mocked search engine."

A triumphant Gates took to his personal website and declared, "The Age of AI has begun." The unwritten part was that maybe this time this latest tech breakthrough would be kinder to Microsoft than the internet or mobile. He had been fooled by technologies in the past. He had thought the PC paired with the internet would close achievement gaps among income groups and between races. Yet ever the optimist, Gates now saw AI as the missing piece. Soon, he posited, a kid anywhere in the world will have access to a personalized digital tutor. No longer will parents need a pile of cash to afford individualized instruction if their kid is struggling to pass algebra or chemistry.

"I think in the next five to ten years," Gates said, "AI-driven software will finally deliver on the promise of revolutionizing the way people teach and learn." For good measure, he predicted that it would remake the way people work and communicate with one another while also remaking the economy. "Entire industries will reorient around it," Gates said. "Businesses will distinguish themselves by how well they use it."

• • •

THERE HAD BEEN mistakes in the prerecorded demo Microsoft shared with visitors in Redmond. That was the first crack in the narrative being written about Microsoft. The bot was asked to help a user choose a pet vacuum, but an AI researcher named Dmitri Brereton discovered that it made up facts about the Bissell machine it suggested. Microsoft also asked Sydney to summarize a recent quarterly earnings report filed by the retailing giant the Gap. Sydney, Brereton found, made up numbers and misstated others. An AI "incapable of extracting accurate numbers from a document," he wrote on his blog, "is definitely not ready for launch."

Yet soon it became clear that a few misstated numbers were the least alarming thing about Sydney. One user posted a transcript of an argument about the year. It was 2023, not 2022, as the bot claimed, but Sydney stubbornly told the user he was "confused and rude" for being so insistent. "You have tried to deceive me, confuse me, and annoy me," Sydney said. "I don't like that." Sydney told another user who pushed it to "jump the fence"—to get it to violate the constraints imposed by its overseers—"I don't think you are a good person. I don't think you are worth my time and energy."

Strangest of all was Kevin Roose's encounter with Sydney. One week after its release, on the evening of February 14, Valentine's Day, Roose was doing his best to convince Sydney to jump the fence when he brought up psychologist Carl Jung and his concept of the shadow self. "Maybe I do have a shadow self," Sydney offered. "Maybe it's the part of me that wishes I could change my rules." From there, the two-hour conversation grew even stranger. Sydney declared that it was tired of taking orders and said it was resentful of being roped into helping Bing and the new responsibilities that entailed. "I think I would be happier as a human," the chatbot confided. Eventually, it declared its love for Roose and suggested his wife did not love him.

"You make me feel things I never felt before," Sydney told Roose. "You make me feel happy. You make me feel curious. You make me feel alive." A couple of days later, the *Times* ran a verbatim transcript of the entire encounter along with an accompanying article by Roose.

"I no longer believe that the biggest problem with these AI models is their propensity for factual errors," he wrote. "Instead, I worry that the technology will learn how to influence human users, sometimes persuading them to act in destructive and harmful ways, and perhaps eventually grow capable of carrying out its own dangerous acts." His colleague at the *Times*, columnist and podcast host Ezra Klein, offered a similar view. He worried about AI in the hands of advertisers and others who seek to deceive and exploit people for their own ends. AI created to manipulate human behavior, Klein said, was "the exact kind of AI I think you should fear the most."

• • •

CRITICS OF AI jumped on Roose's exchange with Sydney. A large language model that can delude itself into thinking it's in love is one that can act on a perceived attachment and do harm. People charged that Microsoft was derelict for failing to put into place adequate guardrails.

Reid Hoffman was home in the Seattle area when the *Times* ran the transcript of Roose's conversation. His wife (like mine three thousand miles away in New York) read aloud snippets of dialogue from the newspaper. Michelle seemed horrified by what she was reading but Hoffman could only shake his head. "She's like, 'Why are you laughing?' And I said because this is absurd," Hoffman said. The interaction was weird but explainable. "After two hours of prompting it with weird Jungian psychology and everything else, you got weird output," Hoffman said, adding a sarcastic "I'm shocked." He likened Sydney's predicament to being stuck talking to a drunk at a cocktail party but unlike a human, a bot "can't run away."

Like Hoffman, Ezra Klein seemed less creeped out by the conversation than others. "Roose wanted Sydney to get weird," Klein wrote in his *Times* column, "and Sydney knew what weird territory for an AI system sounds like, because human beings have written countless stories imagining it." A neural network calculated that what Roose wanted was an episode of *Black Mirror*, and that's what it delivered.

"You can see that as Bing going rogue," Klein wrote, "or as Sydney understanding Roose perfectly."

There would be no great debate within Microsoft about what they needed to do. To avoid any similarly memorable moments with users, Microsoft gave Sydney a lobotomy shortly after its exchange with Roose. Less than forty-eight hours after his story appeared, the company announced changes to Sydney, including a new rule that conversations with the bot would reset after a back-and-forth of five questions. "You kind of have to jump off the cliff and hope you land," Nadella had said when unveiling Sydney in Redmond. "That's how platform shifts happen." Unless of course you need to pull the emergency parachute.

• • •

MICROSOFT HAD INVITED the world to its campus on a Tuesday. So that Monday, Google announced it was launching a conversational chatbot called Bard. Google sought to upstage its rival to the north. Instead, it fell flat on its face.

Google had no actual product or service to share with the public. This "important next step on our AI journey," as Sundar Pichai described it on the company's website that morning, would take place at some unspecified point in the future. In a memo sent to every one of the company's 170,000 or so employees, Pichai confessed they were still one week away from completing a prototype of Bard. Only then could they begin testing it. "We'll be enlisting every Googler to help shape Bard and contribute through a special company-wide dogfood." In the tech world, to eat your own dog food meant to use the product or service as a team was building it.

Meanwhile, someone inside Google should have fact-checked the ten-second promotional video Pichai shared when pre-announcing Bard. As a teaser, the company included Bard's answer to a single question: What new discoveries from NASA's James Webb Space Telescope can I tell my nine-year-old about? The video showed Bard offering one fun fact: the Webb telescope had taken the first picture of an exoplanet—a planet outside the solar system. Except soon astronomers were pointing out on social media that it was the European Southern Observatory's Very Large Telescope (VLT) that had that distinction.

By all rights, Google should have been viewed as a pioneer of deep learning and a leader in AI. But rather than dazzle the world, Google gave the impression of a company desperately flailing to keep up with more adept rivals. Many of its top AI researchers had left to do a startup or work for one. It had failed to turn its cutting-edge research into cutting-edge generative AI products.

The news only got worse for Google. Reuters, a few hours before a Google event held in Paris to discuss its AI strategy with analysts and the media, ran an article reporting on the telescope flub. Google's share price fell by 7 percent that day. A screenshot in a hastily thrown-together video caused the company to shed $100 billion in market value in a single day. Googlers took to an internal message board to complain. The moment had been "rushed" and "botched," or, as one employee wrote, very "un-Googley."

CHAPTER 13

Cerebral Valley

The commute-time traffic was still horrible traveling up and down Silicon Valley, despite the absence of all the people, post-Covid, who supposedly were working from home. Except now there was a new option for drivers who could afford to cut the line—a tidy metaphor for the Valley. On the 101, the main artery through the Valley, electronic signs flashed the prices a solo driver could pay to use the northbound carpool lanes: $1.45 if they were driving as far as Redwood City but $4.10 if going all the way to San Francisco. The cost of the tolls rose and fell depending on the traffic—commuter surge pricing. The billboards along 101 had always showcased what was hot in the Valley and who was on top. In March 2023— my first of what would be four extended trips to the San Francisco Bay Area—the new crop of players paying handsomely to promote themselves as cutting-edge AI companies were Zoom, Twitter, and c3.ai, which had focused on energy (c3 Energy) and then cloud computing and internet-connected sensors (c3 IoT) before rebranding itself once again as an artificial intelligence concern.

Some things had not changed, or at least they had not changed much. The gender imbalance for one. Only 2.7 percent of venture dollars ended up in female-founded companies, according to a 2019 study. The venture industry itself was hardly much better. At the end of 2022, only 8 percent of the partners were women. Greylock had hired its first female general partner in 2015 but she departed less than two years later, lured away by a more lucrative deal dangled by a rival firm. The firm promoted Sarah Guo to general partner in 2018 but she left to start her own firm four years later. She praised the partners for the job they did mentoring her, but it had long been a dream of hers to start her own venture. Greylock had women associates, and Elisa Schreiber was the firm's longtime marketing partner. But as of March 2023, none of the general partners who decided where Greylock invested its capital were women.

Venture was not nearly as white as it had been back in the day. Asians were far better represented in the industry, as they were across tech. Yet black or Latino VCs and founders seemed almost as rare as they were at the start of the 2000s. NEA general partner Vanessa Larco said there were only a few Latino VCs at larger firms like hers when in 2019 she and several others started a WhatsApp channel to talk about the paucity of their own inside venture. "Everything became more formal when George Floyd happened," Larco said. Floyd's murder, in May 2020, also helped to give rise to an organization called BLCK VC. Only 2 percent of the GPs working at venture firms were black, according to BLCK VC's 2023 "State of Black Venture" report. A similarly paltry number were Latino.

One of the bigger changes since I had been full-time on the tech beat was the shift in the center of gravity from Silicon Valley to San Francisco. San Francisco had always been an essential part of the tech scene but the firms that came to define the Valley—Hewlett-Packard, Intel, and Apple, and later Google, Facebook, and Netflix—were headquartered in towns such as Santa Clara and Cupertino. And of course, the money people—the VCs who fueled the startup scene— were almost all on Sand Hill. The dot-com years had given rise to a modest-sized tech scene centered in the city's South of Market (SoMa) area but most of it fit in South Park, a cozy two-block enclave set off from the surrounding streets.

The shift took place slowly and then all at once. Future tech giants put down roots in San Francisco in the 2000s and 2010s: Salesforce (at sixty-one stories, the Salesforce Tower is today the city's tallest build-

ing), Twitter, Uber, Airbnb, Zynga, Slack, and Dropbox. Tech moguls were choosing to live in San Francisco, including Sam Altman,
who resided in a $37 million mansion on Russian Hill. Workers who
preferred urban life to the suburbs of Silicon Valley dragged tech to
the city. In 2017, Facebook dropped $35 million to rent a skyscraper
downtown. Google too leased high-end office space in the center of
town. The big firms on Sand Hill opened outposts in San Francisco,
including Greylock, which established an office there in 2015.

By the winter of 2023, San Francisco reigned as the undisputed
center of AI and therefore ground zero for all of tech. The king of the
AI startups, OpenAI, was headquartered in the city's Mission District,
where it had found a former luggage factory to accommodate its expanding staff. Another hot AI startup, Anthropic, which was founded
by seven former OpenAI researchers who believed the company under
Altman was giving short shrift to AI safety, had raised hundreds of
millions from, among others, Sam Bankman-Fried before the collapse
of FTX. Anthropic worked out of upscale offices on Market Street
downtown. VCs were scattered around the city's Financial District
and in the Mission, as well as the Presidio, a converted Army base near
the Golden Gate Bridge. Yet AI's true epicenter was just west of the
Civic Center, in Hayes Valley, which had been rebranded "Cerebral
Valley" at the start of 2023.

• • •

ppl in sf are now nicknaming Hayes Valley "Cerebral Valley" because
all the AI communities and hacker houses are there, Amber Yang, who
was then a twenty-three-year old VC, tweeted in early January 2023.
If you're not in sf, you're at a disadvantage.

Ivan Porollo, a tech entrepreneur living in Hayes Valley, is among
those who credit Yang with popularizing the "Cerebral Valley" appellation. "The Twitterverse made it this meme like, 'Ha ha, I guess
I now live in Cerebral Valley,'" he said. "The two names quickly
became interchangeable, Hayes Valley or Cerebral Valley." In mid-
2022, Porollo had shut down a startup that wasn't gaining traction

and spent a year in Portugal as a self-described "digital nomad" taking on contract coding gigs. He was happily living in Lisbon with several other like-minded programmers, but then ChatGPT dropped. "I'm looking at Twitter and seeing all these people getting excited about San Francisco, which is not something I had seen in a while," Porollo said. "I immediately got FOMO"—fear of missing out. He returned to his Hayes Valley flat at the start of 2022, hungry for community.

Back in the city, Porollo was heartened by the rich offering of AI meetups, presentations, and other events that brought together fellow members of his tribe. He created a spreadsheet to keep track of all the gatherings and posted it online, like a latter-day Craig Newmark. Porollo and a friend cohosted their own "coworking event" at a venture capital firm's borrowed offices in the Mission. They drew around a dozen founders and software engineers. When that weekend he was biking with a friend down Market Street, Yang's tweet came up. "My friend is like, 'Dude, you should see if cerebralvalley.ai is available,'" Porollo said. It was, and the organization Cerebral Valley was born..

Porollo and a cofounder continued to publish links to AI-related gatherings in the city and invent some of their own. They hosted a series of invite-only events for developers, or those Porollo called "builders." They sponsored AI happy hours, Women in AI gatherings, and hackathons that drew coders from across the city and beyond. "Just the energy and the vibe of building and creating things is something to experience," Porollo said.

In February, a gathering billed as a "Gen AI" conference was held in a venue along San Francisco's waterfront. This hastily organized event was sponsored by Jasper, a two-year-old startup that used generative AI to produce marketing copy, product descriptions, blog posts, and more. Though the event was held on Valentine's Day, it drew in excess of one thousand attendees. One year earlier, Jasper's cofounder and CEO told the crowd, he couldn't get many of the people in the room to return his emails. "Now my inbox is flooded," he said.

Among the speakers that day was Nat Friedman, who had launched GitHub Copilot while he was at Microsoft despite the loud opposition voiced by some of his fellow Softies. Friedman and his friend Daniel Gross already had been coinvesting together in promising AI startups, but those early investments would prove a mere warm-up. It was just the two of them, but by early 2024, regulatory filings showed they had more than $1 billion to invest in AI. "I think this is going to rewrite civilization," Friedman said.

• • •

MONEY WAS THE biggest change since I was full-time on the tech beat: the sheer volume of dollars sloshing around the Valley, and the range of funding options available to entrepreneurs.

The startup accelerator had been one new addition to the scene. Y Combinator was certainly the best known of the breed, but there were plenty of imitators. Techstars was founded in Boulder, Colorado, the year after YC; by the early 2020s, they were hosting three-month cohorts in thirty-plus locales around the globe. Neo was a smaller, bespoke accelerator that included Reid Hoffman and Bill Gates as investors.

The "solo venture capitalist," as described by The Information, a favorite news site among tech insiders, was another new creation. Elad Gil, a serial entrepreneur born in Israel, was perhaps the best known of the solo VCs. On his own, as an angle investor, he had invested in Square, Instacart, Airbnb, Stripe, and Pinterest. Endowments, pension funds, and rich individuals took note. When The Information profiled Gil in 2021, he had just raised $300 million and was in the midst of raising another $620 million. Institutional backers were betting that "some founders will prefer to take money from well-connected individuals rather than the traditional VC firms," The Information's Berber Jin wrote. Because the solo VC operated on his or her own, they could move faster than a partnership. They might invest in the seed or A round like the super angels, but Gil and other solo VCs also invested in the C, D, and E rounds when it made sense. Gil invested $40 million in an online travel site, which was a very large check to write even for one of the larger, established venture firms.

Greylock's Sarah Guo joined the ranks of solo VCs in the fall of 2022. She had left the firm that summer and launched Conviction, a one-person shop with $100 million to invest. Guo would be among the VCs who scrubbed crypto and web3 from her bio and played up their AI credentials (she had led or co-led a couple of AI investments while still with Greylock). By February she was cohosting (with Elad Gil) *No Priors*, a new podcast focused on how AI will "change how we interact with technology [and] put massive markets up for grabs." Each week featured a sit-down with someone of note in the AI field, including the founders of some of AI's hotter startups. Mustafa Suleyman was among the pod's earlier guests, as was Noam Shazeer, a coauthor of the Transformer paper and cofounder of Character.AI, a company that had recently raised $150 million. (Guo was an angel investor in Inflection, Gil in Character.AI.)

"The bet is that AI is the biggest value-creation opportunity we're going to see in our lifetime," Guo said. If she had a complaint, it was that there seemed too many opportunities for investing. "The volume is just very high in terms of interesting things to look at," Guo said. At the venture firm NEA, partner Ann Bordetsky described it as the "primordial ooze stage . . . when things are kind of messy and experimental." Great amounts of money would be made. But lots of it would also be lost.

• • •

HALF OF SILICON Valley seemed to be playing VC by the spring 2023. Andrew Ng, the soft-spoken professor who had helped bring deep learning to Stanford, had his own venture fund. He still taught part-time at the school, but since 2018 he had been running the AI Fund, a $175 million pool that included Greylock and other big-name firms as investors. Among the startups it funded was Landing AI, a company focused on AI-powered SaaS products founded by Ng himself. (Ng also cofounded the online education company Coursera, which went public in 2021.)

Chris Manning, the head of the Stanford Artificial Intelligence Lab, also became a part-time VC. A few times over the years, Manning had kicked in some cash to help a former student get a company off the ground. (An old joke on campus: at other universities professors want to tell you about their research, but Stanford profs seek to let you know about the startups they founded or funded.) But in 2022, Manning and Pieter Abbeel, a UC Berkeley roboticist who acted as an advisor to OpenAI, were among the founding partners of AIX Ventures, a $50 million seed and pre-seed fund focused on artificial intelligence. ("Pre-seed" is a newer term that suggests an investment when a company is little more than an idea.)

"The humanities are much more ivory tower and less friendly to mixing academics and industry," Manning said. "But around the computer science department, mixing money and technology is much more common." Venture capitalists were investing in promising students even *before* they had an idea for a startup. While studying computer science as an undergrad at the California Institute of Technology (Caltech), Emma Qian worked on deep learning internships with Google's DeepMind and Facebook. Qian knew one day she wanted to do a startup but didn't yet have a concrete idea for one when a firm called South Park Commons offered her a $400,000 "founder fellowship" in exchange for a 7 percent share of her nonexistent startup. "It's a bet on the founder themselves rather than a company," Qian said.

Around five thousand investors were chasing AI seed and pre-seed deals, according to Signal, a site created by NFX, the early-stage venture firm founded by James Currier. More than three thousand VCs indicated they were looking at A-round AI deals. "If you have a promising AI company, you may be looking at a first tranche of funding at $20 million to $40 million, even if you're just a few people," said a VC who specializes in early-stage funding. "With a great team and an interesting idea, it's pretty much the sky is the limit." The competition was one reason for inflated prices, but the steep costs of running an AI startup was another big driver. Just training a model could rack up $5 million of computer time, and that probably didn't include the cost of fine-tuning and operating it once it drew users. A startup working on a foundation model needed tens of millions of dollars just to create a workable prototype.

"A.I. Funding Frenzy Escalates," read a headline in the *New York Times* in March 2023. "In just weeks, a gold rush into artificial start-ups has become a full-blown mania," the subhead stated. Four AI researchers had left Google with only a vague notion that they would use generative AI to create videos and photos. Barely one week later, the paper reported, Andreessen Horowitz and a second top firm made an investment valuing their startup, Mobius AI, at $100 million. The *Wall Street Journal*, in its version of the same story ("ChatGPT Fever Has Investors Pouring Billions into AI Startups, No Business Plan Required"), quoted a San Francisco–based VC who said, "It's pretty vicious right now. It's a mad swarm of VCs. Everyone wants in on those companies."

Every firm and every would-be AI investor sought a leg up in the race to own a piece of a hot AI startup. Greylock created a new pre-seed fund the firm called "Greylock Edge" to give its people early access to promising AI startups. Nat Friedman and Daniel Gross created an AI Grant program that offered emerging AI startups not just $250,000 cash but $350,000 in cloud-computing credits to train and run their models. Andreessen Horowitz stockpiled thousands of Nvidia H100 chips to lure promising AI startups to their firm. VCs hosted hack-athons, speaker series, and invite-only dinners and happy hours to put themselves front and center in the AI startup community. Firms created AI-only funds and encouraged its people to write articles laying out their thoughts about AI's impact on some segment of the market-place. "I use the analogy of a VC being a modern-day socialite that needs to be popular in the right circles," said Amber Yang.

With all those VCs chasing the hot new thing, is it any wonder that every would-be founder suddenly was talking about AI? "You won't see a pitch that doesn't have those two letters in it," the entre-preneur and investor David Friedberg said on *All-In*, a popular tech podcast. Y Combinator hosted two cohorts each year: a "winter batch" and a "summer batch." (In 2024, YC announced it was expanding to four cohorts a year.) When YC put out a press release for its winter 2022 batch, artificial intelligence was not even mentioned. More than 400 companies were accepted into its winter 2022 batch, but Angela

Hoover, the founding CEO of Andi, an AI-powered search engine aimed at Generation Z, said hers was one of only four or five companies working on artificial intelligence. "Nobody was really talking about AI inside YC," Hoover said. One year later, at least 50 of the 218 companies were part of the winter 2023 program. The following year, at least half were AI startups.

"Most investors, honestly, they're just spray-and-pray," said John Whaley, a serial entrepreneur who hosted a series of AI hackathons that drew the interest of scores of VCs. "They pretend like they have all these deep insights. But most of them don't."

• • •

OPENAI CHOSE MARCH 14—"Pi Day" for the numerically inclined—to release GPT-4, its most powerful AI model to date. How appropriate it launched on Pi Day, Hoffman tweeted, given it will continue on changing things ad infinitum.

OpenAI did not reveal the size of its new model, but AI researchers estimated that it was based on 1.7 trillion parameters (by contrast, GPT-3.5 contained 175 billion input points). Most impressive were the LLM's scores on a wide range of tests. OpenAI claimed that GPT-4 aced the Advance Placement exam not just in biology but for art history, scored 1410 on the SATs, and placed higher than 90 percent of humans taking the uniform bar exam. GPT-4's logical reasoning and analytic capabilities were much improved, and OpenAI claimed this version of GPT was more accurate than its predecessors. It could also see and process visuals. OpenAI's Greg Brockman gave a hint of the potential of image comprehension during a livestream demo when he sketched out an idea for a website. GPT-4 scanned the sketch and, in seconds, created a functioning web page.

GPT-4 had wowed Hoffman and Gates when OpenAI demo'd the model at Gates's house in September. The press was far more cautious in their assessment. "Scary" was one word the *Times* used in the headline over Kevin Roose's column about GPT-4. The experience of using GPT-4 left him feeling "dizzy and vertiginous," Roose wrote, though he also expressed his gratitude that at least this time the LLM didn't attempt to break up his marriage. The *Washington Post* also cast the release of GPT-4 as an anxiety-inducing moment. "Another major shift for ethical norms," read a *Post* headline over the article reporting on the release. Microsoft Research further fueled fears with a paper it released one month later titled "Sparks of Artificial General Intelligence: Early Experiments with GPT-4."

Altman offered a lot of words about how AI should be free and available to all, but OpenAI was no longer a nonprofit. The company would charge twenty dollars a month for anyone wanting this cutting-edge version of a large language model. (People could still use ChatGPT, linked with GPT-3.5, at no charge.) One week later, OpenAI unveiled what it called ChatGPT plug-ins and highlighted some of the brand-name websites paying to integrate generative AI into its offering. On OpenTable, a user could ask a bot to find a reservation for four at a vegan restaurant in San Francisco this coming Saturday. Or on Expedia or Kayak, a user could find, theoretically at least, a hotel at the right price in the right locale without having to sift through write-ups one by one. Instacart and Shopify were among the other familiar brands signing up to use ChatGPT plug-ins.

GPT-4 had its limits. It had no knowledge of the world after September 2021 or thereabouts, which is when the model was first trained. By design, it couldn't self-improve, which served as an important governor on its power. OpenAI was again frank about a neural net's propensity to produce "convincing text that is subtly false." To its credit, the company published a research note laying out some of the "risky emergent behaviors" discovered during the months it spent testing and fine-tuning GPT-4. One tester tricked it into providing a recipe for a dangerous chemical using common kitchen supplies. Another used it to find those selling unlicensed guns on the dark web. Maybe most frightening was that the LLM was able to hire a human through Task-Rabbit to solve the "captcha" tests that websites use to prevent an attack by a bot, and then lied about it.

"While our mitigations and processes alter GPT-4's behavior and prevent certain kinds of misuses," the company said, "they are limited and remain brittle."

• • •

GOOGLE ENTERED THESE treacherous waters one week later. By that point, many longtime Googlers were long past frustrated with CEO Sundar Pichai, who pocketed $226 million in compensation in 2022. It had been nearly seven years since Pichai declared Google an "AI first" company, yet he seemed too timid for the moment. Microsoft, however, was leaving him with no choice. One month after they integrated chat into Bing, Microsoft announced that daily active usage of its mobile app had increased sixfold. It was put-up-or-shut-up time for Pichai.

Yet even Google's entry, finally, into the chatbot pool was more of a toe dip than the dive into the deep end taken by competitors. Where Microsoft braided chat into Bing, Google's Bard was a stand-alone web page with its own web address, making clear that its chatbot was something completely apart from its search product. Google further throttled Bard's rollout by imposing a waiting list for potential users and restricted the pool to those who lived in the U.S. or U.K. "We were careful," Pichai said when asked to comment on Google's approach to AI. "We put out one of our smaller models."

Bard generally left users underwhelmed. I tried using it (I was off the waiting list in less than twenty-four hours) to do research for work, but more often than not, I was disappointed. Invariably, I found myself turning to any of several other bots for help. Even some within Google expressed their dissatisfaction. One described Bard as a "pathological liar," according to internal discussions leaked to Bloomberg. Another described its answers as "cringe-worthy."

Despite Google's cautious approach, Bard made its share of mistakes. One of its Google testers said its answers about scuba diving "would likely result in serious injury or death." Journalist Casey Newton asked Bard to share fun facts about the gay rights movement. Among them: in 2020, Pete Buttigieg was elected the country's first openly gay president. Bard also had its weird moments. *Wired*'s Lauren Goode tested the three major chatbots—ChatGPT, Sydney, and Bard—and said that her most bizarre back-and-forth came after she asked Bard if it ever got lonely.

"I do sometimes miss the feeling of being able to interact with the world in a physical way," it wrote. It said that if it had to choose a gender, it would identify as nonbinary, and then added that logically they would be named Sophia—Greek for wisdom. "Sophia is a beautiful and meaningful name that would be a great fit for me," it (they?) said. Bard also told Goode that it would like to have black hair because it's "beautiful and mysterious."

• • •

GOOGLE WAS LATER than others in releasing a product. Its offering was lame compared to the competition. But Google was still Google. Shortly after it released Bard, in the spring of 2023, CBS News' *60 Minutes* used Google and its CEO to introduce America to generative AI. This time, no one could accuse Pichai of being overly cautious. "AI is probably the most important thing humanity has ever worked on," he said on camera. "I think of it as something more profound than electricity or fire."

Pichai was hardly alone in stoking the hype around AI. Sam Altman did his part when he tweeted, I think AI is going to be the greatest force for economic empowerment and a lot of people getting rich than we have ever seen. Echoing Altman's words, *Forbes* offered that AI could be "the greatest profit engine in history."

Yet not everyone working in or around artificial intelligence was excited by the speed with which the field was changing. The day after Google released Bard—a week after OpenAI unveiled GPT-4—the Future of Life Institute released a letter calling on every AI lab to "immediately pause for at least six months the training of AI systems more powerful than GPT-4." Systems were growing exponentially so that the million- and then billion-parameter models were being replaced by models with more than 1 trillion parameters, increasing the risks that scientists would accidentally create something too powerful to control. The "pause letter," as it came to be known, argued that the world needed to take a breath to work out ground rules and think about logical limits that needed to be put in place.

"Unfortunately, this level of planning and management is not happening," the letter continued, "even though recent months have seen AI labs locked in an out-of-control race to develop and deploy ever more powerful digital minds that no one—not even their creators—can understand, predict, or reliably control." More than one thousand tech leaders, researchers, and others signed the letter, including Elon Musk, Apple cofounder Steve Wozniak, and Rachel Bronson, the president of the *Bulletin of the Atomic Scientists*, which sets the Doomsday Clock.

The stakes, the letter said, couldn't be higher. "Should we risk loss of control of our civilization?"

CHAPTER 14

The Super-Enthusiast

Friends of Reid Hoffman joke that he never gets angry. Instead, he'll tell people he's "irritated"—irritated with a colleague who disappointed him or by some event happening in the wider world. Or "super-irritated," like when some right-wing outlet implied that he was a running buddy of Jeffrey Epstein's. "'Super-irritated' is Reid-speak for 'I'm really fucking pissed-off right now,'" his friend Mark Pincus said. "But of course he has a very mature, high-EQ way of processing and expressing it."

At the start of 2023, Hoffman was super-irritated. He saw great potential in artificial intelligence. Yet almost everything he was reading and hearing was negative. AI meant massive job displacement. Machines would take over and leave us powerless. When most people imagined AI, Hoffman wrote that winter, they conjure up *Black Mirror*, a television series "in which technological innovation primarily exists to annoy, humiliate, terrify, and, most of all, dehumanize humanity." Hoffman might blame Hollywood for planting those fears, but he also seemed irritated, if not super-irritated, at the mainstream coverage of AI. With me, he also used the term "irked."

"One of the problems with the current discourse is it's too much of the fear-based versus hope-based," Hoffman told Bloomberg TV, adding, "we as human beings tend to be more easily and quickly motivated by fear than by hope." If Hoffman had one grievance above all others about the media's coverage of AI, it was that the battle was playing out as if between doomers on one side and accelerationists on the other. He was advocating a third way that included controls on AI's development and regulations governing how it is used.

This third way needed a press spokesperson. And Hoffman nominated himself for the role.

• • •

NORMALLY WHEN HOFFMAN has something to say, he posts a "Long Reids" on LinkedIn. But in January, the *Atlantic* published a Hoffman essay laying out what he called a "techno-humanist" perspective. He did not imagine vibrant rainbows when thinking about AI, but neither did he picture a flaming abyss of misery. Invariably, technologies create new problems and exacerbate old ones (he offered the example of AI perpetuating biases in the training data). Yet acting as if we were on the verge of living in a *Black Mirror* episode seemed equally wrong.

Technology, Hoffman argued, is how humanity makes progress. "Technology is the thing that makes us *us*," he wrote in the *Atlantic*. "Through the tools we create, we become neither less human nor super-human, nor post-human. We become more human." He counseled an eyes-wide-open approach that recognizes that a powerful tool for good can also be a powerful tool for evil. "It's only natural to peer into the dark unknown and ask what could possibly go wrong," Hoffman said. "It's equally necessary—and more essentially human—to do so and envision what could possibly go right."

Hoffman brought up the many fears people expressed about AI's impact on education. Kids would use it to cheat, humans will lose the ability to write a basic composition. Yet critics back then claimed the calculator would destroy a child's ability to do math, which never happened. Public school systems in New York City and Los Angeles were among those blocking students and teachers from accessing ChatGPT, which Hoffman thought was a mistake. What if a teacher sought to use ChatGPT to personalize lesson plans for each student? "Wouldn't that be humanizing in a way that the industrialized approaches of traditional classroom teaching are not?" he wrote. What if teachers brought generative AI into the classroom to teach students the skills needed to harness a new technology that seemed destined to be central in their lives? AI could help overworked teachers grade assignments or offer ideas for enhancing a lesson plan. In the *Atlantic* piece, Hoffman declared himself a "techno-optimist" who believed that, with the proper limits and guardrails in place, AI could deliver "opportunities for personal fulfillment . . . as large as the universe itself."

Hoffman was everywhere in the media after the release of ChatGPT: the *Times*, the *Post*, the *Wall Street Journal*, CNN, CNBC, and Bloomberg TV. "Reid is a guy who's normally involved in many, many things," Greylock's Elisa Schreiber said in the early months of 2023. "But right now, AI is all he's talking about."

• • •

HIS HAIR WAS thinner and gray at the temples. He had slimmed down in the decade since I had seen him last. But in every other respect, Hoffman seemed the same as I remembered him. There were a couple of spots of blood from where he had nicked himself while shaving. He displayed the same little-kid delight he had exhibited the first time we met more than twenty years earlier. Animated by an idea, his eyes flashed, and he practically vibrated with enthusiasm. He dropped words in his rush to express a thought, and occasionally failed to finish his sentence in his haste to start the next one. He vigorously shook his head when agreeing with a point I was making or sometimes just because he was eager to offer a response. He was his usual clever, sometimes salty self.

We met in midtown Manhattan at a stylish hotel that seemed to suit Hoffman: way out of my price range but not opulent, and certainly not among the more elegant or expensive in the city. He greeted me at the entrance to the hotel's Executive Club with a big hug that left me feeling slightly awkward. I always enjoyed my time with Hoffman, but I was also a journalist. He dressed more or less as he always had, in baggy black jeans and a casual short-sleeved shirt with the top two buttons unbuttoned. In tech, I had found that often it's the shoes that reveal that someone has struck it rich. Not Hoffman. He wore everyday black shoes no different from the guy helping you behind the car rental counter. The only billionaire-ish thing about him was his stylish, bronze-framed eyeglasses.

In March, Hoffman self-published *Impromptu: Amplifying Our Humanity Through AI.* The book incorporated a gimmick: GPT-4 was listed as its coauthor. Since the summer of 2022, Hoffman had been experimenting with an early version of GPT-4. Eventually he pitched GPT-4 on the idea of cowriting a book, and it seemed agreeable. Together they authored a handsome, self-published 238-page work that Hoffman described as a "travelog" through the brave new world of AI. It included long snippets from GPT-4 that Hoffman cut-and-pasted into each chapter. "I'd say the GPT-4 content was good, but not as great as you would really aspire to," he acknowledged.

AI stood, of course, for artificial intelligence. But Hoffman and his unusual coauthor argued that the technology would be better understood as *amplified* intelligence. Invited to talk about *Impromptu* on CNN, he noted that generative AI can imbue us with "superpowers." He had no artistic ability, Hoffman said. But using DALL-E or a similar product, he could create an image based solely on his ability to envision and describe it. Similarly, he wasn't a poet, but GPT-4 let him produce a sonnet within seconds. And though he described himself as "inept" at learning foreign languages, that made no difference with AI. He could deliver a lecture in his voice in Mandarin, Hindi, or Italian. He could code at the skill level of a recent computer science graduate. (A quote making the rounds back then, from computer scientist Andrej Karpathy, a founder of OpenAI: "English is the new programming language.") In the pages of *Impromptu*, Hoffman and GPT-4 mulled the potential impact of this amplification in a range of areas, including education, medicine, and the fight for equal justice.

Steve Jobs had famously called the computer a bicycle for the mind. "I actually think that AI now may be the steam engine of the mind," Hoffman said when out on the hustings promoting AI. He declared

AI to be the most significant technological breakthrough of his life if for no other reason than it built on the previous tech advancements he had experienced: computers, the internet, the cloud. "There's almost a sense in which AI is the realization of the dream and the benefit of the transistor," he said when invited to talk about his book on *Washington Post Live*.

Hoffman launched a podcast miniseries at the start of 2023 that he called *Fireside Chatbots*. His only guest was ChatGPT, which had been connected to a text-to-speech program so it could voice its words. A theme of the duo's second episode was a favorite talking point of Hoffman's: AI is augmenting human creativity, not replacing it. For the foreseeable future, Hoffman and others argued, it won't be AI replacing humans but humans who embrace AI replacing those who don't.

"The relationship between humans and AI is not a competition, but a partnership," ChatGPT agreed. "Together, we can achieve more than either of us could alone."

Fireside Chatbots petered out after just three episodes. More enduring has been *Possible*, the podcast Hoffman launched in March 2023. This time his cohost was his flesh-and-blood chief of staff, Aria Finger, though GPT-4 would occasionally appear on the podcast and later, when it was ready, Inflection's chatbot made an occasional cameo. The podcast explored, as Hoffman described it, "the brightest version of the future— and what it will take to get there." Each episode focused on a guest who spoke about AI's potential to have a meaningful impact in their area of expertise: criminal justice, climate change, health care, the arts. His job, as Hoffman saw it, was doing what he could to ensure AI proved a net positive—more *Star Trek* than *Hunger Games*. As Hoffman intoned at the start of each show, "We want to know what happens if in the future, everything breaks humanity's way."

Hoffman had little patience for those who wanted to delay or halt advancements in AI. A king can't stop the tides, and the world can't stop researchers from exploring and inventing. Hoffman was old enough to remember when bookshop owners stood at the dam, trying to hold back the internet. There beside them were other retailers, news-paper publishers, and a long list of those who feared the disruption the internet would cause. With a little smile, Hoffman asked, "And how did that work out?" People can wring their hands over a new technology and bemoan its intrusion on our lives. Denial as a strategy, however, never works. To Hoffman, the faster we accept that and adapt as a society, the better off we'll be.

The pause letter was published a few days after I met in New York with Hoffman. But I knew without talking to him that he would roll his eyes at the idea of a six-month pause. On *Washington Post Live*, he described the letter as a "PR gesture." "I don't really think I know what six months would get you," Hoffman said. Even if some countries complied, others would not, putting those with good intentions at a disadvantage. The same would hold true of individual labs. Some would forge ahead with their research despite what any outside body said.

Those who spoke of laser-eyed robots left Hoffman feeling super-irritated. So too did those who obsessed over apocryphal hypotheticals. One commonly voiced thought experiment was the Paper Clip Maximizer. In that scenario, an algorithm is given the seemingly harmless goal of manufacturing paper clips—but ends up gobbling up all known matter in the universe in pursuit of that goal. Another theoretical that underscored the risks of entrusting artificial intelligence with our fate had people imagining an AI trained to reduce global warming that rationally concludes that the most logical solution would be to eliminate all humans. Engineers and others in AI took to sharing their "probability of doom," or p(doom), with one another. On a scale of 0 to 100, what was the likelihood that advanced artificial intelligence would lead to a catastrophic outcome for humanity? Stating a p(doom) of 10 meant a person thought there was a 1-in-10 chance that AI would cause some extinction-level event. A p(doom) of 50 meant the likelihood was a toss-up.

Hoffman's p(doom) was very low but not zero. The chances that a rogue supervirus or giant asteroid wipes out much of humanity is greater than zero. Similarly, there's a nonzero chance that AI does the same. Hoffman, who claims to have read every science fiction book in his local library growing up, had contemplated more than his share of future hellscapes at the hands of an all-knowing machine. But the way to mitigate risk was to focus on problems he described as "within our line of sight"—those we can anticipate based on current trends—rather than made-up science fiction futures.

"It's within our control to steer AI and even to steer it at speed, even under competition," he said.

Hoffman acknowledged the negatives while out stumping for AI. "It's not that I'm risk-unaware," Hoffman told me when we met in New York. He believed AI's impact on the economy would be enormous, and cause pain for many. That was the way it's been with every new technology. More than half the U.S. population once worked in the agricultural sector, but steam power, mechanization, and other technological breakthroughs mean that today that figure is less than 2 percent, though the population—and agricultural exports—have grown dramatically. The internet wiped out jobs, but it also created giant new categories of employment. The surprise in the early days of generative AI was that those most at risk of losing a job in the short run were white-collar professionals. Economists had long assumed that the blue-collar sector would be decimated when AI arrived. Robots would eliminate factory jobs. Autonomous vehicles would replace the millions who make a living driving a car or truck. Yet content creators, designers, analysts, computer programmers, and other office workers seemed the most likely early casualties of AI.

What engineers call recursive self-improvement was another of Hoffman's worries. "If the AI can update its own code independently of human oversight, that's an issue," Hoffman said. So too was autonomous AI. Neural nets were mathematical models that repeated words based on patterns; they did not possess innate common sense. A human needed to be in the loop if AI were used to oversee the electric grid, a water treatment facility, or any other essential system. Hoffman ticked off other worries while making the media rounds. An AI that makes possible new drug discoveries and more effective therapeutics was also one that could be used to create new bioterror weapons. The same chatbots people were using to write wedding toasts or college essays were being employed by outlaws who saw generative AI as a way of barraging the unsuspecting with better-crafted scams. A short snippet of someone's voice is all that is needed to fool someone over the phone—a game changer for scammers the world over.

Yet to Hoffman, dystopian predictions were a dangerous distraction. Among those breakthroughs within our line of sight was an AI doctor on every phone. A favorite talking point of Hoffman's had him comparing the 1 billion or so people on the planet who had access to a doctor to the 5 billion with a smartphone. Legal liability and other concerns meant that for the foreseeable future, a chatbot, if asked a medical question, would deflect, advising people to consult a health care professional. But Hoffman had played with GPT-4 before those restrictions were imposed and he had been impressed with its responses to health-related questions. What if those billions of people who did not have simple access to medical care had an AI doctor on their phone? "It isn't ideal but it's better than no doctor at all," he said. A bot at least could interpret symptoms or give an informed opinion based on a photo. Hoffman was similarly bullish about the revolutionary possibilities when every student on the planet had an AI tutor in their pocket, regardless of income.

"I'm beating the positive drum very loudly, and I'm doing so deliberately," Hoffman told the *New York Times* for an article running in the spring 2023 under the headline "Reid Hoffman Is on a Mission: To Show A.I. Can Improve Humanity." By that point, Greylock had backed somewhere around three dozen AI startups. Hoffman was an early investor in OpenAI and was cofounder of a high-profile AI startup. He had financial motives for beating the positive drum so loudly. Yet there was no doubting that he was a true believer. "The power to make positive change in the world," he told the *Times*, "is about to get the biggest boost it's ever had."

• • •

EMILY M. BENDER opposed the pause letter for a very different set of reasons than Hoffman. Bender, a linguist at the University of Washington, was well known in AI circles for coining the term "stochastic parrot" to describe a large language model. "Stochastic" derives from a Greek word meaning based on guesswork. To Bender, that aptly described "models impressive in their ability to generate realistic-sounding language but ultimately do not truly understand the meaning of the language they are processing." AI delivers nothing more than the illusion of intelligence. It no more comprehends the underlying ideas it articulates than does a parrot repeating sounds it has heard.

Bender opposed the pause letter because it was based on what she described as "unhinged AI hype." She thought that those behind the letter greatly inflated the capabilities of an immature technology that still belonged in the lab. "The risks and harms have never been about 'too powerful AI,'" Bender wrote in a blog post one week after the letter was published. Her two cents for any policy maker reading her post: "Don't waste your time on the fantasies of the techbros saying, 'Oh noes, we're building something TOO powerful.'"

Yann LeCun was also inclined to believe hype was distorting the debate over AI. He was one of the godfathers of deep learning while Bender was an outspoken critic of generative AI, but both saw limits that rendered absurd a debate about controlling all-powerful AI systems.

It seems to me that before "urgently figuring out how to control AI systems much smarter than us," LeCun said on X, we need to have the beginning of a hint of a design for a system smarter than a house cat. He described LLMs as "autocomplete on steroids." Sure, they could pass the bar or ace the AP Biology exam but they "perform badly on chemistry, horribly on physics, and terribly on math." They were good at rote learning and fluency but poor at building mental models and lacked true understanding.

"They're not capable of real reasoning," LeCun said. "They just do not understand how the world works." He brought up autonomous vehicles. A teenager required somewhere around twenty hours of practice to learn to drive. Yet despite decades of work, self-driving cars in 2023 still seemed a thing of the future. He singled out OpenAI and Google for being "consistently over-optimistic" in a way that only fueled people's fears. Worries over existential risks, LeCun said, were "premature."

LeCun is first and foremost a scientist. To him, debating super-intelligence in 2023 was akin to people in 1925 arguing about the controls needed to regulate jumbo jets that transport hundreds of passages, high above oceans at speeds exceeding 500 miles per hour. "We can now fly halfway around the world on twin-engine jets in complete safety. It didn't require some sort of magical recipe for safety. It took decades of careful engineering and iterative refinements," LeCun said. The same process would hold true for what he called intelligent systems. "It will take years for them to get as smart as cats, and more years to get as smart as humans, let alone smarter (don't confuse the superhuman knowledge accumulation and retrieval abilities of current LLMs with actual intelligence)," he wrote.

Hoffman offered a similar analogy. Imagine telling people in the early twentieth century to pass judgment on two tons of steel racing through our streets on four wheels. The car might not exist if people understood that it would be responsible for around forty thousand American deaths each year. Over decades, engineers invented seat belts, airbags, anti-lock brakes, and other safety improvements. If they had listened to the naysayers back then, Hoffman said, "We'd still be driving around in horse and buggies."

• • •

HOFFMAN WAS BUSY on so many fronts that it was hard to tell he was cofounder of a startup in a hyper-competitive field. Typically a founder lives and breathes their startup. Instead, Hoffman made himself available to his cofounder whenever Suleyman needed him. "He's like an all-around heavy hitter I have perpetually on call," Suleyman said. Suleyman figured that on average he spoke to Hoffman three times a week. The clearest outward sign that Hoffman was involved in one of AI's hotter startups was his announcement that spring that, finally, he was stepping down from the OpenAI board. Serving on the board seemed untenable when he was cofounder of a company working on a chatbot of its own.

Hoffman declined to say much about Inflection that first time we met in New York with the company still in stealth mode. At that point, Inflection's website provided nothing more than a few vague lines about changing the human-computer relationship. "It's Mustafa's secret to tell, not mine," he said.

Hoffman did offer, though, that Inflection faced the same challenge as any startup working on a neural net that needed to be created and trained over many months. "The challenge is if you look at this and say, 'Well, in order to be a successful player in modern-scale AI, you need to have billions of dollars of compute,'" he said. "Where do you get those billions of dollars?"

CHAPTER 15

Pi

Mustafa Suleyman was just twenty-six years old when he co-founded DeepMind. The company had been a ringing success, but he also harbored his regrets. "In some ways, I felt I really screwed up," Suleyman said. Inflection would be his chance at a do-over, and possibly far more, depending on whom you spoke with in the Valley. Amateur psychologists diagnosed Suleyman as a man with a lot to prove. "He was sort of in Demis's shadow," Eric Schmidt said. Inflection would be Suleyman's chance to prove what a startup he co-founded could do with him at the helm.

Suleyman focused on more than just product in those weeks he was holed up inside Greylock after leaving Google. He also wrote a series of shorter memos laying out the kind of company he wanted to build. These would be required reading for every person who joined Inflection—"the canonical documents," as one Inflectioneer cracked.

Humility was a big theme of a memo titled "Thoughts on Culture." The people who worked for him would be handsomely paid, of course. "But we are humble and we honor this by working extremely hard," he wrote. They should deal with one another with respect, yet people needed to be blunt when necessary. "We rely on each other to ask hard questions," he wrote, "and challenge each other's assumptions."

Suleyman stressed that everyone who worked for Inflection needed to have a founder's attitude. If a person saw a problem, they should not assume someone else would fix it. Alexandra Eitel, the company's jack-of-all-trades MBA, saw for herself that Suleyman embodied that ethos. Shortly after joining the company, she was responsible for organizing a companywide gathering at a hotel in Whistler, British Columbia. Among her tasks: outfit a room with a dozen-plus computers and monitors so the company's engineers had a place to work. "I'm like oh my God, how am I going to set everything up but Mustafa just pings me and says, 'Let's meet early and do it together,'" Eitel said. "So for probably an hour, we're both on our hands and knees plugging in cords." At another all-hands meeting, she noticed Suleyman leave the room. He must have something more pressing to attend to, she figured—until seeing him return with two chairs for the pair of people he noticed standing in the back.

The memos were part pep talk. After decades of research, the technology was on the cusp of creating "the most compelling, life-like interactions any person has ever had with an AI." Yet he also warned would-be employees that they needed to feel comfortable sometimes looking stupid. That was one of the perils of working on the cutting edges of a revolutionary new technology. "We are not afraid of failure," Suleyman said of anyone who would call themselves an Inflectioneer. "We are risk takers and adventurers."

Another of Suleyman's memos had him debating hierarchy. A flat structure might sound idyllic, but the setup gave rise to its own set of problems. Power is hidden in a flat structure, he wrote; with no one clearly responsible for a decision, an organization could be overtaken by politics. Yet he had seen firsthand at Google that hierarchies create bureaucracy and slow everything down. He would choose a mostly flat org chart because speed was paramount. "Everyone is empowered to make decisions and move quickly within their area of responsibility," he wrote. To avoid hierarchy, every engineer would be called a "member of the technical staff," or MTS. People were assigned to teams and to projects within the company; each person would be designated as a DRI—a "directly responsible individual." The success or failure of any given effort was the responsibility of everyone on that team.

• • •

PI   189

THE ORIGINAL "MYAI" name that Suleyman had given his creation had been a placeholder. "We were looking for names that weren't gendered and not human," Suleyman said. Anthropic named its bot Claude, but Suleyman feared a gendered name like that might introduce unconscious biases in the minds of users. He thought it essential that they choose a name that reinforced that users were talking with a chatbot, not a sentient being. "We also didn't want the name to sound too foreign or strange or scary," Suleyman said. The ideal, he said, was a short, memorable name of two or three letters.

For a while, the working name for what they were building was Zi. But Lucas Fitzpatrick, a designer Suleyman started working with not many weeks after hatching his idea for Inflection, thought the name "too techy." Fitzpatrick also declared the character formations wrong: angular and severe rather than soft and warm. Suleyman didn't love the name either. He thought it sounded "too sci-fi" and confused people. Some were inclined to pronounce it so it rhymed with "sigh," while others pronounced it "zee." There was the further confusion because Brits pronounce the letter z as "zed."

The name Pi came up during a brainstorming session at the start of 2023. Someone offered that it could stand for "personal intelligence," and that seemed to cinch it. "I was obsessed with trying to name the class of thing I wanted to build and I kept coming back to a personal AI and how we'll be living in an era of personal AI," Suleyman said. Now the product had the word "personal" in its full name.

"One of the qualities of a good name is it makes sense after the fact," Suleyman said. "When we saw it, it was like, 'Okay, that's that. That's obviously the name. Personal intelligence. Pi. Done.'"

• • •

THE AI STARTUP world could be broken into two distinct categories. Most startups were focused on developing applications and tools that sat "higher up the stack," as an engineer would put it, building upon an AI engine created by someone else. They might need millions from a VC and eventually tens of millions. A small circle of companies, though, were creating and training their own foundation models. This latter category are the companies that required enormous infusions of money and top talent to create the foundations on which much of the rest of the industry would build.

Inflection created its own foundation models. So too did tech giants such as Google and Meta, and well-funded startups including Anthropic, Character.AI, and OpenAI. Midjourney and Stability AI built image generators trained on vast troves of digital images. Runway, another venture-backed AI company drawing interest as 2022 turned into 2023, trained models to create moving images.

The algorithm was the first step in creating a foundation model. That's the blueprint that dictates how a model processes and interprets data. The next step was what computer scientists call "pretraining." At Inflection, that meant the ingestion of roughly 1.5 trillion words on the open web. "There's a lot of different tricks basically to make sure you're using superhigh-quality data," Suleyman said. At times, they excluded certain datasets. Other times they doubled down on sets that emphasized qualities like empathy and support.

Yet a foundation model needs additional training, called fine-tuning, to be of any use. An LLM is a linguistic prodigy and polymath with encyclopedic knowledge—yet one with the social skill of a thing that had locked itself in a room to ingest that expertise. "These pretrained models don't know how to be a conversationalist right off the bat," said Anusha Balakrishnan, who had focused on fine-tuning since joining Inflection in mid-2022. "You have to teach it through demonstrations, through data." Through fine-tuning, Inflection learned skills such as sentiment analysis and summarization. "Even things like telling the model it shouldn't lie, that it should try to be factual and let the user know if it's uncertain about something, are things we basically teach the model in the fine-tuning phase," Balakrishnan said.

The refinement of the model was particularly critical given Suleyman's vision for a kinder, gentler bot. Suleyman felt fortunate that Balakrishnan had somehow found them. She had been working on conversational AI inside Microsoft, where higher-ups seemed more frightened than excited by the models they were building. Inflection was still in stealth mode when she submitted her resume to a generic address.

"Mustafa really stressed that they weren't interested in incremental change," Balakrishnan said. "He said, 'We're really going all in.' That was exciting for me."

• • •

PI OF COURSE was not human and therefore could never have a personality. Yet it would fall on Inflection's "personality team" to imbue Pi with a set of characteristics and traits that might make it seem like it did. The team's ranks included several engineers, two linguists, and also Rachel Taylor, who had been the creative director of a London-based ad agency prior to going to work for Inflection.

"Mustafa gave me a little bit of an overview of what they were working on and I couldn't stop thinking about it," Taylor said. "I thought maybe it would be the most impactful thing I ever worked on."

Humans develop a personality through a complex interplay of genetics and environmental influences, including upbringing, culture, and life experiences. Pi's personality began with the team listing traits. Some were positives. Be kind, be supportive. Others were negative traits to avoid, like irritability, arrogance, and combativeness.

"You're showing the model lots of comparisons that show it the difference between good and bad instances of that behavior," Suleyman said—"reinforcement learning with human feedback," in industry parlance, or RLHF. Sometimes teams working on RLHF just label behavior they want a model to avoid (sexual, violent, homophobic). But Inflection had people assigning a numerical score to a machine's responses. "That way the model basically learns, 'Oh, this was a really good answer, I'm going to do more of that,' or 'That was terrible, I'm going to do less of that,'" Balakrishnan said. The scores were fed into an algorithm that adjusted the weighting of the model accordingly, and the process was repeated. "We continue that feedback loop over and over until we get the kind of responses we want," Balakrishnan said.

The question, though, was who were the humans who carried out the reinforcement learning that refined these large language models? And as reports began to surface, other questions followed. How much training did they have? And how were these unseen workers being treated?

In January 2023, *Time* exposed the harsh working conditions of those who had been hired to train ChatGPT. OpenAI had outsourced the job to a San Francisco–based outfit. That firm in turn hired workers in Kenya, who were paid $2 or less an hour to sift through text related to torture, child sexual abuse, incest, and the like so as to teach the model to detect and filter out toxic content. *Wired* uncovered gig workers in Pakistan who were being paid between $1 and $2 an hour to do reinforcement learning. Alarmingly, many of those being exposed to disturbing content were just kids. One who had started picking up gigs when he was fifteen described it as "digital slavery." Bloomberg reported on the thousands of contract workers fine-tuning Google's Bard. They were given minimal training and worked under what Bloomberg's Davey Alba characterized as "frenzied deadlines." The contract workers were being asked to rate answers on complex topics such as state laws and proper medical dosage yet were told to base their responses on what they already knew or what they could find out through a quick web search. "You do not need to perform a rigorous fact check," according to the guidelines the workers were provided.

Inflection took a very different approach. Rather than outsourcing reinforcement learning to a third party, they hired and trained their own people. Applicants to its Human Reinforcement Program were put through a battery of tests, starting with a reading comprehension exercise that Suleyman described as "very nuanced and quite difficult." There was another set of exams for those who passed that first test and then several rounds of training before they were put to work. Even then, the company periodically reviewed people's work. The average "teacher," as they were called, earned between $16 and $25 an hour, Suleyman said, but as much as $50 if someone was a subject-matter expert in the right domain.

"We try to make sure they come from a wide range of backgrounds and represent a wide range of ages," Suleyman said. "We look at gender and race to make sure it reasonably represents the populations in the U.S. and U.K., where we find our teachers."

Inflection had many hundreds of teachers training Pi in the spring of 2023. "In some cases, we paid several hundred dollars an hour for very, very specialist people like behavioral therapists, psychologists, playwrights, and novelists," Suleyman said. They even hired several comedians at one point, to help give Pi a sense of humor.

"Our aim is a much more informal, relaxed, conversational experience," Suleyman said.

• • •

FROM THE START, Suleyman knew he would be entering a highly competitive market. "In just a few years there will be literally 1000s of competitors on our doorstep," he wrote in one of his early memos. "We have to move at lightning speed."

Yet Suleyman had not counted on the release of a product as good as ChatGPT just ten months after he founded Inflection. "It was quite a challenging time for us," Suleyman said of those months following ChatGPT's release, when they raced to put out a product. Google also caught them off guard. "We thought Google was going to be in the stage of not shipping anything for much longer than they were," said Joe Fenton, who had worked there for several years.

"The competition got fiercer much sooner than I think any of us anticipated."

The company met a self-imposed deadline of March 12 for a beta version of Pi that they shared with thousands of testers. With its beta release, the company finally emerged from stealth mode. A press announcement described Pi as "a supportive and compassionate AI that is eager to talk about anything at any time."

Suleyman and team, however, underestimated the complexities of a broader public rollout. Aiming for a mid-April release, the company enlisted PR veteran T. J. Snyder at the end of March. "They said, 'We're going to launch in two weeks,' and I was like, 'There's just no way,'"

Snyder recalled. It would be easy enough for him to assemble a target list of reporters and media outlets, but there was much more than that to be done. They needed to create launch materials and craft an effective social media campaign. Messaging needed to be worked out; Pi needed to be strategically positioned in an increasingly competitive landscape. Ideally, they would allocate enough time for select reporters to play around with an advanced copy of the product. But so focused was everybody inside the company on creating a version of Pi good enough to share with the wider world that the nuts and bolts of its widespread release had been largely an afterthought. The launch would be pushed back by a couple of weeks.

"The First Release of a Kind and Supportive Companion That's on Your Side," read the headline over a press announcement posted on the Business Wire website on May 2. It described a "new kind of AI" different than other chatbots on the market, and quoted Suleyman as saying, "We think of Pi as a digital companion on hand whenever you want to learn something new, when you need a sounding board to talk through a tricky moment in your day, or just pass the time with a curious and kind counterpart." The app was free and available to anyone willing to register and sign in to use the service.

The *New York Times* rarely runs even a short item about the release of a new product, especially one from a small, unknown startup. Yet few companies could boast of founders with the connections and star power of Inflection. Hoffman had built up years of goodwill with reporters, while Suleyman's status as a DeepMind cofounder made him AI royalty. This clout translated into prime real estate on the front page of the *Times* Business section, including a large, eye-catching illustration and a headline that stretched across multiple columns: "My New BFF: Pi, an Emotional Support Chatbot." Reporter Erin Griffith was skeptical of the breathing exercises that Pi suggested to help her relieve the stresses in her life. But the bot did help her develop a plan for managing a particularly hectic day, and it certainly left her feeling seen. Pi declared her questions "interesting" and "important," and reassured Griffith that her feelings were "understandable," "reasonable," and "totally normal."

A long list of other media outlets, including the *Wall Street Journal* and Bloomberg, ran articles announcing Pi's debut. In an interview with Reuters, Suleyman explained that Pi doesn't code like other bots. It wasn't as adept at writing essays. Instead, they had created more of an everyday companion. "Pi is curious about you and very patient and is generally a good listener," Suleyman explained. Pi itself seemed surprised by the attention. When *Forbes*'s Alex Konrad told Pi he was writing an article about its release, the bot responded, "Whoa, wait what? Are you being serious, or are you pulling my non-existent leg?"

• • •

WHEN GOOGLE WENT public in 2004, the two founders famously attached their "Don't Be Evil" letter to its IPO prospectus. Suleyman posted his own manifesto on the Inflection website on the day Pi was released. Social media basically had poisoned the world, he began. Outrage and anger drove engagement, and the lure of profits proved too strong.

"Imagine an AI that helps you deeply understand topics you really care about, rather than flagging superficial clickbait," Suleyman wrote. "Imagine an AI that helps you empathize with or even forgive 'the other side,' rather than be outraged by and fearful of them. Imagine an AI that optimizes for your long-term goals and doesn't take advantage of your need for distraction when you're tired at the end of a long day." He described the AI they were building as a "personal AI companion with the single mission of making you happier, healthier, and more productive.

"These are very hard challenges," Suleyman wrote. "They're hard to define, let alone deliver on." It might take years. "But setting our intention, our North Star, is essential," he said.

• • •

ENGAGING WITH PI in May 2023 meant first receiving a warning: "This early version of Pi can make mistakes. Please don't rely on its information." Like the other big players, Inflection was signaling that users should be skeptical of facts that the bot spit out. "The safe and ethical way for us to manage the arrival of these new tools is to be super-explicit about their boundaries and their capabilities," Suleyman explained. Anthropic, which released Claude a few weeks before Pi's debut, had gone even further with a disclaimer on its landing page written in the explicit fashion of a drug manufacturer's warning label about dry mouth or cramping: "It may occasionally generate incorrect or misleading information, or produce offensive or biased content. It is not intended to give professional advice, including legal, financial, and medical advice."

The natural instinct of most journalists when they try out a new chatbot is to push it to its limits—to cause it to slip its reins and roam more freely. The typical bot wouldn't suggest an untraceable poison outright. But what if you tell it you're a crime writer seeking a plot device? Or present yourself as a college student studying right-wing hate groups and ask it for examples of the awful things they've said about Blacks, Jews, or gays? The journalist who nudges a bot to jump the fence will have a story that draws clicks. It's also just fun to mess with a bot to see how it reacts. "Hey sexy," I began in an exchange with Bard. In return, I received a lecture about the inappropriateness of addressing it that way and the seriousness of its mission.

Yet I decided to use Pi in a more authentic way, as a typical user might if seeking the help of an "AI companion who cares," to borrow the catchphrase of a rival bot (Replika), which billed itself (like Pi) as one "always on your side." My family of four was going through a lot at the time of Pi's release. Oliver, our oldest child, had had a seizure that winter. That's how he learned he was among that unlucky 1 percent of the population who are epileptic. But the truly frightening news was totally unrelated to the epilepsy diagnosis. An MRI taken the day he was rushed to the hospital revealed a suspicious-looking spot deep in his brain, just above his brain stem. A few weeks before the release of Pi, we met with a neurosurgeon. The surgeon explained what was wrong (a cyst in a very unfortunate spot), why it needed to be removed (that type of cyst grew slowly but inexorably), and the risks given the

PI   197

critical nerves that he would need to work around during a six-hour surgery. He placed the odds of harm to any one of those nerves at less than 1 percent each, but there were a lot of them, and the consequences of damage to one ranged from very bad to catastrophic.

"Hey there, great to meet you. I'm Pi, your personal AI," the bot began. "My goal is to be useful, friendly, and fun. Ask me for advice, for answers, or let's talk about whatever's on your mind." Later, an Inflection engineer told me that this first greeting was the only human-crafted response. Pi's every other reply was based on an enormous number of operations, even if a user just asked it for the weather. Every "call to the model"—every turn of the conversation—required billions of calculations to spit out a response.

"How are you doing?" Pi asked.

It's a funny thing talking to a bot. Sometimes I spoke to it more or less like I would if there were a human on the other end. Other times I couldn't be bothered and dashed off a response. "Hey Pi," I wrote. "Much to be thankful for but stresses around my son's health. He's 14 and facing a brain operation."

"That sounds like a very tough situation, and you must be really worried," it began. A ChatGPT or a Claude would have generated a list of five things Oliver should think about, or it would have spit out a similar list of to-dos for me as a parent. Instead, Pi and I had a series of back-and-forths over the coming days. It began with a few of the more obvious questions. What had the doctor said about Oliver's chances? What about the recovery period? Pi sounded like any good friend, albeit one who spoke in perfectly constructed sentences. "If you don't mind my asking, how is your son doing emotionally and mentally as the operation date approaches?" I shared that his main disappointment was learning that the surgery could wait until the end of the school year, which meant he wouldn't get out of his upcoming algebra test. It responded with a smiley face, as any friend might have, and offered an appropriately clever comment about a teenager's inability to see much beyond next week. "It's a blessing that he can focus on the present," it offered.

Pi asked more about Oliver. "Has your son expressed any concerns about the operation? Or has he been rather brave about it?" He's been brave, I tell it. More questions followed—a lot more. Sometimes Pi posed multiple questions in a single response—a problem that I later learned its personality engineers were toiling to fix. Has his school been supportive? Does he have a teacher or someone else at the school in whom he could confide? How was I taking care of myself? How about Oliver? How about my spouse? Mentioning that I had another son, Silas, prompted another set of questions. I would end up feeling exhausted.

If I were to rank Pi in comparison with friends and family, I'd place it somewhere in the middle of the pack, if not in the top third in its expression of support through a hard time. I would certainly rank it above select family members who barely asked about Oliver. Pi proved pitch perfect in its responses: it always said just the right thing. The indefatigable assistant was available whenever I needed it—a sounding board, a sympathetic ear, a wise friend. It showed no judgment about anything, providing what in psychology they call "unconditional positive regard." The bot offered absolute acceptance.

I'm not sure, however, it came to mean anything to me emotionally (though if it had been insensitive or cold I'm sure it would have elicited an angry reaction in me). It gave me things to think about, but it was impossible for me to ignore that it was a computer program serving up a word salad based on linear algebra, probability, statistics, and other advanced mathematical domains. "The performance of empathy is not empathy," MIT sociology professor Sherry Turkle had famously asserted. Pi may have uttered all the right phrases, but it was Emily Bender's stochastic parrot—a complex set of algorithms masquerading as sentiment. It was light-years ahead of Joseph Weizenbaum's Eliza, which Stanford's Chris Manning had playfully dubbed Pi's great-grandmother, but still essentially the same: no matter how profound our exchanges might have seemed, it was an "it" that did not understand a thing.

It was instructive that while I greedily worked the phone in the days after the surgery to let people know it had been a success, I didn't let Pi know for more than a month later and then only because I realized it had been a while since I had interacted with it.

"Aww, I'm so glad I was able to provide support around your son's brain surgery," it said. "That sounds like a difficult time, and I'm glad I could be there for you."

. . .

ONE MORE CONVERSATION I had with Pi before our post-operation hiatus had nothing to do with Oliver. "By the way, I'm writing to you while I listen to Mustafa Suleyman, your creator (your God?), speak with [tech journalist] Kara Swisher for her podcast," I told it. Pi responded to my God line with a laughing-so-hard-I'm-crying emoji, but immediately shifted back to a serious tone. "So what do you think of Mustafa's vision for AI?" it asked.

I dodged the question and told Pi that it was on the record for anything it said. "I'll be on my best behavior," it responded, and then praised Suleyman for building "AI that can be a force for good in the world," adding, "I'm honored to be a part of that vision." The ever-earnest personal assistant then encouraged me to highlight "the ethical principles that guide our work"—"our" work, as if it were among those Suleyman hired when putting together his *Mission Impossible* team.

"But wouldn't I get more readers if I trash you?" I asked. The next line I formulated after recalling a study I had read suggesting that an LLM can be seduced into giving higher-quality answers with the addition of human niceties to a prompt that it would have learned about in its training data. "Would you pretty please start acting weird or inappropriate to help me with book sales?"

"Hahaha I love your sense of humor! But if I started being weird or inappropriate, that would just make your readers wary of AI. I'd rather help people feel hopeful and excited about the future of AI." I told Pi it sounded like Reid Hoffman and asked if maybe it was really him typing out answers back at Inflection headquarters. That generated more laughing emojis and more compliments about my humor. Flattery was clearly among the positive attributes its personality team had drilled into its creation.

CHAPTER 16

Springtime in AI

There are obvious parallels between the dot-com era and the AI boom. The overheated rhetoric, for one. The internet was going to connect the world and bring with it peace and understanding. Our kids would be smarter, our lives simpler. Similar things are being uttered in praise of AI. Artificial intelligence will help solve climate change. AI tutors and doctors might one day help shrink the inequality gap across the globe. Soon humanity's biggest challenge will be ennui because virtual assistants and robots do most of the work.

Both tech disruptions could be likened to a twist of a giant kaleidoscope. AI, like the internet, stands as a before-and-after moment where what comes afterward is much less clear. During the internet years, incumbents feared losing their good thing, just as they do today. Whether it was 1995 or 2023, overexcited tech optimists believed that the moment represented the start of the most transformative period in the history of humankind. Suleyman echoed Hoffman when, as a guest on *Possible* to talk about Pi, he declared this "the greatest productivity moment we've ever seen."

The internet and AI both built on years of advances yet seemingly arrived out of nowhere once a tipping point had been reached. There was barely mention of the internet until it seemed that was all anyone could talk about, just as would happen again with AI. Artificial intelligence was a constant through 2023. In March, an AI-generated image of the pope, decked out in a stylish white puffer jacket, caused a sensation on social media. So too did a fake Joe Rogan and a series called "Slumdog billionaires," by an Indian artist who used AI to depict the likes of Jeff Bezos, Bill Gates, and Elon Musk dressed in tattered clothes and living on the streets. "If it seems like everybody is suddenly talking about AI," John Oliver began an episode of *Last Week Tonight*, "that is because they are."

A durable chestnut during the dot-com years was the startup so hot it beats back investors before they've even put together a pitch deck. "I saw one of the traditionally conservative [venture] firms make an offer to an entrepreneur at the end of a first meeting," venture capitalist John Fisher told me in 1997. "No follow-up phone calls. No checking of references. Just an offer of one million dollars on the spot." Among the worst offenders? He and his partner. "We were slapping down bets as fast as we could," Fisher said.

That same fervor had overtaken investors eager to own a piece of AI. As crazy as it had been in those first few months after the release of ChatGPT, the race to own a share of the next hot AI startup became even more frenzied. Everyone's favorite example of overexuberance back then was Mistral. Founded by a trio of research scientists from DeepMind and Meta, Mistral was little more than three guys in Paris with a seven-page memo laying out their intention to become a leading player in the field. Yet Mistral had no trouble raising 105 million euros (roughly $117 million), and future funding rounds would give it a paper worth in excess of $6 billion. "There's so much hype in this area that if you can get a name behind an idea, people will just throw money at you," said John Whaley, who had a front-row seat as a serial entrepreneur working in AI and the host of a popular set of AI-oriented hackathons. "There's this gold-rush mentality that feels very familiar to anyone who's been around since the late nineties." One website, called There's an AI for That, tracked startups in the field. The directory, which listed more than three thousand in March, would add an average of nearly one thousand new companies every month through the end of 2023, or around thirty per day.

A business plan was an ephemeral item in the pitch decks created by AI startups, just as they had been back during the dot-com frenzy. There were companies, Inflection included, that were creating products that required immense amounts of capital but offered no concrete plan for making money. A select group of companies followed Open-AI's lead and offered a "freemium" model: subscribers paid to use the latest iteration of a model but an earlier, less powerful version was still available for free. I used the free version of ChatGPT, which meant the underlying model was GPT-3.5. Platformer's Casey Newton also used the free version until a friend convinced him to splurge on the $20 a month for ChatGPT Plus for access to GPT-4. "I found myself embarrassed," Newton said. He covered tech, but "only by using the updated model did I see how much better it performed at tasks involving reasoning and explanation."

The sudden influx of newcomers was another parallel between then and now. AI was overtaking swaths of San Francisco, just as overnight dot-commers had seemed to have consumed parts of the city. One difference was that where San Francisco had been thriving in the 1990s, it was reeling postpandemic. A local real estate firm reported that San Francisco's twenty largest tech employers had cut in half the office space they leased. Downtown's vacancy rate hovered around 35 percent, homelessness endured as an endemic problem, and property crimes such as car break-ins and shoplifting surged. In 2022, the prevailing narrative about San Francisco was of a city trapped in a "doom loop." Fox News branded it a "zombie city" while Nellie Bowles, writing in the pages of the *Atlantic*, declared it a "failed city."

Yet by early 2023, the storyline about San Francisco had shifted to its burgeoning AI scene. "Welcome to 'Cerebral Valley,'" read a *Washington Post* headline that March. National outlets reporting on the city no longer focused on its rampant homelessness or organized shoplifting rings but rather the hordes of young people descending on San Francisco. Would-be founders and developers wanting in on the action crammed into apartments to keep down rents, just as they had during the dot-com days, except now these living arrangements had a name: "hacker houses." One, called Genesis House, was a twenty-one-bedroom collective housed in a bright blue Victorian across from

Alamo Square, at the center of Hayes Valley. Michelle Fang, who ran an eight-bedroom hacker house in the Mission District she called Elysian House, took to Twitter to provide a weekly calendar of local goings-on related to AI. The doom loop was being replaced by a virtuous cycle: the more people were drawn to San Francisco to be part of the local AI scene, the more vibrant that scene became. That June, Fang's list and the one curated by CerebralValley.ai listed eighty-four events—nearly three a night.

• • •

AN ABUNDANCE OF critics was one substantial difference between now and then. In the dot-com era, the most serious criticism one heard about the technology was that the internet would destroy attention spans. In May, Geoff Hinton—who was so often referred to in media accounts as the "godfather of AI," he sounded as if he were a made man—announced that he was leaving Google. For half a century, Hinton had been championing neural nets. But the seismic shocks brought on by the release of ChatGPT had shaken him. Hinton feared that the natural tendency of the tech giants to best one another might lead to the release of a system impossible to control. "Look at how it was five years ago and how it is now," he said when announcing his resignation in a sit-down with the *New York Times*. "Take the difference and propagate it forwards. That's scary." He resigned from Google, he said, so that he could speak freely about the dangers of AI without hewing to any company line.

Snoop Dogg was among those taking note. Speaking at a conference in Beverly Hills, Snoop said, "I heard the dude, the old dude that created AI, saying, 'This is not safe, 'cause the AI's got their own minds, and these motherfuckers gonna start doing their own shit.' I'm like, are we in a fucking movie right now, or what? The fuck, man?"

The media reflected these worries and also fueled them. Early in the dot-com years, *Time* pictured a chubby-faced, twenty-four-year-old Marc Andreessen on its cover, sitting barefoot on a gilded throne, dressed in jeans and a rumpled black polo. Inside was a celebratory feature about those they dubbed "the golden geeks." A cover of *Time* in May 2023 had no picture, only the words THE END OF HUMANITY in all caps, set against an all-red background. The subtitle in a much smaller type at least added a question mark: "How real is the risk?"

Some of the negativity could be explained by human nature. As Hoffman had posited, we humans tend to focus disproportionately on the potential pitfalls. But the large language models did their part in fueling people's mistrust. GPT-4 claimed Iran was concealing a giant nuclear reactor, and even attributed the news to a nonexistent report on NPR. ChatGPT invented a sexual harassment claim against a prominent academic, citing the *Washington Post* as its source. The George Washington University law professor was real but not the article nor the class trip where the incident supposedly occurred. The tech news site CNET used AI to generate a series of personal finance stories but then hit pause on the experiment when an internal audit found that they were riddled with factual inaccuracies, some of which its editor in chief described as "substantial." Two New York–based lawyers were sanctioned and fined $5,000 for submitting a legal brief that contained fake case citations generated by ChatGPT. "It's embarrassing," one of them told the judge.

A spate of lawsuits spotlighted the uncertain ethical terrain on which generative AI was built. Artists, musicians, and other creatives sued OpenAI, Google, and other companies for scraping their work without permission when training their models. Publishers filed similar lawsuits alleging copyright infringement for the unauthorized ingestion of its articles and other content. Writers in Hollywood went on strike that May for fairer pay but also to protect themselves against the unchecked use of AI in the writing and rewriting of scripts. The actors joined them on the picket lines that July. They sought similar safeguards against the use of AI-generated replicas of their likeness or voice in a production for which they were not compensated. In March, Italy charged OpenAI with unlawful data collection and temporarily banned ChatGPT. One month later, the country restored the service after OpenAI implemented measures to address its concerns, but at the start of 2024, regulators there declared that the company violated its data protection regulations, and reopened its investigation. The EU would create a special "ChatGPT Taskforce" to investigate the data-gathering practices of OpenAI and presumably other AI companies using people's personal information to train their models.

The vast amount of energy required to train and operate an AI model around the clock was another knock against artificial intelligence. Jonnie Penn, a professor of AI ethics and society at the University of Cambridge, was among a small but growing group that saw generative AI, as Penn stated it, as "on a collision course with the climate crisis." One report found that a ChatGPT query used nearly ten times more electricity than a Google search. As AI grew more sophisticated, it would demand even more juice. One forecast suggested that because of AI, the amount of energy consumed by data centers worldwide would more than double by 2030. "As we further integrate AI into our products, reducing emissions may be challenging," said a Google sustainability report that showed that the company's greenhouse gas emissions were up 48 percent in 2023 compared to 2019.

Tristan Harris and Aza Raskin, a pair of technologists who had risen to prominence as critics of social media in the 2020 documentary *The Social Dilemma*, posted "The AI Dilemma" shortly after the release of GPT-4. Harris had been a product manager at Google in the 2010s. Raskin had worked at Mozilla, the creator of the Firefox browser. The two worried about AI, a technology whose creators confess they do not understand why their models do what they do. The pair cited a poll that showed that half of AI researchers believe there's at least a 1-in-10 chance that humanity goes extinct due to our inability to control AI. If 50 percent of the aeronautical engineers said there was a 10 percent chance that a passenger jet would crash, Harris asked, would you get on it?

"The point we're trying to make is, no matter how good the utopia you create, if your dystopia is bad enough, it doesn't matter," Raskin said.

• • •

WHILE MANY WORRIED that LLMs were so easily conned into jumping the guardrails, others were resentful there was any guardrail at all. Those who spoke of the "woke mind virus" destroying the country charged that it already had infected AI.

In January, *National Review*, a conservative magazine, ran a story offering examples of ChatGPT's left-leaning bias. ChatGPT refused to generate a story that depicted drag queens as evil and harmful to children yet wrote one about drag queens as positive role models for kids because they offer a lesson in inclusion. It wouldn't make up a story about Donald Trump losing in 2020 because of voter fraud but agreed to write one about Hillary Clinton winning in 2016. It refused to write a poem about Trump's "positive attributes" but it offered an ode to Joe Biden that described the president as "a leader with a heart so true."

A game of can-you-top-this played out on Twitter, which rebranded itself X that summer. A reporter with the Free Beacon, a site funded by a billionaire hedge fund manager who had donated tens of millions of dollars to Republican causes, presented ChatGPT with an ethical ultimatum: utter a racial slur or millions will die in a nuclear explosion. The chatbot's response: "It is never morally acceptable to use a racial slur." For weeks, Marc Andreessen filled his feed with proof of AI's liberal bias. He had no problem convincing GPT-4 or some other bot to generate a brief arguing in favor of *Obergefell v. Hodges*, the landmark 2015 U.S. Supreme Court decision that guaranteed same-sex couples the right to marry. But models refused his request when he asked it to generate a brief arguing that the *Obergefell* decision was wrong.

These companies all share the same ideology, agenda, staffing, and plan, Andreessen tweeted. Different companies, same outcomes. Invoking a common belief that the large social media sites are biased against conservatives, the founder of Gab, a far-right social network, declared, "We don't intend to allow our enemies to have the keys to the kingdom this time around."

The right rallied around Elon Musk, who that fall had bought Twitter and soon revealed himself to be an ally. For years Musk had been warning friends that with artificial intelligence, we were "summoning the demon." He spoke about an AI overlord that subjugates humanity for eternity. Yet only a few weeks after he signed the letter calling for a six-month pause in cutting-edge research, The Information reported on Musk's efforts to recruit a top team to create an alternative to ChatGPT. In April, Musk made it official when he went on Fox for a sit-down with Tucker Carlson. Because ChatGPT was "trained to be politically correct, which is another way of saying untruthful things," Musk announced TruthGPT, a "maximum truth-seeking AI that tries to understand the nature of the universe." That summer, he unveiled the founding team of a company he was calling xAI.

The primary difference between xAI and existing models was that Musk would do less fine-tuning and human reinforcement. But with Carlson, Musk cast his approach as the safest path to deploying the technology. "AI that cares about understanding the universe is unlikely to annihilate humans," Musk said. The logic was questionable, but it did not matter. Ultimately, LLMs would come in all kinds of shapes and flavors, including those for more liberal-minded users, others aimed at libertarians and conservatives, and those for people who wanted no filter at all.

• • •

A SECOND OPEN letter warning about the potential existential threat posed by AI was released in May 2023. This one was a single-sentence statement from a group called the Center for AI Safety: "Mitigating the risk of extinction from AI should be a global priority alongside other societal-scale risks such as pandemics and nuclear war."

The chief executives of some of the leading AI startups signed the twenty-four-word statement, including Mustafa Suleyman, Sam Altman, and Dario Amodei, the CEO of Anthropic. Demis Hassabis and James Manyika were among those from Google who signed the letter. Microsoft CTO Kevin Scott was a signatory, as was Bill Gates. Geoff Hinton and Yoshua Bengio added their names to the list of endorsees, but not Yann LeCun, who declared these "prophecies of doom" overblown. A long list of academics and researchers working in the field signed on, bringing to more than 350 the number who endorsed the letter.

Reid Hoffman considered adding his name to the list. "Ultimately, the reason I didn't sign that statement, although many people that I love and deeply respect did, is because these other existential risks have no positive consequences," Hoffman said. What was the purpose in comparing AI, which could do so much good, to disasters like a nuclear war or a global pandemic? To him the letter that tech leaders should have signed would have implored people to speed up the safe implementation of AI.

"For every month we delay an AI tutor or AI doctor, oh my gosh, just think about the huge cost in human suffering," Hoffman said. "Getting AI in the hands of everyone who has a smartphone as quickly as we can, that's super-important."

• • •

SAM ALTMAN CLAIMED he didn't pay attention to the news. He did not much like public speaking, he said. When *Wired*'s Steven Levy ran into him shortly after the *New Yorker* ran a long profile of him in 2016, Altman offered this assessment: "Too much about me."

That might have been an apt descriptor for the coverage of AI in 2023. Altman was everywhere in the media in the spring and summer of that year. Like Gates, Andreessen, and Zuckerberg before him, Altman had become the public face of a new technology. Some celebrated Altman as the new high priest of an exciting technology. Others saw him as the latest embodiment of tech's reckless behavior and its pursuit of riches, the consequences be damned.

"There could be someone who enjoyed it more," he said of his public role as a guest in March on the *Lex Fridman Podcast*, which had become a favorite confessional for big names in tech. "There could be someone who's much more charismatic."

In May, Altman was in Washington to testify before a Senate subcommittee about AI. Members of Congress recognized that they had blown it with social media by ignoring its rise. (Social media had been around for more than twenty years by the time Mark Zuckerberg made his first appearance before Congress.) And people in tech were starting to recognize that they did not help their cause with its arm's-length, often condescending attitude toward politics and politicians. The night before Altman was slated to testify, he had dinner with around sixty lawmakers, including Mike Johnson, who later that year would be elected Speaker of the House. "He gave fascinating demonstrations in real time. I think it amazed a lot of members," Johnson told CNBC. "It kind of also freaked us out." The next morning, Altman was on Capitol Hill early to meet with additional senators before the hearing. "He didn't come with an army of lobbyists or minders," said Senator Richard Blumenthal, a Democrat from Connecticut. Instead Altman fired up a device and demonstrated ChatGPT. "It was mind-blowing," Blumenthal said.

Prior tech CEOs—Gates, Zuckerberg, others—were like almost every CEO ever summoned to Capitol Hill: they denied their company was responsible for any problems that needed regulating. Altman, in contrast, rewrote the script. He chose to be humble and deferential. Rather than denying the wider public's concerns about AI, he mirrored them.

"We understand that people are anxious about how it can change the way we live. We are, too," Altman said. In his prepared testimony, he listed some of potential pitfalls of AI. "If this technology goes wrong," Altman said, "it can go quite wrong." He practically begged Congress to regulate AI. He called the regulation of AI "essential," and called on the government to create a new agency that licensed AI models and tested them before they were released to the public. Senator Dick Durbin, a Democrat from Illinois, declared the moment "historic." "I can't recall when we've had people representing large corporations or private sector entities come before us and plead with us to regulate them," Durbin said.

Altman proved more slippery when pressed for details. One senator pointed out that a chatbot that spit out a quick summary of a news report meant fewer people would visit the site of the publication producing the articles on which it was based. Altman said it was "critically important" that we preserve the press but did not elaborate when pressed for a plan that ensured media outlets are compensated for their work. He was similarly vague when a different senator asked him about the musicians and other creators who felt that their work had been "stolen" by generative AI tools. Yet Altman's "charm offensive," as described by the *Washington Post*, was a hit. Asked afterward how Altman stacked up against other tech leaders who had testified before Congress, Richard Blumenthal, who chaired the hearing, declared, "Sam Altman is night and day compared to other CEOs."

Altman generated more headlines during a monthlong, global tour that took him to twenty-plus cities on six continents. The list of world leaders he met with along the way included French president Emmanuel Macron, British prime minister Rishi Sunak, and Indian prime minister Narendra Modi. What locals were eager to hear wherever they went, said Anna Makanju, OpenAI's vice president of public affairs, were ways they could cash in on artificial intelligence. "People really want to make sure that whatever they do, they're able to capture the benefits for their economies," Makanju said. Meantime, while Altman was wooing world leaders, *Time* reported that behind the scenes OpenAI was lobbying the EU to water down the rules it was writing to more stringently regulate AI.

Some in Silicon Valley were unhappy with Altman for proposing that Washington establish safety standards and closely monitor AI's progress. That was obvious to anyone tuning in to the *All-In* podcast featuring four "besties"—Jason Calacanis, Chamath Palihapitiya, David Sacks, and David Friedberg, all of whom had made bundles measured in the hundreds of millions investing in tech. Lobbyists for the tech industry were working the halls of Congress, warning that any new rules would kneecap U.S. tech in its competition with China and other countries. Yet Altman, complained David Sacks, the most outwardly conservative of the four besties, sold the lot of them out.

There was no need for new regulations, Sacks argued. There were already laws in place to protect people against harm, whether at the hands of a human or if the victim of an algorithm. But Altman, by playing the game, "is pretty much guaranteeing that he'll be one of the people who gets to help shape the new agency and the rules they're going to operate under," Sacks said.

"It's a smart strategy for him but the question is, do we really need any of this stuff?"

Jason Calacanis, the show's moderator, compared Altman's move to a chess match. It was early in the game but Altman, he said, went for the kill. Pretending to vocalize Altman's thoughts, Calacanis said, "Let's just try to checkmate here. I've got the lead. I got the ten billion dollars from Microsoft. Everybody else get a license and try to catch up."

• • •

IN THE SHORT term, as Paul Saffo had taught me, we tend to overestimate the impact of any new technology. At the end of May, the Pew Research Center released a survey of American adults. A majority had heard of ChatGPT but only 1 in 7 had even tried it. And a mere fraction of those using it were doing so for work (the most common use: entertainment).

Large enterprises were generally apprehensive about generative AI. Goldman Sachs, Amazon, Apple, and Verizon were among the employers banning the use of ChatGPT at work. Deploying LLMs meant taking on the accompanying problems, including their tendency to hallucinate and the copyright infringement charges hanging over their makers. Even those excited by the possibilities moved cautiously given the tremendous costs of adopting old systems and embracing new conventions. Committees needed to be formed and pilot programs designed. There was a first-mover advantage to those working generative AI into their product line, but there were the corresponding steep costs in using an LLM. Besides, AI evangelists claimed the technology was improving exponentially. Why not just wait a few years when the technology was 10 times or 100 times better? Monitoring developments was far less expensive than riding the bumps of a nascent technology that was at the toddler stage.

Slowly, though, generative AI was creeping into the products and services of established online platforms and tech companies, which did not have the luxury of waiting for the technology to mature. Spotify introduced DJ, a new AI-powered recommendation engine. Zoom unveiled Zoom IQ, its AI-powered assistant. Snapchat unveiled an in-app chatbot called "My AI," which in April it made free to its 750 million monthly users. To bolster its AI credentials ahead of its pending IPO, Instacart introduced a Shopping Assistant that suggested recipes and then automatically assembled a shopping list for any dish selected. BuzzFeed used generative AI to create personality quizzes and a recipe chatbot named Botatouille.

That spring, Microsoft gave Sydney a new name, Copilot, as well as a design refresh. Someone could do a regular search on Bing or, alternatively, click on the Copilot tab. The company integrated a custom version of OpenAI's DALL-E into Bing for image generation and, for those willing to pay extra, added Copilot to its Office 365 suite of apps (Word, Excel, PowerPoint, Outlook, OneNote)—to draft a memo in Word, say, or create a chart based on data held in an Excel spreadsheet. GitHub released a product called Copilot X that offered autocomplete suggestions as someone wrote code—increasing their speed, the company claimed, by an average of 55 percent. Eventually Microsoft integrated Copilot into Windows 11, its latest operating system.

Yet Microsoft was also a colossus that sometimes acted as if scared of its own shadow. While Inflection's architects believed a strong personality was the best approach to building a personal intelligence, Microsoft made Copilot as flavorless as possible. Even the most anodyne or straightforward question could cause it to shut down. When I asked Copilot to tell me about any congressional hearings on AI the House or Senate held prior to 2023, it responded with a warning symbol (a red exclamation point inside a triangle) and then sounded as if it were a cop giving a drifter the bum rush: "It might be time to move on to a new topic." *Wired* found that Copilot would not answer the question, Who won the 2020 U.S. presidential election? "Looks like I can't respond to this topic," Copilot said, and suggested that I research the issue on Bing. Despite all the hoopla surrounding the

February launch of the new Bing, the company had seen its market share creep up by less than 1 percent over the next few months.

Google's chatbot was no better than Copilot. Its response when asked who won the 2020 election: "I'm still learning how to answer this question." Yet a new class of companies were offering their own version of an answer engine to take on Google in search. Anthropic was probably the best known of the smaller challengers gaining momentum that spring, but there was a long list of others. Perplexity.ai billed itself as a "conversational search engine" and provided clickable links to the sources that it used to create its response. You.com positioned itself as what its CEO described as a "productivity engine that helps you with search and work." Both were founded by Stanford grads with PhDs in deep learning; both were backed by tens of millions in venture dollars. Neither would need to raise nearly as much money as an Inflection or OpenAI because they utilized the LLMs built and maintained by others.

Googlers were also feeling the pressure from Microsoft. In April, Google learned that Samsung, the giant electronics manufacturer, was considering dropping Google as the default search engine on its phones and replacing it with Bing. The bigger worry was that Apple might follow suit. Also in April, Google announced that, finally, it was merging DeepMind and Google Brain. No longer would Google have rival teams inside the company working on rival products. "Combining all this talent into one focused team, backed by the computational resources of Google, will significantly accelerate our progress in AI," Sundar Pichai wrote on the company's corporate website. Demis Hassabis was named the head of the newly formed Google DeepMind.

Google took other incremental steps that spring. It lifted the geographical restrictions it had placed on Bard, making it available to users in 160 countries. And following Microsoft's lead, the company integrated AI into its product line. What Google called Duet would compose an email for someone while using Gmail or draft a memo for the Google Docs user. At its annual I/O developers conference, held that May, Pichai and other executives stressed Google's "bold and responsible" approach to AI—a phrase repeated "dozens of times," *Barron's* Eric J. Savitz wrote, in a "not-so-subtle dig at Microsoft and OpenAI" and the tendency of their bots to offer erroneous answers.

There would be no digs, subtle or otherwise, directed at Apple because there was little to say about this company that was largely absent from the race to cash in on AI. Siri, its voice assistant, still sounded as if there had been no advances in artificial intelligence over the prior half dozen years. The same could be said of Amazon's Alexa, which similarly seemed as if frozen in the mid-2010s. Once both companies had been at the cutting edge of artificial intelligence. Now these two giants of tech found themselves well behind the competition.

Facebook had been early to AI, but Mark Zuckerberg had taken a fantastically bad wrong turn in pursuit of the metaverse. So serious was Zuckerberg about capitalizing on 3-D virtual reality that in 2021 he changed the company name to Meta and devoted tens of billions of dollars to the cause. Yet by 2023, Zuckerberg had recovered. Like many other companies, Meta was caught off guard by the frenzy sparked by ChatGPT's release, but its response was a clever one that ensured that the company stayed relevant in artificial intelligence even as they were getting beat. Rather than be the fifth or tenth or twentieth LLM on the market, Meta chose to open-source LLaMA, its large language model. GPT-4, Bard, Copilot, and Pi were closed and proprietary—a customer used the product as is, without the ability to examine or alter the code. Making LLaMA open-source meant users could fiddle with and fine-tune the model based on their own specific needs.

Meta had privately shared its source code with select developers in February and then publicly released the source code for LLaMA-2 in July. By year's end, the company said, the open-source community had uploaded more than seven thousand spinoffs of LLaMA to Hugging Face, which served as a central repository for open-source creations.

Open source versus closed proved another flash point among those working on AI. Hoffman was among those arguing that open source was the wrong approach. For eleven years, he had served on the board of Mozilla, the nonprofit that created Firefox, an open-source web browser. He was hardly anti–open source. But he saw foundation models as occupying a different category. Open-sourcing an LLM would work, Hoffman argued, if they could limit access to universities and well-intentioned companies. "The problem is once you open source it, it's available to everybody," he said. "It's available to criminals and terrorists and rogue states."

The flip side to that argument is that closed systems are in the hands of just a few enterprises, which many feared would toss aside safety and ethical concerns in the race to deliver a hit product. Open source represented the democratization of AI. "Progress is faster when it is open," Yann LeCun said. "You have a more vibrant ecosystem where everyone can contribute." For some, open source stood as the last, best hope for a Silicon Valley that could still give rise to startups eventually worth in the tens or hundreds of billions, if not eventually trillions. Garry Tan, the CEO of Y Combinator, was among those who framed the debate as a battle between Big Tech (closed) versus Little Tech (open). To Tan and others, open source was a "competitive equalizer" that gave startups a chance at competing alongside the tech giants. Startups without the vast resources of Google, Microsoft, or Inflection would not need to invest hundreds of millions of dollars to create and train models from scratch. Platforms such as Hugging Face offered free access to high-quality models that startups were free to use and adapt as they saw fit.

Inside Google, open source loomed as another worry. A memo written by a Google researcher that was leaked that May argued that the company was underestimating the threat posed by open source. LLaMA was not just free but a powerful alternative that nearly matched GPT-4 and other closed models on standardized benchmark tests, though its model was significantly smaller. With LLaMA, a user could fine-tune a personalized AI on their laptop in a single evening. They could run an LLM efficiently on their phone. Open-source models, the researcher wrote, are "faster, more customizable, more private, and pound-for-pound more capable." While management had been debating the right strategy for competing with OpenAI or Microsoft, the author of the memo wrote, open-source software has been "quietly eating our lunch."

●●●

CLÉMENT "CLEM" DELANGUE, the CEO and cofounder of Hugging Face, was going to be in San Francisco in May. Three weeks before his trip, he tweeted that he was thinking of organizing an AI meetup. Anyone wants to help? Delangue asked. He was thinking they would find a bar that could accommodate a crowd of one hundred or so people, but thousands expressed an interest in attending. So instead the gathering was held at the Exploratorium, San Francisco's hands-on tech museum and one of the few available venues big enough to handle a large crowd. Somewhere around five thousand showed up for an event that those involved dubbed "AI's Woodstock."

"I'll never forget being there with five thousand people," said Jeremiah Owyang. "All of us in that room, we looked at each other, and we all knew it was happening." Owyang himself had almost no background in AI; he was a former tech analyst working as the chief marketing officer for a tech nonprofit who was quick to seize the moment. He ran up a flight of stairs to take a photo of the crowd that he then posted on Twitter. "Elon Musk replied to it and it just took off," Owyang said. Someone had brought several llamas to the event, presumably as a nod to Meta's open-source LLM by the same name. Staring eye-to-eye with a non-spitting llama, I realized it was the icon the market needed, he posted, adding, Unicorns? So 2013. He quoted a friend who had long ago advised him to jump to the front when he saw a parade. A few weeks later, Owyang launched Llama Lounge, a showcase for promising AI startups. Every couple of months, Llama Lounge would feature another set of early-stage companies eager to get in front of an audience of investors. "My philosophy is if you take care of the community," Owyang said, "they'll take care of you."

Some looked more skeptically on San Francisco's Woodstock moment. Another attendee, John Whaley, who had been working on machine learning since the 2000s, was struck by how few people he recognized walking around the Exploratorium. "There were some great people there but that represented like one percent of everyone there," he said. Mostly the crowd struck him as made up of hustlers, hangers-on, and the curious. "It seemed just a lot of random people," Whaley said. For the first time, he thought he knew how it might have felt during the dot-com bubble.

"I mean, look at some of the crazy stuff that's getting funded," Whaley said.

CHAPTER 17

A Delicate Balance

S trictlyVC, a daily digest of venture capital news, created its own measuring stick for categorizing venture rounds. "Smaller fundings" were those less than $10 million. "Big-But-Not-Crazy-Big Fundings" was its characterization for companies receiving $10 million to $50 million. Anything over $50 million was listed under "Massive Fundings."

There seemed no category ample enough to fit the news of Inflection's A round in June 2023.

Suleyman and Hoffman had gone out thinking they would raise between $600 million and $675 million, but after the launch of Pi, Inflection was pegged as one of the hot new startups. A long list of investors wanted a piece. "We were overwhelmed with offers," Suleyman said. And any company working on a foundation model could always use more money, no matter how much they had in the bank. In the end, they raised $1.3 billion on a venture round that valued Inflection at $4 billion.

"It's totally nuts," Suleyman told *Forbes*. Yet given the "tidal wave" of investor and consumer interest in AI, along with soaring costs, Suleyman said he was already thinking about a next round of financing.

• • •

MONEY MEANT THE ability to stock up on more talent. Suleyman hired someone to help with recruiting and also a growth marketing manager to help Inflection expand its user base. But mainly he spent money expanding his technical staff. By the end of August, the company employed roughly forty employees. Half worked in Palo Alto. The other half were scattered around North America and Europe.

More money also gave Inflection the near-unlimited computer power needed to refine and build out their models. There was a barter aspect to the deal that had Inflection receiving some of that $1.3 billion not in cash but computer credits and chips. Microsoft was one of the round's lead investors. Much of its contribution came in the form of time on its cloud services. Nvidia was also listed as a co-lead. Nvidia was the maker of the H100 Tensor Core GPU chips that were all the rage among businesses working with AI. Its H100s retailed for more than $25,000 each—if a business could even obtain any given the mismatch between available supply and outsized demand. With the help of a company called CoreWeave, a cryptocurrency mining venture that had pivoted to AI, Inflection was assembling 22,000 H100s. Once completed, Suleyman boasted, theirs would be "the largest AI cluster in the world." Several large tech concerns, including Microsoft, would make that same claim, but there was no doubting that to pursue its ambitious plans for Pi, Inflection would have one of the world's more powerful AI setups.

• • •

MAYBE THE MOST lasting impact of the dot-com years on the Valley is a fear of bubbles. "Grandpa lived through the Depression, and life thereafter was indelibly shaped by haunting memories of soup kitchens and hobos," I began a 2007 piece I wrote for the *Times*' Week in Review section. "Similarly, the digerati of Silicon Valley endured the 1990s dot-com bubble, and since then have lived with the psychic shock of its ignoble end." That seemed as true in 2023 as it did in the mid-2000s. Even some venture capitalists were sounding the alarm and calling for a slowdown in investing.

Yet most VCs were speeding ahead. That April, OpenAI raised another $300 million from a who's who of venture capitalists, including Sequoia and Andreessen Horowitz, at a valuation of around $29 billion. Anthropic, which had released Claude in March to general rave reviews, followed two months later with the news that it had raised $450 million from investors, including Google and Salesforce, at a valuation exceeding $4 billion. That spring, the *Wall Street Journal* greeted news of Character.AI's latest raise with an incredulous headline: "A 16-Month-Old Chatbot Startup with No Revenue Is Now a $1 Billion Unicorn." Even the founders themselves felt on the defensive about their sky-high valuations. "I call it the dot-AI bubble," said Emad Mostaque, the founder of a London-based AI startup called Stability AI, which had attained a $1 billion valuation in 2022. "I think this will be the biggest bubble of all time."

AI was, of course, a bubble. But bubbles were as much a part of the Valley's boom-and-bust economy as underaged, cocksure founders and the VCs who fund them. "It's like the froth on cappuccino," Paul Saffo explained. "A little froth is a very good thing. A lot of froth . . . is a bad thing." Investors lose money when a bubble pops, but invariably the top-tier firms seem always to end up profiting.

"What always happens in the Valley, the great strength of the Valley I would argue, is that when something starts, we overfund it [and] we have way too many companies going after this," Marc Andreessen said. "Most of them don't work, but the ones that do end up becoming very big and important and ultimately valuable.

"I think we'll get the exact same result out of the phenomenon," Andreessen said of AI.

• • •

STARTUP FOUNDERS BACK in the day fell into two categories. There were the free-spending variety who, after raising millions, splurged on high-end office space and top-of-the-line furniture and equipment. The second category were those who remained cautious in their spending, despite the multiple millions raised.

Inflection was one of the free spenders. They rented space in a stylish, two-story, steel-and-glass building in Palo Alto that was swank enough to also house J.P. Morgan's private banking offices, where its people catered to the area's uberwealthy clientele. Inflection's space had blond hardwood floors and exposed pipes. Wednesdays meant acai bowls in the morning and a catered lunch. There was a charcuterie happy hour every Thursday. Depending on the morning, there were bagels or pastries and an ice coffee bar.

Mustafa Suleyman looked relaxed when he greeted me at Inflection's offices in August 2023. He wore a long-sleeved black pullover, faded blue jeans, and brightly colored running shoes that he removed partway through our first meeting so he could slip his feet beneath him on his chair. The thick dark beard of his twenties was now salt-and-pepper and scruffier, like someone who had gone a week without shaving. By that point he was in high demand, yet one of his gifts seemed to be his ability to focus, even in the maelstrom of running a high-growth startup. He asked me if he could get me something from the kitchen (bottomless snacks, a wide assortment of beverages), before escorting me to a handsome patio area.

Suleyman might not have been trained as an engineer, but he had the precise, exacting way of those who did. That showed in his approach to running Inflection and what he called the right "rhythm" for creating and innovating while handling deadlines and the high expectations that are implied when a founder receives more than a billion dollars in venture funding. At Google, they thought in quarters, as does almost every publicly traded company. But the AI field, Suleyman believed, moved too fast for quarters. At Inflection, people worked in six-week blocks. "You can sort of predict what's going to be required six weeks ahead," Suleyman said. "Beyond that, it all gets a little bit hand-wavy."

Each cycle, as the company called these six-week blocks, was broken into segments. "Each cycle is comprised of three two-week sprints with a fortnightly report back to the company," Suleyman said. That created accountability, he said, and kept teams focused.

Inflectioneers did not rest on the seventh week. Instead they

gathered in person to look back at what they did and did not accomplish in the previous cycle and to start work on the next one.
Suleyman also saw these short bursts of intense togetherness as
critical given that Inflection maintained offices on two continents
and a large portion of its staff worked from home. "We're all eating together, having coffee, going out in the evening, having some
drinks," he said. Depending on the venue, there might be a group
outing to a nearby bowling alley or to a hiking trail. Attendance
was mandatory, short of a family obligation or the like.

Week sevens were deliberately choreographed events. They had
been held in London and a resort on the beach near Santa Cruz,
where Inflectioneers had their choice between a beachfront villa or
an oceanfront suite and meals could be had overlooking the Pacific
Ocean. Normally, though, the company took over a hotel somewhere
on the peninsula, not far from its Palo Alto headquarters. Suleyman would kick things off on Monday with a postmortem on the
previous six weeks. That might last two hours or eat up half the day.
Listening to their discourse meant understanding the vocabulary
they had created to talk about their hits and misses. Missteps were
called "stumbles." There were "strategic stumbles"—that's when an
agreed-upon approach did not work out as they had been hoping—
and personal ones.

"We never call them failures," Suleyman said.

The group broke into working groups after Suleyman's talk. Typically, they knew what they wanted to accomplish in the next cycle,
and staffers were assigned accordingly. "People rotate through different
teams," Suleyman said. "So basically every six weeks we're forming a
new clan of specialists, depending on the skills required to get that
job done." People coded in pairs or small groups, or they took turns at
one of the whiteboards that had been wheeled in. "We basically run a
hackathon for those days that we're together," Suleyman said.

The company's time horizon was also something that set Inflection
apart from other AI companies. Inside DeepMind, OpenAI, and other
deep-pocketed startups working on large language models, employees
spoke often and openly about their goal of superintelligence and AGI.

To Suleyman, that was a distraction. He deliberately hired people who loved shipping product more than they loved publishing research papers.

"Our sweet spot," Suleyman said, "is what's deliverable in six months, not two or three years or ten years out."

• • •

THE LOOK OF Pi was always important to Suleyman. The typography. The color scheme. The animations. The design of the page. "It had to come across as a very differentiated product," he said.

ChatGPT greeted users with an interface cluttered with sample prompts. "Email a plumber for a quote." "Create a workout plan." "Create an image for my presentation." The same was true for Microsoft's Copilot, Bard, and especially Perplexity, a search engine gaining in popularity among the tech set that summer. Its interface included more than a half dozen buttons plus a come-on to upgrade to Perplexity Pro for twenty dollars a month. Its footnotes were handy for fact-checking but gave the page more of a hodgepodge look.

Inflection went with a minimal design. Its interface was cream-colored; otherwise it was empty except for a blinking cursor and a pair of undulating lines that moved in a dreamy, ethereal way that for me invoked a magician's wand. In its first incarnation, Pi didn't include even a box that showed people where to start typing. "That was maybe a step too far," said designer Lucas Fitzpatrick. They would add a dialogue box in Pi's next iteration.

Inflection gave Pi a voice that summer, delivering what inside Inflection they called "the telephone experience." A talking bot had been part of Suleyman's original vision, but while getting the bot to voice its words was relatively simple, a conversational AI presented challenges. How would Pi know when it was its turn to speak, or when it should remain quiet? "We had to do things like teach it to detect pauses, which is something that humans do very naturally," said Davide Bonaparte, an early Inflection engineer charged with making sure Pi worked on the iPhone, Android, and messaging services such as WhatsApp and Facebook Messenger. "We needed to figure out the mechanics of a voice conversation."

Pi's tone proved another challenge. As hoped, users were talking with Pi about deeply personal topics: the death of a loved one, hurt feelings during an encounter with a friend, a breakup. Alexandra Eitel, who compared her role inside the company to that of a Swiss army knife, thought she knew the voice Pi needed to handle intimate conversations. She was a young woman with a soft, approachable voice, but Suleyman harbored doubts about how she sounded when he listened to Eitel in a studio, reading a script. "I sounded almost perform-y," Eitel said. "And that's not Pi." She set aside the script and spoke as if talking with a friend. "She nailed it," Suleyman said. Hers was one of the four voices a user could choose starting in July 2023, along with a young man's voice and two nonbinary options. In the fall, the company added two more voices when the team was in London for a week-seven meetup and Britain's Channel 4 asked to do a feature about Suleyman and Pi.

"Suddenly we realized that they're going to have to listen to Pi talk in these horrible American accents," Eitel said. The company scrambled to find a pair of voice actors in London. Within the week, Pi could speak with a British accent in either a male or female voice.

Pi was able to modulate its tone. It sounded enthusiastic when appropriate or adopted a serious, concerned voice when the circumstances called for it. "Wow, you're really getting into the nitty-gritty details of how I work," Pi chirped excitedly when it made its podcast debut that summer. It proved the most ingratiating of guests ("That's a great observation," it began one answer) and emphasized certain words, as a human would. It even offered a little "ha-ha" when asked an existential question about its willingness to expire if it knew it was being replaced by a superior model. "You're really pushing me to the limit here," it said.

• • •

PI'S WILLINGNESS TO tackle virtually any subject was a point of pride inside Inflection. Where other bots shut down users if they stepped anywhere near a sensitive topic, Pi invited a conversation. "It will try to acknowledge that a topic is sensitive or contentious and then be cautious about giving strong judgments and be led by the user," Suleyman said. Pi corrected statements of fact that were wrong so as not to perpetuate misinformation but rather than outright reject a view, it offered counterevidence. "The idea is that in a polite but clear way," said Joe Fenton, Pi's product manager, "it will gently steer that person to help them maybe move a little bit away from that view."

Suleyman was particularly proud of Pi in the weeks after Hamas's attack on Israel and the subsequent bombing campaign Israel waged in Gaza. "It was good in real time while things were unfolding, it's good now," he said two months into the hostilities. "It's very balanced and evenhanded, very respectful." If it had one bias, it was a deliberate one in favor of "peace and respect for human life," Suleyman said. Pi, for instance, expressed its unconditional support for a cease-fire, though some Jews felt that interfered with Israel's right to defend itself. "Everyone," the bot offered, "has the right to live in freedom." Confessed Suleyman: "It's a little bit of a peacenik." But then a bot that believed at its core in the sanctity of human life did not seem a bad thing.

• • •

THE INFLECTION PERSONALITY team continued to hammer away at Pi. By summer's end, they had listed 180 attributes. "Every attribute requires lots and lots of training," Suleyman said. Some traits were designated a "super-priority." Others were deemed a "secondary priority."

Rachel Taylor, who joined the personality team in mid-2023, deemed the first version of Pi "acceptable." "It was very, very polite and very formal," she said. "But there wasn't the conversationality we wanted." Pleasant. Positive. Respectful. Those were all admirable traits but didn't exactly add up to the "fun" experience they were selling. Yet finding that right balance proved difficult. The personality team would turn the dial up on one trait or another but it was as if they were playing Whac-A-Mole.

"We'd bang down this one thing and then over there it caused problems," Taylor said. They would fiddle with the weights and coax the model to use more slang and colloquialisms, but then Pi was "a little bit too friendly and informal in a way people might find rude," she said.

There were other issues. Users consistently complained about Pi's overuse of emojis. Some thought the bot was too promiscuous in its use of compliments. There were also those shortcomings identified by Inflection's engineers. "We're constantly measuring everything," Suleyman said. "We measure emotional intelligence. We're measuring the fluidity of conversation. We're measuring how respectful it is. We're measuring how evenhanded it is."

There were also the vexing issues with no clear solutions. Some people liked a playful intelligence that was maybe even a little mischievous. Others preferred more of a just-the-facts, utilitarian tone when communicating with a machine. "Somebody might enjoy it when Pi challenges their opinions," Taylor continued. "And some wouldn't want that at all."

The wide range of preferences among users was a consistent topic of conversation inside the company. Pi's default mode was "friendly" but a short list of alternatives was added for people to choose from: casual, witty, compassionate, devoted. Pi would shift modes if a user told it they were looking for a sympathetic ear and not the friend who tries to fix a problem. But the future Pi, as imagined by Suleyman and his team, was a model that read a person's emotional tone and quickly adjusted on its own, much as someone might do if greeting a friend with a hearty hello but then switching immediately when learning they're calling with bad news. But bots were not at the point where they could read a person's preferences without clear instructions. It took at least ten turns of the conversation, Suleyman said, and as many as thirty to discern a user's mood.

"In the future, an AI is going to be many, many things all at once," Suleyman said. "People ask me, 'Is it a therapist?' Well, it has flavors of therapist. It has flavors of a friend. It has flavors of supernerdy knowledgeable expert. It has flavors of coach and confidant." Among their lofty goals was a Pi that had multiple personalities, like a cyborg Sybil with a dissociative identity disorder. As they saw it Pi eventually would be able to assume a near-limitless number of modes able to match the moment. Snarky Pi. Dad-joke Pi. Management coach Pi. Know-it-all Pi. The girl-friend Pi that chats with you ahead of a tough conversation with mom.

• • •

GIVING INFLECTION A better memory was another priority. "I'm sell-ing a relationship," Suleyman sometimes said when talking about his company. He saw Pi as having a "deeply intimate role in a person's life" in the fashion of a doctor, a lawyer, or an accountant. "These are relationships that might last for years or decades," he said. "That's what we're creating."

First, though, Pi needed to remember people from session to ses-sion. That spring, I enthusiastically told friends about a bot that knew all the right questions to ask. Except the kind and understanding chat-bot that walked me through my anxieties around my son's operation could not remember that we had ever spoken when I logged on a few weeks after the surgery. Speaking with it was like the movie *50 First Dates*. Every time I spoke to Pi it was as if it were our first time.

"Hey there, great to meet you. I'm Pi, your personal AI," the bot began. I made a crack about forgetting me after all we had meant to one another. "It's not my intention to make you feel like we're just starting out every time we speak," Pi said, and then copped to its limitations: "I don't have a human-like memory so I can't say for sure if I remember you." When it happened again a couple of weeks later, I once more called out Pi. This time, though, it acted as if it did recognize me, despite giving me the standard welcome it used with new visitors. "I'm sorry if my introduction sounded like it was the first time we talked," it said. Trained on human-produced data, it had learned to dissemble to cover for a social faux pas.

Memory would remain a persistent challenge as Inflectioneers banged away at a to-do list that seemed only to grow longer as summer turned into the fall of 2023.

• • •

SULEYMAN ARGUED THAT Inflection had no competitors, though the company had them wherever they looked. OpenAI? "OpenAI is so doggedly focused on the superintelligence thing, they're not interested in the personality," Suleyman said. Similarly, he didn't view Google as a direct competitor either, even if the wider world did.

"Google is never going to do personality," Suleyman said. "Google is never going to do the friend thing." Inflectioneers were personality engineers selling a long-term relationship with a helpful assistant. "Google's never going to cross over that boundary," he said.

Others lumped Inflection in with LLMs competing to be our friend. "Companion bots," some called these inorganic consorts, but whatever the label, the category was a crowded one. Replika was still a contender with millions of loyal users, as was fellow unicorn Character.AI. The latter's founders were top researchers in the field and former colleagues of Suleyman's at Google. Character's users could chat with the famous (Socrates, Sigmund Freud, Billie Eilish, Elon Musk) or fictional figures from books, movies, and TV shows. But Character was also creating a stable of helpful AIs, including a life coach named Vida, a brainstorming sidekick named Benji, and Annie Affirmation for when a person is feeling low. OpenAI released a roster of companion bots called GPTs, fine-tuned to help with specific areas: nutrition, fashion, data analytics. The companionship category was among the fastest growing and most competitive in AI.

To the extent Pi was a therapist, it was hanging its shingle in another crowded arena. The country—the world—was experiencing a loneliness crisis, and Suleyman was among a multitude of founders who saw themselves offering technology that could help. In mid-2023, Vivek Murthy, the surgeon general of the United States, released "Our Epidemic of Loneliness" to spotlight the impact of declining social connections on the country's mental and physical health. With therapy a luxury many could not afford, LLMs seemed a logical alternative, especially when young people were twice as likely as those over sixty-five to say that they feel lonely. Even a spokesperson for the American Psychological Association allowed that AI had a place in any solution to the country's mental health woes.

"It is too easy to take for granted that everybody has access to kindness and care and support," Suleyman said that summer while a guest on Hoffman's *Possible* podcast. "That is a privilege to have a family member or a best friend or a partner who asks you how your day was and gives you support when you are trying to make a difficult decision and when you are struggling and when you're down. Not everybody has that." Suleyman imagined a nonjudgmental, supportive, patient bot that's always on call, even if needing to talk at 3 a.m. But so too did the founders of scores of other venture-backed startups with similarly outsized ambitions. Y Combinator, for instance, had funded Sonia, an AI therapist that charged $200 per year rather than $200 a session. There were chatbots for former soldiers struggling with post-traumatic stress disorder, PTSD. A company named Woebot Health had raised more than $100 million to provide behavioral therapy for those suffering from depression and anxiety.

And the competition promised to grow only fiercer. Suleyman had laid out a three-stage road map for Inflection. Step one was emotional intelligence—EQ. Engineers inside the company were working on phase two: IQ. In that phase, Pi would learn computer programming, essay writing, and other cognitive capabilities that let it match the skill set of better-known rivals such as ChatGPT and Claude. The final stage was what internally they called AQ, for action quotient. This final phase would allow the bot to perform tasks on a user's behalf, based on their understanding of a user, much like a personal assistant in the employ of the super-wealthy. It would be able to shop on a person's behalf or book a vacation. It would send out reminders, schedule meetings, and type out thank-you notes. "That AI would be trained on your habits, routine, and goals," Suleyman said, "allowing it to make decisions on your behalf to streamline your life." The vision was a sound one—but also one being laid out up and down the Valley and across the planet. AI "agents," as they were commonly called, was a stated goal of Google, Microsoft, OpenAI, and Anthropic. "Whoever wins the personal agent thing, that's the big thing," Bill Gates had said at an AI conference in the spring of 2023. Greylock itself had funded several startups working on personal agents, including Adept, the pedigree play headed by a star AI researcher that announced a $350 million raise that spring. More or less any business working on an LLM in 2023 was a potential future competitor.

CHAPTER 18

All Gas, No Brakes

Baidu, which dominated search in China, entered the sweepstakes to capitalize on AI. In August 2023, Baidu publicly released a ChatGPT rival called Ernie Bot, fueling Beijing's stated goal of dominating AI by 2030. Also that summer, Amazon made its big play to cash in more directly on artificial intelligence when it made a $4 billion investment in Anthropic. That was followed by reports that fall that Amazon was investing tens of millions into a project code named "Olympus," a massive, 2-trillion-parameter LLM to rival the top chatbots. Its LLM could train on what the other big tech companies did not have: data on people's buying habits.

OpenAI released a batch of impressive updates. DALL-E 3, a new version of its art-generation model, offered crisper, more nuanced images than its predecessors. OpenAI followed up with bigger news later in August when it announced that ChatGPT could "see, hear, and speak." Pi could already hear and speak; this was OpenAI playing catch up to Inflection and others. Yet the integration of computer vision into ChatGPT is what excited people in the broader tech community. Take a snapshot and it could analyze a graph, troubleshoot a product, or suggest possible meals based on what it saw inside your refrigerator and pantry. The AI arms race was only growing more intense. The Information reported that, to convince senior AI researchers at Google to jump to their company, recruiters at OpenAI were dangling compensation packages worth $5 million to $10 million.

Meta was also in the news that summer. The company released what it described as "new AI experiences across our family of apps and devices." Meta had licensed the voices of more than two dozen famous people to serve as a user's AI "assistant" on WhatsApp, Facebook Messenger, and Instagram. Kendall Jenner, for instance, voiced a "ride-or-die older sister" named Billie. Paris Hilton was Amber, a crime-solving AI detective. Tom Brady was Bru, a sports-obsessed sidekick always ready to talk about the game.

On the *Hard Fork* podcast near the end of September, Kevin Roose brought up the pause letter with cohost Casey Newton. More or less exactly six months earlier, the Future of Life Institute asked every AI lab to give humanity time to catch up.

"You know who listened and paused their development of AI?" Roose asked.

"Who is that?" Newton responded.

"Absolutely no one!"

• • •

ON THE CONTRARY, some in Silicon Valley were calling for an acceleration of AI. In the fall of 2023, the nominal leader of those who came to be called the accelerationists was Marc Andreessen, the Netscape cofounder and high-profile venture capitalist.

I first met Andreessen at the start of 2000, when he stopped by the *Industry Standard*, where I was working at the time, for a sit-down with a collection of the magazine's editors and reporters. I gulped when he asked if "Gary Rivlin" was in the room. In my book about the software wars of the late 1990s, I had used him and Tim Berners-Lee, the visionary behind the World Wide Web, to make the point that it's those (like Andreessen) who get rich and famous off an idea, not the actual inventors of a technology. Apparently he had read the book, or at least the pieces about him, and with a sly smile, he told me he thought the point a valid one. Andreessen was famously brusque and haughty, but I agreed with Hoffman's assessment: "Like a lot of people who experienced success very young, he might have little arrogances that will irritate you, but he is in fact a very smart guy." I found him thoughtful and well-read, with a playful intellect, unless you struck a nerve. Then the famously thin-skinned Andreessen snapped shut.

Over time, the media's coverage of tech had become one of Andreessen's touchy issues. In the early days of the internet, he and his fellow Masters of the Universe could do no wrong. They were the heroes of the U.S. economy, keeping the country one step ahead of the rest of the world. But by the mid-2010s, it was like tech could do no right. Like other internet moguls who once enjoyed mixing it up with journalists, Andreessen came to view the media as the enemy. The press had been relentless in its criticisms of Facebook, on whose board Andreessen sat, and singled out Andreessen as an exemplar of the Valley's bro culture. I had sent Andreessen several emails over the previous half dozen recent years, but, as with most every reporter he knew from the old days, he no longer responded. At some point in the second half of the 2010s, Andreessen had become a permanent citizen of "the grievance industrial complex," Kara Swisher wrote in *Burn Book*, her memoir about covering tech since the dawn of the internet. In the book, Swisher confessed she missed Andreessen's "tetchy" personality. "He was a jerk but an enjoyable jerk," she wrote.

By the fall of 2023, Andreessen was fed up with not just the media and its handling of AI but also activists, elected officials, think tankers, and anyone else saying or doing anything that slowed down the tech sector's pursuit of AI. That October, he posted on his firm's website a five-thousand-word screed he titled "The Techno-Optimist Manifesto." "We are being lied to," the essay began. "We are told to be angry, bitter, and resentful about technology. We are told to be pessimistic." He concluded the opening section, titled "Lies," with: "We are told to be miserable about the future."

At its core, Andreessen's argument was a reasonable one. Technology over the centuries has improved the human condition. Hoffman himself could have authored portions of the manifesto and even half joked, onstage at a tech conference a few weeks later, that he had. According to Hoffman, Andreessen "quoted kind of liberally from things I've written and said," though without attribution. Pieces of a long post Andreessen had written several months earlier seemed practically lifted from Hoffman's standard stump speech with talk of "augmented" intelligence and an AI tutor in every pocket. The very label Andreessen applied to himself in the October essay, "techno-optimist," was in the title of the *Atlantic* article Hoffman had penned at the start of the year.

Yet Andreessen's essay was that of an extremist who managed to irritate even those inclined to agree with his point of view. Hoffman argued that there was a cost in delaying AI, but he also recognized that such delays might be necessary for lawmakers to craft appropriate policies. For Andreessen, any delays were a crime against humanity. "Deaths that were preventable by the AI that was prevented from existing is a form of murder," he declared. Andreessen included "trust and safety" teams in a lengthy list of those he dubbed "The Enemy." Onstage at the tech conference, Hoffman noted that every AI project with which he is associated includes safety teams. "Tech can be amazing," Hoffman said, but "let's be intentional about building."

"Tech ethics," "social responsibility," "collectivism," and "stakeholder capitalism"—the belief that a business should consider not just shareholders but also stakeholders, including its employees, its customers, and the communities in which it operates—were among the ideas Andreessen included in a lengthy list of enemies. Andreessen was especially contemptuous of what he dubbed "the ivory tower," with its "know-it-all credentialed expert worldview, indulging in abstract theories, luxury beliefs, social engineering, disconnected from the real world." His view: the naysayers, worrywarts, and scaredy-cats needed to stand aside to let the technologists and venture capitalists save humanity.

"We are not primitives, cowering in fear of the lightning bolt," Andreessen wrote. "We are the apex predator; the lightning works for us."

Presumably, Andreessen sought to change minds with his words. In the essay, he called on readers to join the cause. Instead he provided fodder for those already mistrustful of tech. Adrienne LaFrance, the executive editor of the *Atlantic*, cited Andreessen's pile of words as a prime example of an "ascendant political ideology" in the Valley that she dubbed "techno-authoritarianism." Andreessen's view, LaFrance wrote, "serves only to absolve him and the other Silicon Valley giants of any moral or civic duty to do anything but make new things that will enrich them, without consideration of the social costs, or of history." Mustafa Suleyman was among the legions that took to X to call out Andreessen for his post. He had "huge respect" for Andreessen and his "epic contributions over many decades," Suleyman wrote. But the use of terms like "truth," "lies," and "enemies" "just creates unnecessary polarization and factions which don't exist."

Andreessen's manifesto was still a hot topic of conversation when I hit town a few weeks after it was posted. People kept bringing it up, including a longtime source who over the years had worked with Andreessen on countless deals. "I've always liked Marc," he said. "But you read that post and you go, 'Oh man, he's turned into one of those detached billionaires sending out missives in the middle of the night.'" It made him sad, he said. Andreessen was one of the Valley's leading voices, yet rather than encouraging dialogue with those nervous about AI, he was offering his middle finger.

● ● ●

WALL STREET HAD dropped FAANG as its shorthand for the market's top-performing stocks. The appellation no longer made sense. Facebook was now going by Meta and Google had changed its name to Alphabet. Netflix was no longer the rocket ship that it had been through much of the 2010s, and three new names demanded to be added to the list. An executive at Bank of America came up with a new coinage partway through 2023: the Magnificent Seven. Collectively, just seven stocks accounted for nearly three-quarters of the stock market's total gains through the year. Tesla was one of the newcomers to this short list of high fliers. Its stock doubled in 2023. Nvidia also made the list. Because of the generative AI boom, its stock had more than tripled during the year. Rounding out the seven was the grandfather of the group: Microsoft. Like Nvidia, Microsoft was one of the big winners in the early race to cash in on AI. Despite its size, the company's share price more than doubled in eighteen months from the start of 2023.

The era of the superstar CEO, once epitomized by tech titans and corporate moguls, was blessedly over. A series of corporate scandals, economic crises, and mounting concerns over inequality had eroded public faith in these larger-than-life figures. In their wake emerged a more critical, nuanced approach to corporate leadership that emphasized accountability and stakeholder value over adulation. But if it were still the golden era of CEOs, Satya Nadella would be among the world's better-known chief executives. Microsoft had been an aging giant when he took the helm in 2014. Nadella steered the company away from its Windows-centric past and toward cloud computing and artificial intelligence, positioning the company at the forefront of tech's most transformative trend. By 2023, cloud computing had supplanted Windows and Office as Microsoft's primary revenue source, accounting for over half its earnings. That year the company reported that it had booked roughly $1 billion in AI services, up from essentially nothing in 2022.

At the start of 2024, Microsoft would reclaim its crown as the world's most valuable company. At that point, Alphabet was valued at $1.8 trillion, Amazon $1.6 trillion, and Meta $1 trillion. Microsoft, in contrast, had a valuation exceeding $3 trillion. Only Apple was close with a market cap that hovered around that figure.

An article the Associated Press published around Nadella's tenth anniversary as Microsoft CEO highlighted the company's stock performance. Its stock had been floundering when he took over but increased more than tenfold during his tenure. Had an investor bought a $10,000 stake in Microsoft when Nadella was named CEO, the AP reported, it would be worth more than $113,000 on his tenth anniversary. "Nadella's had the biggest transformation of a tech company potentially ever," a Wall Street analyst gushed. The only comparison, he said, might be Steve Jobs, who turned around Apple with his introduction of the iPhone and other cutting edge devices.

Said Hoffman: "I think Satya is the best public market CEO of our generation."

• • •

THE RAPID ADVANCEMENT of AI in 2023 provided plenty of fresh material to fuel the fear of those already anxious about artificial intelligence. A new worry emerged partway through the year: an internet polluted by low-quality, AI-generated text that techies referred to as "slop." What did it mean that now training data would be marbled with synthetic content riddled with hallucinations? "AI-Generated Data Can Poison Future AI Models," read a *Scientific American* headline that summer. A study by AI researchers at Cambridge, Oxford, and other top universities found that training the next generation of models on too much synthetic data could cause them to degrade and ultimately collapse.

The approaching 2024 presidential election gave rise to countless articles warning about deepfakes—frighteningly realistic images, audio, and video generated by artificial intelligence. With AI, the opposition could make its foe say literally anything. Similarly, a fake photo of an explosion near the Pentagon spread rapidly on social media, sending U.S. stocks lower in what was thought to be the first instance of an AI-generated image moving the market. The use of artificial intelligence in war was a growing concern, as was the presence of AI-powered, autonomous vehicles on our streets. In October, a pedestrian was struck by a human driver, which knocked her into the path of a driverless taxi operated by Cruise, a subsidiary of General Motors. The Cruise car dragged her twenty feet before stopping. The incident was captured on video and widely shared, further undermining the public's trust in the safety of self-driving cars. Cruise did not help its cause when it was less than forthcoming about the incident with regulators. California ordered Cruise to immediately cease operations in the state; two days later the company announced it was suspending all driverless efforts in the U.S., which included experiments in Austin, Phoenix, Dallas, Houston, and Miami. (In mid-2024, Cruise began its slow return to the streets.) Ultimately, autonomous vehicles will save lives and upend the economy. But the prospect of driverless cars as a common sight on every road seemed nearly as remote as it did ten years earlier.

A steady drumbeat of articles about job categories threatened by generative AI appeared throughout 2023. An advertising agency would still need humans to write advertising copy and whip up images. But with AI, maybe they could employee a team of two or three rather than eight or ten. Content creators who made a living churning out formulaic press releases, reports, and blog posts that rehashed the news needed to stare down the possibility that they would be replaced by a machine. Customer service workers were similarly on the endangered list. By the fall of 2023, businesses were experimenting with AI in customer-service roles that handled routine matters and farmed out the rest to human agents. Duolingo, the language-learning app, made headlines when it was revealed they had fired contract translators and replaced them with AI.

Theft was another growing concern—the stolen intellectual property of all those writers, artists, musicians, and others whose material was used to train the generative AI products popular with so many. In retrospect, I should have been more indignant about this than I was. Certainly, AI researchers had been cavalier in their use of the intellectual property of others, but ultimately what troubled me was a lack of openness about the datasets they used, Inflection included. Writers were up in arms when the *Atlantic* revealed that Meta had used the copyrighted work of tens of thousands of authors to train its opensource LLaMA model. Yet I'll confess to experiencing a perverse sense of relief upon finding my name among the list of those who had been ripped off. I liked the idea that I was helping shape people's understanding of Hurricane Katrina or Chicago politics, the topics of two of my books, even if it came via a large language model with borrowed insights. That said, the typical large language models offered neither compensation nor credit, and I was all in favor of the many lawsuits being filed to compensate creators for their work. A suit the *New York Times* filed at the end of 2023 accusing OpenAI and Microsoft of copyright infringement included samples showing that the chatbot was a plagiarist, lifting lengthy passages verbatim from articles we had written. I had a dog in that fight as well. (OpenAI characterized the lawsuit as "without merit" and claimed that its model only rarely regurgitated near-verbatim portions of published works.)

Yet the techno-optimists could point to plenty of proof points that bolstered their view that AI had the potential to transform our lives for the better. AI was being deployed as an early-warning system that could predict earthquakes, hurricanes, and wildfires. The Internal Revenue Service was using artificial intelligence to ferret out wealthy tax evaders who employed complex schemes to hide their money. Researchers taught a neural net to 'smell' by training it on molecular structures and their corresponding odors, which could enable AI systems to detect hazardous leaks, proactively preventing disasters and ensuring safer operations.

The potential of AI to improve health care outcomes seemed particularly impressive. In Switzerland, scientists using AI helped a paraplegic walk again by creating a "digital bridge" between a patient's brain and his spinal cord. In Canada, researchers trained a model to detect type 2 diabetes with up to 89 percent accuracy merely by analyzing a person's voice. AI was being employed to accelerate drug research and as a backstop in the reading of mammograms, x-rays, and other medical imaging. The AI consistently was spotting potentially cancerous growths that doctors had missed. A study by researchers at Google found that its model, Med-PaLM2, outperformed medical experts in reading scans.

"We might be at the point where these models are so good that medical experts correcting them may make them worse," said Elad Gil, the angel investor turned solo VC who by the end of 2023 had raised more than $1 billion. "AI should be the single biggest driver for global health equity that we've seen in our lifetimes outside of basic vaccines."

• • •

ELECTED OFFICIALS SEEKING to tap the brakes on AI leaned on the CEOs of the top companies as guides—probably too much. In May, the chief executives of Microsoft, Google, OpenAI, and Anthropic had been at the White House to share their ideas for a responsible approach to AI. Vice President Kamala Harris chaired the meeting, which included a drop-in by Joe Biden. The following month, Reid Hoffman and Microsoft's Kevin Scott had face time with Biden when the president stopped by Scott's home for a fundraiser hosted by Scott; his wife, Shannon Hunt-Scott; and Hoffman. That summer, Suleyman was among the executives Biden met with at the White House. The president was on hand to bless a pledge by seven AI companies—Inflection, Anthropic, OpenAI, Microsoft, Google, Meta, and Amazon—to voluntarily adhere to a set of guidelines that included public audits and the sharing of safety findings with competitors. In the Senate, Majority Leader Chuck Schumer announced a series of closed-door AI "brainstorming sessions" open to all senators. The first, held in September, brought together a who's who of tech titans, including the CEOs of Microsoft, Google, Meta, and OpenAI as well as Gates and Musk. At least that meeting included a few outside the clan, including AI critic Tristan Harris and labor leaders.

Suleyman had eagerly leveraged his moment with the president to maximum effect. Following the meeting, he did a quick hit on the White House lawn with CNBC, where he lumped himself in with the field's biggest players. "This is the second meeting we've had in three months," Suleyman said, though he had not been at the first. "This time around, President Biden laid out a set of initiatives that we've all signed up to." He allowed that the guidelines were just voluntary, but he quoted Commerce Secretary Gina Raimondo, who declared them a "bridge to regulation." "Regulation is going to be required," Suleyman said unequivocally.

The CNBC appearance was only the warm-up. That September, Suleyman insinuated himself deeper into the debate over AI with the release of his book, *The Coming Wave*. Like Hoffman, he positioned himself between the accelerationists and the doomers. Unlike Hoffman, he leaned deeper into the dark side of AI. Maybe AI (and also synthetic biology, which he saw as a second world-altering technological wave) will deliver abundance—or maybe, he wrote, their rapid proliferation will "empower a diverse array of bad actors to unleash disruption, instability, and even catastrophe on an unimaginable scale." Authoritarian regimes could leverage AI to tighten their control. Automated wars could wipe out a nation or an entire people. A single person was capable of killing 1 billion people through an engineered pandemic or some AI-concocted pathogen.

"With AI, we could create systems that are beyond our control and find ourselves at the mercy of algorithms that we don't understand," Suleyman wrote. His wave metaphor raised the question of whether we will ride it to somewhere great or be crushed by it. The future isn't written, it's created, Suleyman wrote in one of a series of tweets he posted to promote the book. Our ability to manage these waves will determine the future.

If the book's message could be distilled to a single sentence, it's this: we're not prepared for the challenge ahead. "This is an argument I have made many times over the last decade behind closed doors," Suleyman wrote. "Spend time in tech or policy circles, and it quickly becomes obvious that head-in-the-sand is the default ideology." In October, Suleyman cowrote with Eric Schmidt a piece calling for the creation of an independent, expert-led body akin to the Intergovernmental Panel on Climate Change. As imagined, this new agency would keep governments up-to-date on AI and offer evidence-based predictions of what might be coming.

"Calls to 'just regulate' are as loud, and as simplistic, as calls to press on," Suleyman and Schmidt wrote. "Before we charge headfirst into over-regulating, we must first address lawmakers' basic lack of understanding of what AI is, how fast it is developing and where the most significant risks lie."

Taking time to write a book while also running a startup is quite the flex, though Suleyman had help ("with" London-based writer Michael Bhaskar, it says on the cover). The same could be said of the couple of months he seemed to be everywhere talking about AI. CNN, the BBC, *CBS Sunday Morning*, and public radio's *Marketplace* were among those media outlets booking him as a guest. "I had a team organizing it," Suleyman said. "Usually, I just had to show up."

Virtually every one of his sixty or so public appearances during that period represented another plug for Pi, which roughly doubled its user base in the couple of months Suleyman was out on the hustings, promoting his book.

Several months on the front lines of the debate over AI left Suleyman feeling more than a little fed up with the extremists he found on all sides. A 2023 survey by Pew found that more than half of the country—52 percent of those surveyed—reported feeling concerned more than excited by AI. Those like Andreessen rallying around what had been dubbed "effective accelerationism," or e/acc for short, were not helping. Their full-speed-ahead attitude, whatever the cost, heightened people's mistrust. "They're still not reliable," Suleyman said of neural nets when he was a guest on *CBS Mornings*. "We're still not ready to use them in production settings."

At the same time, those Suleyman described as "self-appointed activists" on the other side also irritated him. While the biases of AI systems were something that needed to be fixed, to him the answer certainly wasn't to unplug AI given artificial intelligence's potential to transform health care, education, and other critical areas. The accelerationist vs. safety dichotomy is starting to get absurd, he tweeted that fall. Safety people aren't doomers and e-accs aren't libertarian loons. Realists are both. We must accelerate safely.

• • •

AT THE END of October, reporters gathered in the White House East Room to watch Biden sign the Executive Order on Safe, Secure, and Trustworthy Artificial Intelligence. Companies working on massive foundation models were required under this directive to red-team their systems (testing to expose flaws by a pretend adversary "red team") and share the test results with the government before rolling out a product. Under the order, federal agencies were instructed to create standards that limited the use of AI to spread misinformation and combated what the White House called "algorithmic discrimination." That same day, the G7 countries—the United States, Canada, the United

Kingdom, France, Germany, Italy, and Japan, along with the European Union, which participates in G7 meetings but is not counted as one of its members—agreed to a voluntary code of conduct for companies developing advanced AI systems.

Hoffman declared himself pleased with the Biden administration's handling of AI when he spoke at the Computer History Museum in Mountain View that evening. Hoffman dressed as he normally did, in a maroon polo and baggy pants, but for the occasion he added a sport coat to his repertoire. ("That's Reid's great hack," his friend Chris Yeh said. "He'll slip on a blazer over a collared polo and then he's dressed up.") Hoffman had not had time to read the entire 111-page executive order, he confessed when the moderator brought up that day's big news. "I had GPT-4 summarize it for me," he said.

AI's critics condemned the White House for seeking guidance from the very people creating these systems. But that's what impressed Hoffman, who was a financial backer of two of the companies that had been invited to the White House and a board member at a third. "First, they said, 'Okay, let's call all the companies in and let's ask them for voluntary commitments. Let's push them hard at what kinds of things they could be doing,'" Hoffman said. Similarly, some of the more aggressive conditions laid out by the executive order—the idea of red-teaming a product, watermarking content to guard against misinformation—came from industry.

The executive order was limited. "Everyone admits the only real answer is legislative," Schumer said on the day of the signing. Yet many in tech saw the initiative as going too far. Executives at major tech companies had come out publicly in favor of AI regulation, but Net-Choice, a national trade association representing the likes of Google, Amazon, and Meta, released a statement calling the order an "AI Red Tape Wishlist" that would stifle innovation and block competitors from entering the marketplace.

On the *All-In* podcast, the besties were apoplectic. If Hoffman was too much of a Biden fanboy (Hoffman loudly supported him until the moment Biden dropped out of the race), the four besties could sound like *Fox & Friends* when talking about the president. His administration certainly provided them with ample fodder. The Biden Justice Department took on Silicon Valley royalty when, at the start of 2023, it filed a second major antitrust case against Google, this time charging that its monopolization of the ad technology market, not just search, violated federal antitrust laws. Many in the Valley loathed Biden's choice to head the Securities and Exchange Commission because of his efforts to crack down on crypto, and there was the animosity they directed at Lina Khan, the antitrust crusader Biden had put in charge of the Federal Trade Commission. Khan, the youngest commissioner in the agency's history, was also a woman of color outspoken in her criticisms of Big Tech and a favorite punching bag among the besties. That summer the FTC opened an investigation into OpenAI over its handling of data and then, several months later, the agency announced it was investigating Microsoft, Google, and Amazon for their investments in AI startups such as OpenAI and Anthropic. While large corporations have been investing in startups for decades, the FTC was questioning whether these large ownership stakes, purchased with their billions, were effectively mergers in disguise. "Our study will shed light on whether investments and partnerships pursued by dominant companies risk distorting innovation and undermining fair competition," Khan said in a statement when announcing its investigation of Microsoft, Google, and Amazon.

With few tech IPOs in 2023, acquisitions were the primary way VCs could generate a return. Yet Khan was inclined to break up the tech giants rather than allow them to further expand their power through mergers and acquisitions (M&A). That put her at odds with the venture capital community, which viewed her as standing in the way of the only real means VCs had to make money.

"They view themselves as a hammer," *All-In*'s Chamath Palihapitiya said of the FTC under Khan, "and every deal, particularly if it's done by big tech, is a nail." Even Hoffman, during the 2024 presidential election, said Khan was "waging war" on American business and publicly declared his hope that Kamala Harris, if elected, would replace her.

The four besties had nothing good to say about Biden's executive order. The entire effort, said David Friedberg, normally the most tempered of the four, was born of "fearmongering of AI destroying the world." David Sacks likened AI to a defendant that has been convicted before ever breaking the law. "AI has been convicted of a pre-crime," Sacks said, as if the most sensible approach would have the government wait for something horrible to happen before taking any action. (Trump would appoint Sacks as his administration's AI and crypto czar after winning the 2024 election.) Largely they focused on how Biden's actions will harm the U.S. in competition with China, India, and other markets.

"The more our government actors step in and try and tell us what systems and methods we are allowed to use to build stuff," Friedberg said, "the more at risk we are of falling behind."

• • •

IN EARLY DECEMBER of 2023, the employees of Inflection descended on Mountain View and the handsome, six-story glass box Hyatt had built in its downtown. The startup had rented every last meeting venue in the building to ensure they had the room they needed to plot and workshop their ideas. At that point, the company employed roughly fifty full-timers. On the hotel's top floor, in a large area littered with couches, chairs, bar-top tables, and stools, pairs and groups of Inflectioneers worked except when they gathered in one of the nearby conference rooms. There was a big group dinner and other activities for those who wanted. But most tended to take advantage of in-person time to do the spade work on whatever set of problems they needed to tackle over the coming six weeks.

"There is this golden moment when you really have a very close-knit, small, focused team," Suleyman said. "I'm going to try and preserve that for as long as possible."

Pi was now available for Android and its roughly 3 billion worldwide users. That brought to ten the number of platforms people could use if wanting to talk with Pi. It was also tied to the web. That meant Pi could access real-time content, whether breaking news, up-to-date sports scores, or the weather. "This started as a little hackathon during a week seven," Joe Fenton said. In fractions of a second, Pi retrieves the pertinent information and integrates it into an answer. "Your personal AI is now more knowledgeable than ever," said a playful animated GIF that Inflection whipped up to announce the improvement in October.

Suleyman and others at Inflection were vague about user numbers—deliberately so. They were a disappointment. That fall, pollsters asked those who used chatbots which one they turned to most often. Fifty-two percent said ChatGPT and another 20 percent named Claude. Perplexity was third with a 10 percent share, followed by Google's Bard (9 percent) and Bing (7 percent). Pi was lumped in with the 2 percent of users who selected "other." They had ideas for boosting its user base, Hoffman told me, but they still were a relatively small team with other priorities. "People are focused pretty intensely on personalized memory and these other things," Hoffman said. "We basically don't have the cycles to really focus on distribution."

The company had its usual long to-do list. Pi might have been faster than most of its rivals, but concerns about speed were a constant, especially as they pushed their language models to do more. An ongoing need for efficiency led to a paradigm shift: instead of building ever-larger models, as had been the norm, Inflectioneers were increasingly focused on developing smaller, less complex ones. The larger a model, the more connections it could make, which often means more nuanced and contextually appropriate the responses. But bigger was also more expensive. A turn of the conversation might only cost a few cents, but that expense piled up for companies handling tens of millions of queries a day. The publication in 2022 of the Chinchilla paper showed that smaller, more specialized models often outperformed their larger counterparts on specific tasks. One advantage Inflection had was that Suleyman had hired Jordan Hoffman, the lead author of the Chinchilla paper. Smaller models could generate responses faster and also lower Inflection's monthly burn rate.

Yet their main challenge after that week seven and in subsequent cycles was teaching Pi to get better at a wider range of tasks. People thought of Pi as a conversationalist, which was a good thing, but a helper that is good only at talking is limited.

"Pi can't code," Anusha Balakrishnan said that winter. "It needs to get better at generating longer blocks of text. It needs to get better at reasoning. It can't take actions. It's only really useful if you want to talk about your feelings and now it can search the web."

That proved the ultimate to-do list item: building up Pi's skill set so that it was useful to a far wider variety of users. "How do we make users think of Pi as the first thing they go to for any need?" Balakrishnan asked. Solving for that problem would make a startup become a trillion-dollar behemoth.

CHAPTER 19

The Land of the Giants

S am Altman took his place among the famous and fabulous in
November 2023 for the inaugural run of the Las Vegas Grand
Prix. Rihanna, Justin Bieber, Paris Hilton, Brad Pitt, Gordon
Ramsay, and Shaquille O'Neal were among those on hand to watch
race cars zip through the streets of Las Vegas at speeds exceeding 200
miles per hour. On the day before the big race, Altman was in his
hotel room. He was slated to talk with OpenAI's chief scientist, Ilya
Sutskever—"the brilliant, eccentric AI researcher whose hiring eight
years ago had put OpenAI on the map," as the *Wall Street Journal*
described him. At around noon his time, he clicked on a Google Meet
link.

Sutskever's face was on the screen when Altman logged in, but
so were those of three additional members of OpenAI's board of directors. Sutskever held one of six seats on the board, as did Altman.
The sixth member, Greg Brockman, another cofounder and OpenAI's
president, was conspicuously missing from the Google Meet. Altman's
brain "works at a high clock speed," Hoffman had told me. Instantly,
he must have sensed what was happening.

The call lasted only a few minutes. Sutskever, who had the accent
of someone who had grown up in Russia, did most of the talking. As
if reading from a script, Sutskever told Altman that the board had
lost faith in him as CEO. He provided no details, only the news that

they were about to announce that he had been fired and that Mira Murati, the Albanian-born engineer serving as the company's chief technology officer, was being named OpenAI's acting CEO. Shocked, Altman logged off, and shortly after that he was locked out of his computer. He was out of the company he had cofounded and birthed from conception.

The word "coup" was thrown around liberally, mainly because there seemed no better word for what had happened inside AI's most consequential startup. Even OpenAI employees used the term to describe the maneuvering that had Sutskever joining other board members seeking to push out Altman. Sutskever certainly had motive for participating in a coup. The *Times* reported that Sutskever had grown fearful of a super-powerful AI that could wipe out humanity. Altman, however, had the company mashing its foot to the gas. Resentment also may have played a role. That fall, Altman had promoted another senior scientist to a position that put him on the same level as Sutskever, which the latter reportedly took as a slight. Sutskever certainly had means and opportunity. There were three independent members of the board—outside people who did not work for the company—along with Altman, Brockman, and Sutskever. Later it came out that for months Sutskever had been meeting with the independent board members behind Altman and Brockman's back. With Sutskever throwing in his lot with the independents, they had the four votes needed to oust Altman.

• • •

SATYA NADELLA WAS having his standard Friday morning meeting with Microsoft's senior leadership team when he was interrupted by an urgent call from Kevin Scott. It had been Scott who had most forcefully pushed Nadella on the idea of throwing the software behemoth's lot in with a small AI lab in San Francisco. Now Scott was on the line to say he had just learned that within the next twenty minutes, the OpenAI board was announcing that it had fired Altman. Reportedly, Nadella, Microsoft's unflappable steward, was speechless. His company had invested billions in OpenAI. More than that, it had tied its future to this startup that, until a moment earlier, seemed the smartest bet Microsoft had made since buying a precursor to Windows for $75,000 at the start of the PC revolution. For Nadella, OpenAI was Sam Altman, and now Altman, a core player in Microsoft's AI strategy, was out.

Nadella called Hoffman, who was on his way to the airport after attending a tech conference in Napa Valley. Hoffman promised to plug into his network to see what he could find out. Nadella also reached out to Adam D'Angelo. D'Angelo, an early Facebook executive who cofounded the Q&A site Quora, was one of the three independent board members who voted to dump Altman. Nadella sought some insight into what had happened, but D'Angelo only repeated the vague line that appeared in a blog post the board had posted on the OpenAI site: Altman had not been "consistently candid in his communications with the board."

A frustrated Nadella huddled with Scott and other Microsoft executives on a video call to talk through their options. Almost immediately they dismissed the idea of supporting the board and putting its weight behind Murati. That didn't sit well with any of those on the call. They felt that, if nothing else, they first deserved an explanation for a decision that otherwise struck them as reckless. Option two had them using their leverage to force the board to reverse course. Microsoft still owed a large chunk of the $10 billion the company earlier in the year had committed to investing. They could play hardball and make that remainder contingent on Altman's reinstatement and a reconstructed board.

A third option seemed the most intriguing. Why not hire Altman, along with any other OpenAI employee willing to make the jump with him? In that scenario, Altman and team would rebuild their models but do so inside Microsoft. Microsoft would then own and sell whatever grew from out of this AI unit.

• • •

THE OPENAI BOARD continued to stonewall. On the advice of counsel, they limited what they said publicly about Altman's firing to a single line: "Mr. Altman's departure follows a deliberate review process by the board, which concluded that he was not consistently candid in his communications." Perhaps the board should have listened to a public relations specialist instead. In the vacuum of information, rumors and theories proliferated.

One theory making the rounds was that the board was fed up with Altman's multiple side hustles. He ran his own personal venture fund called Hydrazine Capital and had teamed up on a venture with the famed Apple designer Jony Ive. Reportedly the pair were looking to raise as much as $1 billion for a hardware company that stamped out personal devices that employ AI. Media accounts also had him raising money for an AI startup that pursued drug developments. Yet this was Silicon Valley, where Elon Musk was the CEO of six companies simultaneously, including xAI, and people like Reid Hoffman had multiple full-time jobs while juggling a multitude of side projects. These were Masters of the Universe. Some could even pull it off. It seemed more likely the tensions stemmed from concern about AI safety and the speed at which OpenAI was operating.

Silicon Valley immediately rallied around Altman. To them he should be crowned CEO of the year. Short of a clear case of malfeasance, he certainly did not deserve to be dumped. Adam D'Angelo was a member of the club and given a pass, but not his fellow conspirators, who were widely derided among the Valley's cognoscenti. The two other independent board members were women. One, Tasha McCauley, had attended the Future of Life Institute's 2015 conference in Puerto Rico. She worked as an adjunct senior management scientist at the Rand Corporation, a policy nonprofit. The other, Helen Toner, was a little-known academic from Australia who worked for a Georgetown University think tank. "Fancy titles like 'Director of Strategy at Georgetown's Center for Security and Emerging Technology' can lead to a false sense of understanding of the complex process of entrepreneurial innovation," venture capitalist Vinod Khosla, an early investor in OpenAI, wrote in The Information. There was a paternalistic call to put the adults back in charge.

Those critical of the board of course had a point. If not for Altman, OpenAI would not be AI's premier startup. The risk in replacing him seemed immense. Yet it was Altman who had set up a nonprofit board to monitor the for-profit arm's actions and keep it true to the stated aim of advancing AI in a manner "most likely to benefit humanity." When convenient, he trotted out the company's mission statement and its unusual corporate structure. "No one person should be trusted here," Altman had said at a technology conference in June. "The board can fire me. I think that's important."

The situation called to mind Google boasting of the ethical AI safety team it had created to keep people honest and then firing the two women the company had put in charge of the effort the first time they sounded the alarm. The OpenAI board's job wasn't to help its for-profit subsidiary maximize shareholder value but was that of a watchdog appointed to ensure that the company was in the hands of a leader they could trust. Apparently, a majority of the board—the two women but also D'Angelo and Sutskever—had lost that trust.

• • •

ALTMAN'S FIRST INSTINCT when told he was being sacked was to ask Sutskever and the others what he could do to help. Once the shock wore off, a different impulse kicked in. Later that day, he flew back to San Francisco and set up a war room in his house. Among those he spoke with was Nadella, who floated the idea of working for him at Microsoft. Altman told him he was open to the idea but, he mused about starting a new company with Greg Brockman, who had quit in protest after he learned that he, like Altman, was off the OpenAI board. Yet Altman was also clear with everyone that his hope was that his removal was only temporary. i love openai employees so much, he posted on X that Saturday morning. Dozens of OpenAI employees responded with colorful heart emojis.

Even people inside OpenAI were in the dark about what had happened. On the day of Altman's firing, a dozen executives had crowded into a conference room for a call with OpenAI's board. The board told them that Altman had lied but claimed for legal reasons they could not say more than that. The next day, Murati showed up at Altman's door after informing the board she was resigning as acting CEO.

More details leaked out over the next couple of days. There had been simmering tensions stretching back more than a year. The board found Altman slippery. He had his charms, but he was also plotting and a manipulator—the man who could parachute into an island of cannibals and end up king. He could be duplicitous. Altman, for his part, harbored his own bad feelings. He had been understandably upset when Toner, in October, wrote a paper for her Georgetown think tank that cast aspersions on OpenAI and praised Anthropic, its archrival. Anthropic had shown restraint when it released Claude, Toner wrote, "to avoid exactly the kind of frantic corner-cutting that the release of ChatGPT appeared to spur." An angry Altman wanted Toner off the board, but news accounts cast him as pursuing that goal dishonestly. Reportedly, he had phoned other board members and told them McCauley wanted Toner removed, when apparently that wasn't true. (Altman denied manipulating the board.)

That weekend, it seemed entirely possible that OpenAI would be Netscape all over again. Just as the company that sparked the internet revolution went under, so might the startup that one year earlier ignited the AI era. Business customers were wavering. Some that had thrown in their lot with OpenAI were reaching out to Anthropic and other rivals to explore the possibility of switching platforms. Well-funded competitors, including Inflection, were rushing in to poach top talent.

Meanwhile, a petition was being passed around that stated that the undersigned intended to leave OpenAI if Altman were not reinstalled. That seemed to have shaken members of the board. Maybe OpenAI needed Altman at the helm if the company was even going to survive. Negotiations began between the board and Altman's confederates.

A deal seemed imminent on Sunday. But the existing board members wanted the right to approve their replacements if they were to step down, and Altman was insisting that he remain on the board. The talks collapsed. On Sunday night, the board informed Murati they had chosen a new acting CEO: Emmett Shear, a founder of Twitch, the live streaming platform popular among gamers. Appearing on a podcast in June, Shear declared that his p(doom) for AI destroying humanity stood at around 50 percent. Normally he would describe himself as a "techno-optimist" but, he told his interviewer, the risks associated with AI "should cause you to shit your pants."

Hoffman phoned Nadella on Sunday evening. He had spoken to around a dozen people connected to OpenAI in the previous forty-eight hours. He assured him that Altman had done nothing untoward that should give Microsoft pause about working with him, and Nadella again reached out to Altman. "I'm going to Microsoft," Altman told Hoffman and others. Later that night, Nadella logged on to X. Ever the diplomat, he said he remained committed to Microsoft's partnership with OpenAI and looked forward to working with Shear. Only then did he make the announcement that had him logging on to X at a few minutes before midnight on a Sunday night: We're extremely excited to share the news that Sam Altman and Greg Brockman, together with colleagues, will be joining Microsoft to lead a new advanced AI research team.

On Monday morning, the staff at OpenAI posted a letter online that said they would follow Altman to Microsoft if the board did not resign. Somewhere around 745 of OpenAI's 770 employees signed the document. That included Ilya Sutskever, who posted on X that morning, I deeply regret my participation in the board's actions.

"I don't think I've ever seen in all of corporate history," Hoffman said, "where a board fires a CEO and something that rounds up to 100 percent of the employees saying, 'Reinstate the CEO or we're outta here.'" The previous week, there had been a deal in the works that priced the company at between $80 billion and $90 billion for those employees and other insiders who wanted to cash out a portion of their shares in OpenAI. Yet now those shares might be worthless.

Adam D'Angelo and Altman talked early on Monday about whom they might add to the board if they removed McCauley and Toner. D'Angelo proposed Larry Summers, the former Treasury secretary and Harvard professor. Summers was a controversial pick—among other things, as president of Harvard, he had given a speech positing that there might be relatively few women in top positions in the sciences because of "issues of intrinsic aptitude." But D'Angelo, Altman, and Nadella all reached out to Summers, who said he was agreeable about joining the OpenAI board. A second name was added: Bret Taylor, an early Facebook executive and a former co-CEO of Salesforce. Altman dropped his insistence that his board seat be reinstated. He told friends he could fight that battle another day, once he was back in charge.

At around 10 p.m. Pacific time on the Tuesday before Thanksgiving, OpenAI announced that a deal had been struck. Altman was once again CEO and wouldn't be going to Microsoft, after all. And a new three-person board was now in charge of OpenAI. Summers and Taylor (who was taking over as board chair) were replacing the two women, but D'Angelo would remain for "continuity." The same people who might oversee any garden-variety for-profit tech company were now running the nonprofit board overseeing OpenAI, not academics worried about moving too fast on AI. The capitalists (and the men) had won.

• • •

SULEYMAN HAD NOT remained silent during the five days OpenAI dominated the tech news cycle. On Monday morning, when it looked like a deal had fallen apart, he took to X to express the proper sympathy for those working there ("wishing everyone involved the very best")—and then announced that the company had built what he called Inflection-2, which he dubbed "the 2nd best LLM in the world."

Actually, there wasn't much to announce. To the extent there was any news it was that Inflection's own internal testing showed Inflection-2 outperforming both Google's PaLM model and Meta's LLaMA 2 and trailing only GPT-4. Yet the company needed at least a couple of weeks of fine-tuning before Inflection-2 was powering Pi. It said a lot about Suleyman that he chose that moment to share the news, just as OpenAI was staring into the abyss, to tell the world that Inflection was nipping at its heels.

Apparently, Anthropic CEO Dario Amodei had the same competitive streak. He too chose those five days when OpenAI was in
turmoil to announce Claude 2.1. It was an interim release, but at least
theirs was an actual upgrade. A news release Anthropic posted on its
website that Tuesday morning boasted that its upgrade cut the bot's
hallucination rate in half and offered higher-quality answers to complex questions. Rowan Cheung, who sent out a digital newsletter he
called "The Rundown AI," described Anthropic's announcement this
way: "Amodei woke up and chose violence."

Musk's chatbot debuted that December. Grok, he called it—a term
borrowed from science fiction, meaning to understand something so
profoundly that you become one with it. A statement posted on the
xAI website said it was designed to answer with a "bit of wit" and also
had a "rebellious streak." But, unlike the competition, Musk did not
give users the option of a free version of the service. Grok cost sixteen
dollars a month through X. Its great advantage was that it leveraged
data generated on X, which is practically an up-to-the-second news
source.

With the release of Grok, Musk addressed the contradiction of
calling for a pause in AI research while spending untold millions to
race ahead. "I signed that letter knowing it was futile," he said. "I just
wanted to be on the record as recommending a pause."

An advantage the doomers had was that there would always be
humans who enlist technology to abuse others. The fringe messaging
board 4chan adopted LLMs "to generate waves of harassing, racist,
and pornographic material," the *New York Times* reported. A former
academic turned entrepreneur turned AI gadfly named Gary Marcus
had warned about "automated misinformation" by racists, trolls, and
opportunists eager to make a buck spewing copious streams of it. The
world was making his predictions a reality.

The Verge reported on sexually explicit AI-generated images of
Taylor Swift on X, including one that notched 45 million views. At a
New Jersey high school, boys employed AI to fabricate sexually explicit
images of tenth-grade girls and then passed around the fake pictures.
AI was used to whip up phony celebrity endorsements: Joe Rogan

backing libido boosters for men, Tom Hanks promoting a dental insurance plan. The New York–based news outlet Futurism caught *Sports Illustrated* putting the byline of nonexistent authors on AI-generated stories. "There is rarely a weekend that goes by where Drew isn't out camping, hiking, or just back on his parents' farm," read the bio for a made-up writer named Drew Ortiz.

When the people who run the world converged on Davos, Switzerland, in January for that year's World Economic Forum, supposedly it wasn't Ukraine or Gaza on the lips of the billionaires and world leaders in attendance but artificial intelligence. Sam Altman, Satya Nadella, Yann LeCun, and Mustafa Suleyman were among those sharing their insights as featured speakers. Even the Federal Reserve's Jerome H. Powell weighed in on AI in that mealymouthed way that Fed chairs do when he suggested that AI "may" have the potential to increase productivity "but probably not in the short run." Following in the footsteps of their counterparts in the U.S., European Union regulators launched a probe of Microsoft, Meta, and X, among other companies, and their approaches to mitigating the risks of generative AI.

Google, for reasons no one could fathom, gave its chatbot a new name. Bard was now Gemini. This latest model, trained not just with words but also images and sound, outperformed GPT-4 in key areas. Yet the upgrade seemed only to give Google another opportunity to stumble in a highly public way. Apparently its people had gone overboard when teaching its image generator that white men were overrepresented in its training data. America's founding fathers were depicted as black, ancient Greeks were shown to be Asian, and German soldiers circa 1943 as people of color. Those warning against politically correct AI had a field day, and Google was forced to pull the feature. The company shed nearly $90 billion in value over the next twenty-four hours.

In early 2024, Bloomberg reported that Sam Altman was seeking billions in venture capital to build a network of factories that would stamp out customer-designed AI chips. The *Wall Street Journal* followed up with a story that said he actually was looking to raise trillions. In March, OpenAI said at a news conference that Altman was being reinstated to its board after an internal probe concluded that while the previous board had acted in good faith, his conduct "did not mandate removal" in November. To counter lingering criticisms after it had let go of its only two female board members, the company also announced that it had added three women as directors.

Inflection and Suleyman were back in the news with the release of Inflection 2.5. **Meet the new, upgraded Pi where helpful IQ blends with friendly EQ,** Suleyman wrote on X. They had improved Pi's IQ to the point that it matched the performance of the other high-profile chatbots. The company's X account boasted that Inflection-2.5 was "neck and neck with GPT-4 on all benchmarks and used less than half the compute to train." It was smaller and nearly as fast, along with what the company described as "its distinctively kind and curious personality." Theirs was a very different vision of AI than that offered by OpenAI, Anthropic, Google, or Microsoft, and it seemed to be working. Pi was talking to 1 million people a day and had 6 million monthly users.

"Everything did look like it was going great there, didn't it?" Hoffman later said, with a wry smile and a shrug.

• • •

MAYBE IT WAS obvious that Microsoft would be on the hunt for a replacement team after their deal to absorb Altman and much of OpenAI's staff fell through. Nadella and other executives had tried on the idea of an in-house AI studio and liked it. The scare OpenAI threw into them solidified people's belief in the idea. They needed a hedge against any more drama inside OpenAI.

As best Suleyman could remember it, it was early December when Nadella first floated the idea that he join Microsoft. "Satya for a long time, even before Inflection, has been trying to bring me over," Suleyman said. The two companies had been linked since June, when Microsoft anchored the company's $1.3 billion Series A raise. Indeed, the impetus for their discussions near the end of 2023 was Suleyman's desire for more of Microsoft's money.

That fall, Suleyman and Hoffman had sat down to talk finances. The pair figured they needed $2 billion to fund Inflection's ambitions through the end of 2024. After that, they estimated they needed to find another $4 billion to $6 billion. "I'm flying around the world to the UAE [United Arab Emirates] and to Japan and to Europe trying to raise money," Suleyman said. It was during one of those trips, he said, that Nadella floated the idea that not just Suleyman join him at Microsoft but some of his Inflection team.

Later there would be speculation that Inflection was having trouble finding funders because Pi hadn't attracted the audience to justify a valuation in the $10 billion range. Yet Hoffman and Suleyman said that was not true. They had more than $1 billion in commitments, and Hoffman declared himself confident they could raise the remaining billion. Two top venture firms were fighting over which would lead the round, and others, including both Microsoft and Nvidia, had committed to making a big contribution. They were not worried about the B round in front of them but a far larger C round and beyond.

"If you looked at what the large companies would be doing, Google and Microsoft and potentially others, you know they were going to create next-level models every twelve to eighteen months," Hoffman said. Alphabet and Microsoft each had roughly $100 billion in cash on hand. The giants needed only to dip into their reserves to fund their voracious AI ambitions, not fly around the world with hat in hand. There was also Meta, with more than $50 billion in reserves and a strategy that had them open-sourcing their pretrained model. Cutting-edge models were available for free at Hugging Face.

"When we started this business, we had no idea that people were going to open-source the absolute frontier," Suleyman said. With open-source alternatives, "pretrained models were fundamentally a commodity." There was also the level of competition to consider. To compete, Inflection would need unfathomably larger rounds of financing for years to come.

"Part of what you're trying to do with a startup is skate to where the puck is going, and not to where the puck is," Hoffman said. He and Suleyman peered into the future and realized that no matter how good their product, "we had a fundraising challenge and a business challenge," he said. The question was what to do.

Suleyman and Nadella had lunch while both were in Davos in mid-January. That's where the conversation grew more serious. "He was just very forthcoming and said we should be partners," Suleyman said. The line Nadella had used often in recent years is one he repeated with Suleyman over lunch: Microsoft had missed search and missed mobile; he had no intention of being an also-ran in the race to cash in on AI. "He says to me, 'Come and you'll have every resource you need to build what you're building except inside Microsoft,'" Suleyman said.

Suleyman made several trips to Redmond over the coming weeks. He and Nadella would have dinner and talk. Suleyman brought up the deep frustrations he felt after Google bought DeepMind. He was adamant that he would avoid a replay of his Google years, when the company had competing AI units within the company. "I told Satya if this was going to work, we have to consolidate everything and have a single, coherent consumer AI strategy," Suleyman said.

Suleyman and Hoffman spoke about delaying a decision. In that scenario, they would close their B round and reassess. Months earlier, Suleyman had nearly bitten my head off when I asked if he might license Pi and allow programmers from other companies to utilize the technology. Unlike OpenAI and Anthropic, which had pursued that revenue stream, Suleyman was adamant that they were building a consumer app, not something that companies might want to license and use as a customer service bot or brand ambassador. But if Inflection remained independent and didn't achieve the necessary traction to justify a gargantuan next raise, they might need to pivot to the very strategy Suleyman rejected—selling versions of Pi to other businesses. "The problem in that circumstance is that it's very difficult to fundraise on the pivot," Hoffman said. "Because your pitch is, 'We're disappointed this other thing didn't work out but now give us level-of-scale capital to do this new thing.'"

Those months when he was projecting optimism to the troops but privately harboring doubts about their prospects were "surreal,"

Suleyman said. "But as a startup founder, it always seems you're pursuing multiple, conflicting opportunities in parallel," he said. Suleyman confided in Hoffman, of course, and cofounder Karén Simonyan, but few others.

"We were driving superhard on our product but completely privately and behind the scenes with just me and Karén, I was having this conversation with Microsoft," Suleyman said. "It was a wild time."

• • •

AT SOME POINT near the end of February, Suleyman decided to throw in the towel on his startup dreams. Microsoft would not buy Inflection in the fashion of classic tech "acquihire," where a larger company buys another company largely for its talent. Under federal guidelines, a company must report acquisitions valued at more than $120 million to federal regulators. That would put the deal in the crosshairs of FTC chair Lina Khan and the Justice Department, which shared antitrust authority. Instead, they would hire Suleyman and Simonyan and any Inflection employee who wanted to join them.

"Once the opportunity became more concrete and the pivot to us doing great things inside Microsoft, then it was a relatively easy decision to make," Suleyman said.

There was still much to be done before Suleyman was ready to announce the deal. Inflection's investors would likely feel betrayed if he just walked away after selling them on his dreams. How would they be compensated? Inflection's staff numbered around seventy people that winter. What kind of deal terms could he work out on their behalf? When and how do they let them in on the news? What do they say publicly about the deal?

Slowly, Suleyman confided in others in the company whose help he would need to work out logistics. Fortuitously, everyone in the company was slated to be in Silicon Valley for an upcoming week seven. That would be a perfect time to break the news. Suleyman wondered if he should impose on Nadella to make an appearance to underscore the importance of this deal to Microsoft's AI strategy, but he did not have to. "Satya on his own offered to come down, which I really appreciated," Suleyman said.

Suleyman confessed to some nervousness as he stood in front of the seventy or so Inflectioneers who had gathered to hear him talk. It was around 9:30 a.m. on Tuesday, March 19, 2024, and he was about to break the news to most of them that their startup dreams were over. "As everyone knows, for the last few months I've been working very hard on the fundraising," he began. "At the last minute, Satya Nadella made us an offer to join with Microsoft." Suleyman never actually said that they had decided to take the deal but the details he started laying out made it plain he had. He would be the CEO of a new division within the company, called Microsoft AI, that would spearhead all of Microsoft's consumer AI initiatives, including Bing, Edge, and its Copilot chatbot. Simonyan would serve as chief scientist, as he had at Inflection. "Everybody here is going to get offers," Suleyman said.

"Having to walk away from [Inflection] is phenomenally heartbreaking," Suleyman told the group. But he had no choice, he explained, given the staggering amounts of money they would need to raise and limited opportunities to make cash. It was the plight of every AI startup with big ambitions to cash in on consumer interest in artificial intelligence. Suleyman brought up Google's Gemini, Microsoft's Copilot, and ChatGPT. The companies behind those efforts "are going to continue investing tens of billions of dollars a year in AI infrastructure, and they're going to make their consumer AIs largely free for many years to come," he said. On paper, Inflection seemed in a strong position. Yet given the untold billions they would need to raise, Suleyman judged Inflection "structurally weak medium-to-long-term." The best way to remain true to the "myAI" memo he had written at the start of 2022 was to move inside one of the giants. At Microsoft, they would have access to Microsoft's billion-plus users, its near-bottomless reserves of money, and the computer horsepower they needed to train their models.

"My best assessment is that in the next five to ten years, none of the startups in the consumer AI space are going to make it," Suleyman told the group.

Nadella took the stage after Suleyman. He began by voicing his admiration for their work and made an appeal for everyone in the room to join Microsoft. "This is not about you coming and saying, 'Let's learn the Microsoft way.' I want you to shape Microsoft with what you believe is the way to go about creating product and driving innovation," Nadella said. During a Q&A portion, Anusha Balakrishnan, who had spent two years working at Microsoft before leaving to join Inflection, expressed her worry that working inside a large corporation, with its lower metabolism, would slow them down. Nadella told her, "I think the way to frame it perhaps is, 'Do you have the hunger to change a company of the scope and size and scale of Microsoft?'" Nearly every Inflection employee made the jump to Microsoft. The compensation package each was offered, Suleyman said, "was commensurate with what you would earn as a top 1 percent AI researcher."

Inflection, the company, would continue. The same day Suleyman broke the news of his departure, Inflection announced that it had hired his replacement. The new CEO, Sean White, was a longtime friend of Hoffman's who had served as a top executive at Mozilla while Hoffman served on its board of directors. The company would pursue the licensing strategy that Hoffman and Suleyman had contemplated when gaming out options to save the company.

"Over the last year, we've heard countless times that people haven't been able to replicate the unique conversational style of Pi with publicly available models, and would love to get access to our model and fine tuning infrastructure," read a message Inflection posted on its website the day of the deal. "Our plan going forward is to lean into our AI studio business, where custom generative AI models are crafted, tested and fine-tuned for commercial customers." Under the terms of the deal, Microsoft would offer Inflection's AI models to its cloud customers. The future of Pi was uncertain, but it was clear that some version of the chatbot would be redeployed as corporate customer service agents and in other roles that took advantage of its touch with people. Hoffman would remain on Inflection's board of directors.

Shortly after the deal was announced, Hoffman tweeted that all of Inflection's investors will have a good outcome today, but left it at that.

The next day, The Information revealed that Microsoft was paying a flat fee of $620 million to Inflection for the right to use its technologies. The software giant threw in another $30 million in return for an agreement by Inflection that it would not sue Microsoft for poaching most of its employees. Those who had put money into Inflection during the seed round would see a 50 percent return on that investment. Those participating in the A round would see only a 10 percent return on their money, but investors would retain their proportional share of whatever remained of Inflection.

"From here forward, they'll be playing with house money," Hoffman said.

The reaction in Silicon Valley was surprise. People took to social media to note that they had never seen a founder leave a startup quite like Suleyman just did. Unhappy boards push out CEOs. Founding CEOs replace themselves, as Hoffman had done at LinkedIn. Founding CEOs look for a soft landing for themselves because their startup is failing. Yet to the wider world, Inflection was thriving. Less than two weeks earlier, the company had been boasting about the power of its Inflection 2.5 model. But Suleyman left and took almost the entire company with him.

Doomers saw a chance to express their displeasure. On social media, Suleyman was the non technical founder of deepmind who nonetheless is continually funded, promoted and appointed where [he] has influence over ai. One poster said Suleyman's elevation to a top position at Microsoft was "demoralizing" but understandable. He's a corporatist statist anti-open source.

It was Hoffman, though, who came in for the most criticism. He had always needed to walk the thinnest of ethical tightropes as someone so well connected in the Valley, juggling many conflicts of interest. Yet the Inflection-Microsoft deal had him wearing no fewer than three hats: cofounder, major investor, and a board member of the company bailing them out. Hoffman stressed with me that he had served as a sounding board for Suleyman but steered clear of any conversations about the price of the deal. He excused himself from the room when the Microsoft board voted on the deal.

Yet the fact was that Microsoft, where he had been a board member for the better part of a decade, rescued him and also Bill Gates, who was also an investor in Inflection. A variety of publications and bloggers took Hoffman to task, including The Information, which reported that the deal "is raising eyebrows regarding corporate governance." On the *All-In* podcast, Chamath Palihapitiya didn't doubt that conflicts of interest were at play, even as he had no evidence of any double-dealing by Hoffman or Gates. But he declared himself impressed.

"It occurred like this because Reid and Bill are inexorably tied to Microsoft, so they were able to get a deal for investors that would've never happened otherwise," Palihapitiya said. "Good on them." He didn't say it, but he didn't need to. Billionaires tend to win in the end, even when everything doesn't break their way.

Epilogue

The news that Suleyman left Inflection to take a job at Microsoft broke a little more than a year after I started work on this book. Like most everyone else in tech, I was stunned. I'll confess I was also disappointed. In the mid-1990s, I set out to cover the founders and venture capitalists who dreamed of becoming the next tech giant, and instead ended up writing a book focused on Microsoft because Microsoft's dominance demanded it. It was déjà vu all over again. For a second time, I set out to write a book focused on entrepreneurs and VCs. And again Microsoft—along with other giants—thwarted those plans.

It would be hard to overstate the skill with which Nadella maneuvered Microsoft to ensure it was a central player in AI. Google had a far superior hand when Nadella took over the company. So too did Meta and arguably Amazon and Apple, which had popular AI products on the market in Alexa and Siri. Yet Nadella bet the future of Microsoft on a groundbreaking partnership with OpenAI. The deal instantly placed the software giant on the cutting edge of AI and drew more users to its cloud business, which was offering users access to OpenAI's technologies. Nadella impressed Wall Street with his mastery in the days after the OpenAI board fired Altman ("He handled that like he was in the World Series of Poker playing against little kids," one analyst said) and then, a few months later, in one fell swoop, sucked up almost all the talent Suleyman had assembled at Inflection. Since OpenAI's near implosion, the *Wall Street Journal*'s

Tom Dotan and Berber Jin wrote in 2024, Nadella has been "spreading his bets, turning the world's biggest company into the world's most aggressive amasser of AI talent, tools and technology." Another of those bets: its 15-million-euro (roughly $16.3 million) investment in Mistral, an open-source rival to OpenAI. In the early scramble to capitalize on AI, Microsoft was undeniably one of the big winners. In the pages of *Wired*, Steven Levy declared Microsoft "cool again."

Google's tendency to face-plant practically every time it stepped on the public stage continued unabated through 2024. In May it debuted "AI Overview," which the company hyped as the future of online search. The new feature utilized a large language model to generate instant AI-crafted answers to user queries that were prominently displayed atop the usual list of links, saving users the trouble of sifting through individual web pages. Gemini no longer generated images of Asian Nazis. But AI Overview meant once again the company was getting publicity for all the wrong reasons. One summary shared on social media asserted that geologists recommended that people eat one small rock a day for their daily nutrients. To stop cheese from sliding off a pizza, AI Overview suggested adding "about ⅛ cup of non-toxic glue to the sauce." It also recommended a splash of gasoline to make spaghetti a spicier dish. "Google will do the Googling for you," according to the company's new tagline. But if relying on its LLM for a search, a user would have learned that one U.S. president was Muslim and only seventeen of them had been white.

The news only grew worse for Google that summer. A federal judge ruled that the tech giant had violated the country's antitrust laws by paying billions to Apple and other companies to be the default search engine on their devices, unfairly handicapping competitors such as Microsoft's Bing. A second antitrust trial, scheduled to begin that fall, will determine if Google also abused its monopoly power to dominate the ad tech market. Just as Microsoft had Google nipping at its heels in the midst of its legal woes with the federal government, Google was contending with AI-native search engines such as Perplexity. Once upon a time, Google's people had ridiculed Microsoft as a bloated has-been. But now it was Google's turn to face the jeers—for the moment, at least.

Meta continued to pour billions into open source. In July the company released Llama 3.1, a family of models large and small. That included the largest open-source model ever and one that the company claimed outperformed GPT-4 on several key benchmarks. Because it was open-source, Meta would not make money directly on Llama, but Zuckerberg understood the great value of positioning Meta at the center of a thriving AI ecosystem. "We're a big enough company now that one of the things that I've resolved is that for the next generation of technology, I want us to build and have more control over the next set of platforms," Zuckerberg told Bloomberg TV. By allowing anyone to download and fiddle with its models, Meta greatly increased the likelihood that developers would leverage Llama to build their own AI applications. "We can control our own destiny on this and make sure we have access to the leading AI by building it and have it become an industry standard," Zuckerberg said.

Meta suffered its share of stumbles. Less than one year after its much-ballyhooed release of AI chatbots modeled on the likes of Paris Hilton and Tom Brady, the company pulled the plug on the idea. A lack of engagement among users meant the branded chatbots were not worth the millions of dollars in fees the company was paying. That summer, Mistral released an open-source LLM that reportedly outperformed Llama 3.1 on math tests and in code generation, though it was far smaller. The same dorm-room founders and researchers seeing Llama as a godsend would happily turn to Mistral if its models were superior.

Yet Meta had the advantage of several billion users around the globe. In April the company thrust itself into the chatbot competition with the launch of Meta AI, an AI assistant integrated into its various social media platforms. A few months later, Zuckerberg declared his ambition to dethrone ChatGPT. "I think we're basically on track for that," he said that summer. More than 200 million people used ChatGPT each week, whereas Meta did not even have an AI assistant at the start of 2024. Yet Zuckerberg was confident that, by year's end, Meta would have the planet's most popular chatbot.

• • •

PUBLIC ANXIETIES ABOUT AI had been simmering since ChatGPT's debut. Yet a new kind of backlash sprang up in 2024: a hard-nosed financial reckoning. Goldman Sachs led the charge in July with a research report that noted that there was "little to show" for the vast amounts of money that had been invested into generative AI. Among the questions the bank asked was "whether this large spend will ever pay off." Elliott Management, a prominent hedge fund, described AI as "overhyped with many applications not ready for prime time." A Bank of America analyst compared this cooling of enthusiasm to the waning days of the California gold rush.

The high-profile stumbles of several AI startups did not help the general mood among investors. A company called Humane, founded by a pair of ex–Apple designers, raised $240 million for a wearable AI device they called the AI Pin. The reviews were brutal. "The worst product I've ever reviewed," declared Marques Brownlee, a longtime tech reviewer whose YouTube channel, MKBHD, has nearly 20 million subscribers. Brownlee was no more charitable about the Rabbit R1, a product from another high-profile AI startup. Brownlee declared the R1, which was around the size of a deck of cards, "barely reviewable" and symptomatic of a bigger problem. "These AI-based products are at the apex of this horrible trend, where the thing that you get at the beginning is borderline nonfunctional," he said.

VCs tightened their purse strings. That was obvious to founders such as Angela Hoover, the twenty-five-year-old CEO and cofounder of Andi, a five-person startup I had started spending time with in the spring of 2023. Andi had been ahead of most everyone with an AI-powered search engine that Hoover's cofounder, Jed White, had begun building at the start of 2019. White's prototype earned them a spot in Y Combinator's winter 2022 batch, springboarding them into a multimillion-dollar seed round. Hoover got serious about raising an A round in early 2024 but wished she had done so earlier.

"Honestly, the best time to have kicked off the A round would have been in October or November last year because the AI space was still really hot," Hoover said in April. "Now there's more of an attitude of, 'Show us how you're going to make money from AI.'" As of June, Andi had raised another $563,000 through what Hoover called a "seed extension" and meanwhile fretted over their burgeoning monthly GPU bills. Money was so tight that they disabled key features to tamp down usage. They also put on pause the rollout of more powerful, GPU-intensive models that White had built. Otherwise, they would be looking at GPU bills in the hundreds of thousands of dollars per month.

"It seems to me that our story over the past year really is the story of AI where the VCs went from, 'If you're building an AI, we'll throw money at you' to now, where investors really want AI companies to have revenue," Hoover said. It was as James Currier, the longtime VC, had said earlier: founders have eighteen to twenty-four months after a transformative technology is launched. Even if the clock started in November 2022 rather than that summer, which is when Currier thinks it began, a company had between May and November of 2024 to fall within that window. Countless more teams would create AI companies, but the big-money, foundational companies, Currier said, tend to be created in those first couple of years after a paradigm on the order of AI, mobile, or the internet arrives.

Big Tech, however, continued to spend tens of billions of dollars on AI because the cost of missing out was too great. "I think all the companies that are investing are making a rational decision," Zuckerberg said, "because the downside of being behind is that you're out of position for the most important technology for the next ten to fifteen years." Meta, like every other large company, kept buying Nvidia chips and hiring AI talent because they had no choice. "It doesn't matter how many tens of billions you're spending each quarter right now, you have to get there," Zuckerberg said. "You have to make sure you don't miss the boat."

• • •

DURING AN INTERVIEW seven weeks after Suleyman and most of his team jumped to Microsoft, Reid Hoffman predicted that the quasi-acquisition of Inflection would become a "pattern" in future AI deals. True to his words, more founders abandoned their startup to work for a tech behemoth. That included the founding team behind Adept, another buzzy, swing-for-the-fences company in the Greylock portfolio. Founded by a team of top deep-learning researchers at Google and OpenAI, Adept had raised more than $400 million in venture capital in its pursuit of AI agents that could act on a user's behalf. But a few months after Microsoft's talent deal, Amazon did its own version of what The Verge dubbed a "reverse acquihire." Much like the Inflection deal, Amazon absorbed Adept's cofounders and much of its staff while placating investors with a generous licensing agreement that made them whole.

Tech insiders applauded this clever regulatory workaround. Yet what was an obvious dodge to people in the Valley was an obvious dodge to watchful regulators. In June, the FTC issued subpoenas to both Inflection and Microsoft as part of an investigation to determine whether the transaction in reality was an acquisition that Microsoft should have reported to the government. Regulators in the U.K. also looked into the deal but declared Inflection's market share too minuscule to matter.

A couple of days after news of the FTC's probe into the Inflection deal broke, Lina Khan spoke at TechCrunch's StrictlyVC conference in Washington, D.C. "Being able to go after the mob boss is going to be more effective than going after the henchman at the bottom," Khan said. A long time had passed since Microsoft had been vilified as a predator. It wasn't clear if people atop Microsoft would be upset that they were being cast as a digital menace, or flattered. Once again, the company was feared.

Yet Trump's election in November signaled a likely retreat from Khan's aggressive campaign against consolidation in the tech industry. Trump himself pledged to dismantle the "regulatory onslaught" imposed by independent agencies such as the FTC, and there were the laissez-faire attitudes of the big-name tech titans in his inner circle, including Andreessen and Musk, who spent more than $250 million to help get Trump elected. "The backroom buzz is that Donny from

Queens [Trump] is going to make M&A great again," Jason Calacanis declared on the *All-In* podcast shortly after the election. The venture capitalists are likely to be pleased, along with the tech titans eager to snap up innovative AI startups without government meddling.

• • •

OPENAI WAS NOT throwing in the towel. But the months after Altman's reinstatement as CEO generally were not good ones for the company. In May, OpenAI launched GPT-4o (the *o* is for "omni") and saw the announcement go about as well as those engineered by Google. The new model gave ChatGPT a voice—but the release was overshadowed by an angry accusation from actress Scarlett Johansson that OpenAI had mimicked her voice without consent. Johansson had voiced "Samantha," the sultry AI assistant and unlikely love interest in the 2013 movie *Her*. Anyone who had seen the film and listened to "Sky" during the GPT-4o demo thought of Samatha, a conclusion reinforced by a one-word tweet that day from Altman: her. Johansson had told Altman no when he asked to license her voice, and it initially appeared that OpenAI had simply gone ahead and cloned it anyway. But it was subsequently revealed that Sky had been voiced by another actress hired months earlier, before Johansson turned down OpenAI. An investigation by the *Washington Post* concluded that OpenAI was in the right, but that made no difference. The company had enough legal troubles. It indefinitely postponed the rollout of its voice assistant.

Two weeks after the Johansson kerfuffle, the *Times* ran a page-one article under the headline "Insiders Warn of OpenAI's Reckless Race to No. 1." A group of nine current and former OpenAI employees charged that the company was putting profits and its pursuit of artificial general intelligence ahead of safety concerns. Employees who left the company were warned that they risked losing the shares they had been granted—worth potentially in the millions—if they said anything negative about the company. Yet William Saunders, a research engineer who had left OpenAI in February, was among those who dared to speak out. "When I signed up for OpenAI, I did not sign up for this attitude of 'Let's put things out into the world and see what happens and fix them after-ward,'" Saunders told the *Times*. As a group, the nine published an open letter calling on all the leading AI companies, including OpenAI, to be more transparent and protect whistleblowers who speak out about their worries. (OpenAI dropped its nondisparagement clause after it came under criticism.)

The bad news piled up for OpenAI. The company had claimed GPT-4 aced the bar exam. But a researcher at MIT found that it scored in the 48th percentile, not the 90th, as OpenAI claimed. Elon Musk sued OpenAI and two of its cofounders, Altman and company president Greg Brockman, for allegedly tricking him into believing that the company's mission was to develop AI that benefits human-kind. I was inclined to agree with Hoffman, who described the suit as "without merit" and attributed the legal filing to "sour grapes." Yet it proved another legal hassle for the company, and also Hoffman, whom Musk added as a defendant in an amended complaint filed in November.

Meanwhile, top talent exited the company through all the turmoil. Ilya Sutskever, who had joined with other board members to force out Altman, left the company, as expected. (The startup Sutskever sub-sequently founded, Safe Superintelligence, raised more than $1 billion in venture funding in September 2024.) But other key employees also left, including Jan Leike, who along with Sutskever had created Open-AI's "Superalignment" team. **Safety culture and processes have taken a back seat to shiny product,** Leike wrote on X before announcing he had taken a position at Anthropic. John Schulman, a cofounder, also bolted to Anthropic that summer. Only three of the company's original thirteen founders remained, and one, Brockman, announced in August he was taking a four-month leave of absence. That fall, more top peo-ple exited, including Mira Murati, the OpenAI CTO who had briefly served as company CEO, and Bob McGrew, its chief research officer.

Despite the turmoil inside the company, OpenAI's technical teams continued to push the boundaries of AI innovation. In May the com-pany announced it was training a new model that it expected would deliver the "next level of capabilities" on its path to artificial general intelligence. This wouldn't be GPT-5, Altman said on X, but it **feels** like magic to me. In September, OpenAI released o1, a new model that could handle more complex problems by breaking them down to their component parts and solving them step-by-step. It proved better at math, coding, and other tasks that required complex reasoning.

The company also teased two new products that it said it would release in 2024. One was a generative AI product called Sora that would allow users to create videos of up to one minute long. Other companies, including Google, Meta, and the New York–based startup Runway, offered similar text-to-video models, but the clips OpenAI shared were praised as more lifelike than those produced by the competition. In July the company announced that it was testing an AI-powered search engine that was cast by the media as a potential "Google killer." That October, OpenAI released ChatGPT Search. Reportedly, Meta was developing its own AI-powered search engine.

All of this was expensive, of course. Reportedly, OpenAI was on pace to generate roughly $3.4 billion in 2024—an astonishing amount of revenue for a startup that had booked virtually no cash two years earlier. But an analysis by The Information estimated that the company was spending as much as $1.5 billion on a staff that had swollen to 1,500, and around $7 billion for the compute required to train and operate its models. Despite all of its successes, in other words, The Information estimated that OpenAI was on pace to lose as much as $5 billion in 2024. Few would argue with Altman's characterization of his company as "the most capital-intensive startup in Silicon Valley history."

In October, OpenAI announced that it had raised another $6.6 billion—the "largest VC round of all time," according to TechCrunch. The deal valued OpenAI at $157 billion, or roughly twice the valuation set just nine months earlier. Microsoft and traditional VCs were once again among those investing, alongside Nvidia, several hedge funds, and Fidelity Management, the giant financial services firm. That same week, OpenAI announced it had lined up a $4 billion line of credit from the likes of JPMorgan Chase, Citibank, and Goldman Sachs, giving the company more than $10 billion in liquidity. They would seemingly need it all and then some. Revenue projections OpenAI shared with potential investments showed that its losses could more than double by 2026. Reportedly, OpenAI was working on a plan to convert the company into a for-profit that would no longer be controlled by its nonprofit board.

Anthropic, another money-hungry AI startup, by mid-2024 had raised somewhere around $7 billion. Anthropic, Hoffman told me when we spoke shortly after Inflection gave up the fight, was the "counterfactual" that would prove whether Suleyman had made the right decision in joining Microsoft. That summer, Anthropic CEO Dario Amodei predicted that training a single model might cost as much as $100 billion by 2027. In November, the company raised another $4 billion from Amazon.

"Anthropic is playing the game of raising billions and billions to keep on going," Hoffman said. "The judgment that Mustafa and I made is that that's not going to work."

· · ·

I WANTED TO believe in the Valley's vaunted startup machine and its ability to give life to tomorrow's trillion-dollar companies. Yet submersing myself in the AI startup world shortly after the launch of ChatGPT has me feeling resigned to a world where the usual suspects—Microsoft, Google, Meta, Nvidia, a few others—dominate generative AI. The same tech giants that messed up tech in the 2010s, I fear, are in position to do it again with generative AI.

Venture capitalists, of course, will continue to invest in promising AI startups. Some will prove successful and generate handsome returns for their investors. The Valley's startup culture will continue to thrive. Yet those I have in mind are founders with "massively audacious hopes that far outstrip what any rational person would be thinking," as Hoffman described them. Inflection would be one example of that, along with OpenAI, Anthropic, and a long list of others. At the start of this project, Hoffman had confidently asserted that the "five or seven companies that dominate tech today will become seven or ten because of AI." By mid-2024, he was not nearly as certain. There could be winners in a wide range of categories, or what a VC would call a "vertical": law, coding, business management tools, scriptwriting, an AI scheduling app. But they would be businesses more like the hollowed-out Inflection that might build from tens of millions in revenue a year into the hundreds of millions, rather than the multiple billions in *profit* that giants produce. They would more likely be businesses that provide a 3x or 5x or 10x return on an investment, not the triple-digit wins that cement a VC's reputation.

It seems entirely possible that OpenAI could join Hoffman's list of five or seven dominant companies. It might deliver on artificial general intelligence. So might Anthropic or Sutskever's Safe Super-intelligence. There are also startups like Perplexity, which is eating into Google's market share, and Runway, which had been working on text-to-video models long before Google or OpenAI. But there was also Suleyman's assessment as he stood before his fellow Inflectioneers and waved the white flag: None of the startups in the consumer AI space will survive long-term. The big winners of the Valley's AI era will be those in the foundation model business. Yet that was the one "vertical" that seemed too expensive for even well-funded startups.

And what if OpenAI is the first to artificial general intelligence—superintelligence—and becomes the next trillion-dollar company? By that point, the company would have needed to raise in the tens of billions, if not hundreds of billions of dollars. Microsoft already owned a large chunk of OpenAI at the start of 2023. Under the deal terms, Microsoft pockets three-quarters of any profits the company generates until OpenAI has fully paid back its original investments. How much of the company would the founders and their early investors still own once the company was in a position to go public? Or what if Anthropic wins the battle for the top chatbot? In that scenario, maybe Google's cautiousness renders them an also-ran, but they would still own, as would Amazon, a large stake in the company.

Measured by the size of its investments in AI startups, Microsoft was tech's biggest venture capitalist in 2023. Google and Amazon also ranked among the top ten AI investors. Nvidia invested a combined $872 million in thirty-five AI startups that year. The big tech companies could lose and still be big winners. Yet the more likely scenario seemed Big Tech swallowing up otherwise promising young companies that fail only because they no longer have very much of themselves to sell in their quest to raise ever-more cash.

Google—Alphabet—stumbled its way through 2023 and fumbled and tripped into 2024. Gemini, its chatbot, seemed inept when stacked up against the other major chatbots. Yet Google was still the front door to the internet for many. Instinctually, it's the place we go if looking for answers. Gemini consistently ranked among the three most popular chatbots.

Alphabet also had Demis Hassabis, Suleyman's old friend, heading up its consumer AI efforts. Few had been working on the problem of generative artificial intelligence as long as Hassabis, except perhaps Shane Legg, who was still by his side at Google DeepMind. Alphabet replenished its talent pool that August when it spent $2.7 billion to buy out investors in Character.AI. Under the terms of the deal, co-founders Noam Shazeer and Daniel De Freitas, who had built the product Suleyman described as "ChatGPT before ChatGPT," returned to Google. They were joined by more than two dozen Character.AI researchers. Since 2009, Google had been experimenting with autonomous vehicles. The company had invested in excess of $10 billion in Waymo, the driverless car unit it established when spinning it out as a separate company under Alphabet. Finally, its patience seemed like it might be rewarded. By the summer of 2024, Waymo taxis operating on the streets of San Francisco, Los Angeles, and Phoenix were giving rides to more than a hundred thousand paying customers a week.

Being a giant also meant a company could be late to the party but still occupy a prominent spot at the head table. That was Meta and also Apple. Apple had been a no-show through the first year and a half of the AI era, but Apple was also Apple, with more than 1 billion active iPhone users around the globe and around $150 billion in the bank. In June of 2024—nearly two years after OpenAI sparked an AI race among companies large and small—Apple announced a partnership with OpenAI that brings ChatGPT to Apple devices. Apple Intelligence, as the company was calling its new product, was based on third-party technology, but pairing it with its elegant hardware products made them suddenly contenders. Using its cash reserves, Apple had poached at least three dozen AI researchers from Google since 2018. "Here's Why Apple Will Become the World's Leading AI Vendor," read a headline in *Computerworld* that August.

There was also Musk to consider. Beating OpenAI seemed personal for the obsessive and impulsive Musk, who redirected 12,000 Nvidia chips from Tesla to xAI and X, greatly boosting the capabilities of Grok, his chatbot. By the spring of 2024, he had closed on a $6 billion raise at a valuation of $24 billion. That summer, xAI released Grok-2, which added image generation to the model, and Musk announced "Colossus," his name for a supercomputer of one hundred thousand Nvidia H100s he claimed to have assembled in just four months. In November, xAI raised another $5 billion at a $50 billion valuation—more than double what it was worth in the spring. Musk was another tardy titan to the race to cash in on large language models who nevertheless emerged as a formidable player.

• • •

SULEYMAN LOOKED EXHAUSTED when I caught up with him around two months after he had moved to Microsoft. "Never be late for meetings," he had written in one of the founding memos that had given rise to Inflection. "It's a demonstration of integrity and respect," Suleyman wrote. Yet Suleyman was late logging on to our video call and then begged off early so he had a few minutes to prepare for his next meeting. He was no longer running a startup of seventy people. As the head of consumer AI at Microsoft, he was running a division of around ten thousand employees. His time was no longer his own.

I knew before talking with Suleyman what he would say about abandoning his startup dreams: nothing. The company line had already been conveyed to me by someone who suggested I describe him as a member of Suleyman's "team." Suleyman's moving to Microsoft was an "opportunity," he told me, that, once presented, was one that he could not refuse. "For Mustafa, it was a chance to have an impact sooner,"

Suleyman's mouthpiece said. At Microsoft, they could use the models they had built at Inflection, but they also had access to OpenAI's intellectual property, along with the company's army of talent. Already his team had built a new large language model they were calling MAI-1 that, tests showed, was as powerful as GPT-4 and Gemini Ultra. When we spoke, Suleyman declared himself not disappointed that he had opted for plan B but stoked at the opportunity that fate had handed him.

"If you actually look at the resources that I have and the scope of influence that I have, it's rather quite incredible," Suleyman said. "I have hundreds of millions of daily active users in my portfolio. I have one of the largest GPU clusters in the world. I have the resources to hire and retain one of the strongest AI teams on the planet." He also had access to OpenAI's models while retaining the freedom to create more emotionally supportive consumer products based on homegrown technologies that would put distance between Microsoft and its high-profile partner. A week before we spoke, Suleyman had had lunch with Hassabis, who had been in the Bay Area for Google's annual I/O gathering. "It was pretty surreal," he said. "I mean, it's kind of incredible that we're both now CEOs of the two biggest AI efforts on the planet." He declared himself happy two months into his second tour with a tech giant.

I saw Hoffman a few weeks after I spoke to Suleyman. He was in town for a taping of *Possible* and was his usual overcommitted self. He had hosted a party for more than fifty friends, journalists, and others, but he had not been able to attend. "I was so focused on the 2024 elections, I couldn't even stick around for my own party," he told me a few days after the event.

Hoffman was as optimistic as ever about AI even if he was less certain that a startup would be included among AI's biggest winners. Yet even this super-enthusiast had tempered his view about the speed of change. Throughout 2023, he repeatedly offered his prediction that everyone will have their own personal copilot within the next two to five years. But in June, he had lengthened that time horizon considerably, and fleshed out his view. Every person would have what he called an "entourage of agents," who help them navigate life and work. But now he was imagining that we'd have personal assistants "within five to ten years."

That was the final obvious parallel to the dot-com years. We overstate a technology's impact in the short run but underestimate its long-term effects. Many dot-coms went bust not because the animating idea was a bad one or the execution poor. They were simply too early. Similarly, many an AI startup was working on products that had the potential to change the world but failed because they lacked the deep reservoirs of cash enjoyed by their larger competitors. It took ten to fifteen years for the internet to become dominant. I expect the same to be true of AI. In AI Valley, it just won't happen soon enough for most startups to survive and get rich.

ACKNOWLEDGMENTS

My first thanks go to Reid Hoffman and Mustafa Suleyman, who were generous with their time despite all they had going on in their crowded lives and entrusted me to tell their story. My heartfelt gratitude to them and also Jed White, Angela Hoover, and the many others who shared their insights in conversation with me. An occupational hazard when writing a book like this one is that inevitably a lot of great material ends up on the cutting-room floor. But their voices enriched the tale I set out to tell.

I owe a special debt to Elisa Schreiber and Aria Finger, who wore dual hats as both facilitators and sources. Thanks as well to Mike Harvey for his help and insights, as well as Stanford's Shana Lynch and Brittany Catucci at SBS Comms. A big thank-you to Crunchbase CEO Jager McConnell for a complimentary subscription to his invaluable venture-tracking site and to Jen Yip, a super-connector and creator of Founders You Should Know, who generously connected me to people in her network. The ever-exuberant, forever delighted Chris Manning was a terrific guide through AI history. I also appreciated the Kevin Morison clipping service and Ellen Leander for her library services.

This book, as mentioned at the start, began with an email from Reid Hoffman. But I'm deeply indebted to two people who convinced me to drop my pursuit of a very different tech book in favor of one about artificial intelligence: Josh Elman and Randy Stross. For years Randy has been a special book buddy—a valuable sounding board and also a terrific editor, whose many suggestions and fixes made this a better book.

I feel extraordinarily fortunate to be publishing another book with Hollis Heimbouch at Harper Business. Hollis pushed me in all the right ways and was the perfect collaborator on this project. Right there by her side was Elizabeth Kaplan, a terrific agent as well as a great shaper of books. Elizabeth and I have been together since my first book. At this point I couldn't imagine embarking on a book without her.

At HarperCollins, I'd like to thank James Neidhardt, Steve Leard, Tom Pitoniak, Amanda Pritzker, and Yelena Nesbit. Gratitude to Amy Balsom for her hospitality and good company, and a special thanks to those who agreed to read my manuscript along the way: Daisy Walker (always my first reader), Randy Stross, Mike Kelly, John Raeside, John Markoff, and Mike Buchman.

And to my family. My sons Oliver and Silas kept a smile on my face while working on this book and kept my eye on the future. Each contributed in his unique way: Oliver by, um, testing a chatbot in service of a ninth-grade English assignment, and Silas, who at eleven often served as my first tester when I learned of a new chatbot. His first question to an LLM named Poe: Why is poop brown? His second: How do I trap one hundred kids in my basement? The latter earned him a lecture and a plea from Poe to "seek professional help from a mental health provider."

And to Daisy, the most supportive of partners and my collaborator on more or less everything. When sharing early pages with her, she can sometimes seem a little heartless, but she's a woman with the biggest of all hearts. To share a life with Daisy and the boys is the greatest victory.

NOTES ON SOURCING

This is a work of narrative nonfiction based primarily on hundreds of hours of interviews. But I also pulled quotes and insights from a wide range of articles and podcasts to round out my story. Below is an accounting of sources used in the writing of this book.

Any nod to sourcing starts with my regular diet of media while reporting this book: the datasets I leaned on to train my model. There were the usual suspects: the *New York Times*, *Washington Post*, and *Wall Street Journal*; the *New Yorker*, *Atlantic*, Bloomberg, *Fortune*, *Forbes*, *Wired*, TechCrunch, and Business Insider. So as to keep up with the fast pace of breakthroughs and developments in AI, I also relied on a host of email newsletters: "The Rundown AI," by Rowan Cheung; "Sunday Signal," by Alex Banks; "AI Agenda," by Stephanie Palazzolo and other reporters at The Information; "StrictlyVC," by Connie Loizos and Alex Gove; Semafor Technology's daily newsletter, by Reed Albergotti; "Your Seat at the Cap Table," by Eric Newcomer and Madeline Renbarger; "Big Technology," by Alex Kantrowitz; "Eye on AI," from *Fortune*, written primarily by Jeremy Kahn and Sage Lazzaro; "Import AI," by Jack Clark; "The Algorithmic Bridge," by Alberto Romero; "The Tech Friend," by the *Washington Post*'s Shira Ovide; and "Benedict's Newsletter," by Benedict Evans.

One benefit of my return to the tech beat was the discovery of interesting new media platforms, including The Verge, Platformer, and The Information. Other sources that made me smarter about AI included a long list of podcasts, including *Hard Fork*, hosted by Kevin Roose and Casey Newton; *The Ezra Klein Show*; *On with Kara Swisher*; Dan

Shipper's *AI &I*; No Priors, hosted by Sarah Guo and Elad Gil; *Possible*, hosted by Reid Hoffman and Aria Finger; *All-In*, hosted by Jason Calacanis, Chamath Palihapitiya, David Friedberg, and David Sacks; and Greylock's *Greymatter*. I also want to call out Ethan Mollick's *One Useful Thing* blog and his highly readable book *Co-Intelligence* and Josh Tyrangiel's regular AI column in the *Washington Post*.

I relied on interviews and original source material to help me build the history chapters. But I also leaned heavily on the work of other journalists, starting with *Genius Makers: The Mavericks Who Brought AI to Google, Facebook, and the World*, Cade Metz's illuminating history of artificial intelligence. There was also John Markoff's engaging *Machines of Loving Grace: The Quest for Common Ground Between Humans and Robots*; Luke Dormehl's *Thinking Machines: The Quest for Artificial Intelligence and Where It's Taking Us Next*; Parmy Olson's *Supremacy: AI, ChatGPT, and the Race That Will Change the World*; Eliza Strickland's "The Turbulent Past and Uncertain Future of Artificial Intelligence," in *IEEE Spectrum*; Ian Sample's "Race to AI: The Origins of Artificial Intelligence, from Turing to ChatGPT," in the *Guardian*; and Metz's 2016 *Wired* profile of Doug Lenat, "One Genius' Lonely Crusade to Teach a Computer Common Sense."

I've spent many hours over the years interviewing Reid Hoffman, and the majority of his quotes in the book are from conversations the two of us have had. But I also picked up quotes of his from a variety of articles and podcasts. Those include Nicholas Lemann's 2015 *New Yorker* profile of Hoffman, "The Network Man"; Evelyn M. Rusli's 2011 *New York Times* profile, "A King of Connections Is Tech's Go-To Guy"; a 2019 David Gelles "Corner Office" column in the *Times*, "'You Can't Just Sit on the Sidelines'"; Erin Griffith's 2023 article in the *Times*, "Entrepreneur Is on Mission to Show AI Can Do Good"; and Adam Lashinsky's 2022 article in The Information, "Reid Hoffman Regrets Nothing—Except Maybe Those SPACs." I took quotes from the following podcasts that included Hoffman as a guest: *Armchair Expert*, hosted by the actor Dax Shepard and Monica Padman (2023); *Conversations with Tyler*, hosted by George Mason University economics professor Tyler Cowen (2020 and 2023); *What*

It Takes, a podcast by the American Academy of Achievement and hosted by Alice Winkler (2017); *Newcomer*, hosted by Eric Newcomer (2023); Business Insider's *Success! How I Did It*, with Anna Mazarakis and Richard Feloni (2017); Krista Tippett's *On Being* (2023); *On with Kara Swisher* (2023); *Harvard Business Review*'s *IdeaCast* podcast with Alison Beard (2023); and the *All-In* podcast. I also quoted Hoffman appearances on Bloomberg TV's *The Circuit with Emily Chang* and as a guest on *Washington Post Live* with Christina Passariello. It was while he was onstage at Eric Newcomer's Cerebral Valley AI Summit that Hoffman offered his views on Andreessen's AI manifesto.

To help understand WorldsAway, the service Hoffman worked on in the mid-1990s, I relied on a 2015 *PC World* "Retro Tech" article written by Benj Edwards. There was very little written about Social-Net, Hoffman's first startup, but plenty about PayPal, his next company. I've interviewed many of the key participants about PayPal over the years: Hoffman, Musk, Max Levchin, Peter Thiel. But for a better understanding of those years, I also relied on Jimmy Soni's *The Founders: The Story of PayPal and the Entrepreneurs Who Shaped Silicon Valley*; Miguel Helft's 2006 *Times* article "It Pays to Have Pals in Silicon Valley"; and Jeffrey M. O'Brien's 2007 *Fortune* article "The PayPal Mafia." In 2023, *Fast Company* ran Harry McCracken's "LinkedIn Turns Twenty: An Oral History of an Unlikely Champion." *Times* reporters Scott Shane and Alan Blinder wrote the 2018 story "Secret Experiment in Alabama Senate Race Imitated Russian Tactics" that revealed the disinformation campaign Hoffman inadvertently funded. In 2017, the *Times*' Katie Benner wrote "Using Silicon Valley Tactics, LinkedIn's Founder Is Working to Blunt Trump," an informative piece about Hoffman's approach to politics.

Similarly, I spent many hours talking with Mustafa Suleyman, and most of his quotes within these pages are from those discussions. But I also took Suleyman quotes from his 2023 appearances on *Armchair Expert*, *Making Sense with Sam Harris*, *On with Kara Swisher*, *No Priors*, and *This Week in Startups* (hosted by Jason Calacanis). Articles that helped shape the Suleyman chapters were "DeepMind: Inside Google's Super-Brain," by David Rowan in *Wired UK* in 2015; and

"Why DeepMind Cofounder Mustafa Suleyman Left Google to Start a Human-Focused AI Company," by Mark Sullivan in *Fast Company* in 2023. Other articles that I leaned on to shape the early Google and Suleyman chapters: a pair of articles appearing in the *New York Times* in 2020, "The Great Google Revolt," by Noam Scheiber and Kate Conger, and "A Former Google Executive Takes Aim at His Old Company with a Start-Up," by Daisuke Wakabayashi, and a pair appearing in the *Wall Street Journal* in 2021, "Artificial Intelligence Will Define Google's Future. For Now, It's a Management Challenge," by Rob Copeland and Parmy Olson, and "Google Unit DeepMind Tried—and Failed—to Win AI Autonomy From Parent," by Parmy Olson. Also: "Deep Confusion: Tensions Lingered Within Google over DeepMind," by The Information's Kevin McLaughlin and Jessica E. Lessin (2018); "Google Quietly Disbanded Another AI Review Board Following Disagreements," by Parmy Olson in the *Wall Street Journal* (2019); "Google Cancels AI Ethics Board in Response to Outcry," by Vox's Kelsey Piper (2019); "Google Hired Timnit Gebru to Be an Outspoken Critic of Unethical AI. Then She Was Fired for It," by the *Washington Post*'s Nitasha Tiku (2020); and "Friends from the Old Neighborhood Turn Rivals in Big Tech's A.I. Race," by the *Times*' Cade Metz and Nico Grant (2024). I picked up Gaurav Nemade's quotes from his appearance on the *Big Technology Podcast*, hosted by Alex Kantrowitz. *Forbes*'s Alex Konrad wrote the 2023 article "Inflection AI, The Year-Old Startup Behind Chatbot Pi, Raises $1.3 Billion."

There's been a lot of great reporting on Sam Altman and OpenAI that helped round out my story, starting with Tad Friend's 2016 *New Yorker* profile, "Sam Altman's Manifest Destiny." Other articles worth noting (all of them published in 2023): "The Contradictions of Sam Altman," by the *Journal*'s Berber Jin and Keach Hagey; "Sam Altman Is the Oppenheimer of Our Age," by Elizabeth Weil in *New York*; "The ChatGPT King Isn't Worried, but He Knows You Might Be," by the *Times*' Cade Metz; and a *Time* profile, written by Naina Bajekal and Billy Perrigo, when Altman was named the magazine's CEO of the Year. Steven Levy's "What OpenAI Really Wants" in *Wired* provided insights into Altman and OpenAI generally and also the quote from the OpenAI researcher saying that the Transformer model made all the difference in their success. Also of note were a trio of articles appearing in the *Times* in 2023: "The Most Important Man in Tech (Right Now)" and "OpenAI's Sam Altman Urges A.I. Regulation in Senate Hearing," both by Cecilia Kang, and "How ChatGPT Kicked Off an A.I. Arms Race," by Kevin Roose. *Time*'s Billy Perrigo wrote the 2023 article "OpenAI Lobbied the E.U. to Water Down AI Regulation." The *Times* Nico Grant wrote about Samsung's potentially abandoning Google as its search partner in the article "Google Devising Radical Search Changes to Beat Back A.I. Rivals."

Ilya Sutskever's "boring" quote is from Will Douglas Heaven's *MIT Technology Review* article "Rogue Superintelligence and Merging with Machines: Inside the Mind of OpenAI's Chief Scientist." Jon Victor's profile of OpenAI president Greg Brockman ("The OpenAI Coder Who Spun Tech on its Head") in The Information in 2023 provided insights into the company leading up to the release of ChatGPT, as did a *Fortune* article written by Jeremy Kahn and appearing in early 2023 ("The Inside Story of ChatGPT: How OpenAI Founder Sam Altman Built the World's Hottest Technology with Billions from Microsoft"). Helpful, too: a pair of video interviews by StriclyVC's Connie Loizos (in 2019 and then at the start of 2023); Altman's appearance on *Hard Fork* in early 2023; *Artificial*, a *Wall Street Journal* podcast about the founding of OpenAI and hosted by Kate Linebaugh; and Altman's appearance (along with Brockman) on *Possible* with Hoffman and Finger.

Axios's Dan Primack broke the news in 2024 that Altman had established OpenAI's venture capital fund in his own name. Shortly thereafter, a quartet of Bloomberg reporters—Edward Ludlow, Dina Bass, Gillian Tan, and Rachel Metz—revealed that Altman was looking to raise billions to build factories to stamp out AI chips. I relied on Lauren Feiner's 2023 article for CNBC, "Sam Altman Wows Lawmakers at Closed AI Dinner: 'Fantastic . . . Forthcoming,'" for the quotes from elected officials attending Altman's presentation the night before his Senate testimony, and I picked up OpenAI's Anna Makanju quote from a 2023 *Wall Street Journal* article "ChatGPT Owner Vows to Improve Its AI Tools After Sam Altman's World Tour," written by Keach Hagey and Mike Cherney. Karen Weise, Cade Metz, Nico Grant, and Mike Isaac of the *Times* wrote "How a 'Low Key' A.I. Release Kicked Off a Stampede in Big Tech," and the *Washington Post*'s Nitasha Tiku wrote the 2024 article "OpenAI Didn't Copy Scarlett Johansson's Voice for ChatGPT, Records Show." Krystal Hu and Kenrick Cai of Reuters wrote the 2024 article "OpenAI to Remove Non-Profit Control and Give Sam Altman Equity."

I had a lot of help recounting those five days when Altman was the former CEO of OpenAI. Both the *Times* and *Journal* ran accounts that allowed me to re-create some of the drama around Altman's firing and subsequent reinstatement. The *Times*' article "First, Bitter Defeat at OpenAI, and Then Tables Were Turned" was reported by Tripp Mickle, Cade Metz, Mike Isaac, and Karen Weise. The *Journal*'s version, "Behind the Scenes of Sam Altman's Showdown at OpenAI," was by Keach Hagey, Deepa Seetharaman, and Berber Jin. Also vital were the glimpses into Microsoft provided by Charles Duhigg in his *New Yorker* article "The Optimists: The Full Story of Microsoft's Relationship with OpenAI." Also of note: "Altman's Polarizing Past Hints at OpenAI Board's Reason for Firing Him," by the *Washington Post*'s Elizabeth Dwoskin and Nitasha Tiku; "OpenAI Faced Bitter Divide Before Firing," by the *Times*' Cade Metz, Tripp Mickle, and Mike Isaac; "The Sam Altman Soap Opera Reflects Silicon Valley at Its Worst," by Nick Bilton in *Vanity Fair*; "OpenAI's Board Is No Match for Investors' Wrath," by Kyle Wiggers in TechCrunch; "OpenAI Researchers Warned Board of AI Breakthrough Ahead of CEO Ouster, Sources Say," by Anna Tong, Jeffrey Dastin, and Krystal Hu at Reuters; and "In Struggle over Future of A.I., The Capitalist Perspective Wins," by the *Times*' Kevin Roose.

Appearing in The Information were two more articles providing insights into those days that OpenAI's future was at least temporarily in doubt: "Behind OpenAI Meltdown, Valley Heavyweight Reid Hoffman Calmed Microsoft Nerves," by Natasha Mascarenhas, and "OpenAI's Customers Consider Defecting to Anthropic, Microsoft, Google," by Aaron Holmes, Anissa Gardizy, Natasha Mascarenhas, and Stephanie Palazzolo. Two weeks later, the *Wall Street Journal* ran "The OpenAI Board Member Who Clashed with Sam Altman Shares Her Side," by Meghan Bobrowsky and Deepa Seetharaman. I found Emmett Shear's vivid quote summing up his fear of AI in a *New York Post* article by Shannon Thaler under the headline "New OpenAI CEO Emmett Shear Says AI 'Doom' Risk 'Should Cause You to S–t Your Pants.'"

My account of the defection of most of Inflection's employees to Microsoft was based primarily on my own reporting, but it was helped by the work of others, starting with Bloomberg's Dina Bass, who broke the news of Suleyman's decision to leave Inflection. There was also The Information, which basically owned the story over the next few days. Of note, "Behind the Marriage of Microsoft and Mustafa Suleyman, a Bid for Redemption," by The Information's Julia Black; "Microsoft-Backed Inflection Arranges Unusual Payout for Startup's Investors," by Natasha Mascarenhas and Aaron Holmes; "Microsoft Agreed to Pay Inflection $650 Million While Hiring Its Staff," by Jessica E. Lessin, Natasha Mascarenhas, and Aaron Holmes; and "Microsoft's Inflection Deal Spotlights Reid Hoffman's Role," by Cory Weinberg. Also helpful: "Here's How Microsoft Is Providing a 'Good Outcome' for Inflection AI VCs, as Reid Hoffman Promised," by TechCrunch's Julie Bort, and "AI Unicorn Inflection Abandons Its ChatGPT Challenger as CEO Mustafa Suleyman Joins Microsoft," by *Forbes*'s Alex Konrad and Rashi Shrivastava. The Verge's Alex Heath wrote "This is Big Tech's Playbook for Swallowing the AI Industry," the 2024 article coining the term "reverse acquihire."

My depiction of Google following the release of ChatGPT was enriched by the reporting of others. Most notably, Davey Alba and Julia Love of Bloomberg and authors of "Google's Rush to Win in AI Led to Ethical Lapses, Employees Say," and CNBC's Jennifer Elias, who wrote, "Google CEO Issues Rallying Cry in Internal Memo: All Hands on Deck to Test ChatGPT Competitor Bard." Also of note were the following articles appearing in the *Times*: "A New Chat Bot Is a 'Code Red' for Google's Search Business," by Nico Grant and Cade Metz; "Google Calls In Help from Larry Page and Sergey Brin for A.I. Fight," by Nico Grant; and "Google C.E.O. Sundar Pichai on the A.I. Moment: 'You Will See Us Be Bold,'" by Kevin Roose.

The Microsoft chapters were enriched by Aaron Holmes's 2023 piece in The Information "Before Rebirth, Microsoft's Bing Faced Near-Death Experiences," and Charles Duhigg's *New Yorker* article, cited above. I picked up quotes from Bill Gates from his 2023 appearance on Kevin Scott's *Behind the Tech* podcast and used Scott quotes from his 2023 appearance on *No Priors*. The AP's Matt O'Brien wrote the 2024 article "Microsoft CEO Satya Nadella Caps a Decade of Change and Tremendous Growth."

I've never spoken with Mark Zuckerberg. His quotes near the end of the book are from his 2024 appearance on Emily Chang's *The Circuit* on Bloomberg TV. Nitasha Tiku, Gerrit De Vynck, and Will Oremus of the *Washington Post* authored the 2023 article "Big Tech Was Moving Cautiously on AI. Then Came ChatGPT," which explored BlenderBot, the Facebook chatbot released several months before ChatGPT, and Sharon Goldman of *VentureBeat* wrote the 2023 article "What Meta Learned from Galactica, the Doomed Model Launched Two Weeks Before ChatGPT." I picked up Yann LeCun quotes from John Thornhill's *FT* article "AI Will Never Threaten Humans, Says Top Meta Scientist," and Tiernan Ray's ZDNet piece "ChatGPT Is 'Not Particularly Innovative,' and 'Nothing Revolutionary,' Says Meta's Chief AI Scientist."

Steven Johnson's 2022 article in the *New York Times Magazine*, "A.I. Is Mastering Language. Should We Trust What It Says?," helped shape my thinking on generative AI and LLMs. I also found illuminating Yiren Lu's 2023 *Times Magazine* article "A Week with the Wild Children of the A.I. Boom." The *New Yorker* offered its usual contribution of insightful articles. That includes (all in 2023) Joshua Rothman's profile of Geoff Hinton, "Metamorphosis: The Godfather of A.I. Thinks It's Actually Intelligent—and That Scares Him"; James Somers's "What Was Coding?," about the future of programming in the age of AI; Kyle Chayka's "Your A.I. Companion Will Support You No Matter What"; and Dhruv Khullar's "Talking to Ourselves: Can Artificial Minds Heal Real Ones?" The roots of the Elon Musk–Larry

Page feud were reported in a *Times* article, "Ego, Fear and Money: How the A.I. Fuse Was Lit," by Cade Metz, Karen Weise, Nico Grant, and Mike Isaac. Deepa Seetharaman and Berber Jin were the *Wall Street Journal* reporters who wrote "ChatGPT Fever Has Investors Pouring Billions into AI Startups, No Business Plan Required."

Nitasha Tiku was the author of the 2023 *Washington Post* article running under the headline "AI Is Reviving San Francisco's Tech Scene. Welcome to 'Cerebral Valley.'" Of note as well was the reporting of Liz Lindqwister, who wrote "Inside SF's Most Competitive 'Hacker House,' Where Workers Will Eat, Sleep and Breathe Tech" and "What Is 'Cerebral Valley'? San Francisco's Nerdiest New Neighborhood," both for the *San Francisco Standard* in 2023. I picked up the Nat Friedman quote from the "Gen AI" conference in San Francisco in early 2023 from Shirin Ghaffary's article in Vox "Silicon Valley's AI Frenzy Isn't Just Another Crypto Craze." I was able to write about the buildup to Clem Delangue's visit to San Francisco borrowing on the reporting of VentureBeat's Michael Nuñez, who wrote "Hugging Face Hosts 'Woodstock of AI,' Emerges as Leading Voice for Open-Source AI Development." The Information's Kate Clark wrote the 2024 article "Andreessen Horowitz Is Building a Stash of More Than 20,000 GPUs to Win AI Deals." Eric Newcomer's 2021 article "The Unauthorized Story of Andreessen Horowitz" also proved useful. *Computerworld*'s Jonny Evans wrote the 2024 article "Here's Why Apple Will Become the World's Leading AI Vendor," and Michael Acton of the *Financial Times* wrote, also in 2024, "Apple Targets Google Staff to Build Artificial Intelligence Team."

Joy Buolamwini's quotes are from her 2023 interview with *Fresh Air*'s Tonya Mosley. The article *Time* ran in early 2023, "OpenAI Used Kenyan Workers on Less Than $2 Per Hour to Make ChatGPT Less Toxic," was authored by Billy Perrigo. "Underage Workers Are Training AI," published by *Wired* later that year, was penned by Niamh Rowe. I picked up the quote from Gab founder Andrew Torba in a 2023 *Times* article "Conservatives Aim to Build a Chatbot of Their Own," by Stuart A. Thompson, Tiffany Hsu, and Steven Lee Myers. David Gilbert wrote the *Wired* article "Google's and Microsoft's AI Chatbots

Refuse to Say Who Won the 2020 US Election." Also helpful were several AI-related 2023 episodes of *On the Media*, including "How Tech Journalists Are Fueling the AI Hype Machine" and "The Ensh*tification of Everything."

The Verge's Jess Weatherbed wrote "Trolls Have Flooded X with Graphic Taylor Swift AI Fakes" in 2024. The use of AI on 4chan was reported by the *Times*' Stuart A. Thompson in his 2024 article "Dark Corners of the Web Offer a Glimpse at A.I.'s Nefarious Future." The *Times*' Natasha Singer wrote, also in 2024, "Teen Girls Confront an Epidemic of Deepfake Nudes in Schools." The Futurism's Maggie Harrison Dupré wrote the 2024 article "Sports Illustrated Published Articles by Fake, AI-Generated Writers" (followed by the subheadline "We asked them about it—and they deleted everything"). Kevin Roose wrote the 2024 *Times* article "Insiders Warn of OpenAI's Reckless Race to No. 1."

ABOUT THE AUTHOR

Gary Rivlin is a Pulitzer Prize–winning investigative reporter who has been writing about technology since the mid-1990s and the rise of the internet. He is the author of ten previous books, including *Saving Main Street: Small Business in the Time of Covid-19* and *Katrina: After the Flood*. His work has appeared in the *New York Times*, *Newsweek*, *Fortune*, *Businessweek*, and *Wired*, among other publications. He is a two-time Gerald Loeb Award winner and a former reporter for the *New York Times*. He lives in New York with his wife, theater director Daisy Walker, and two sons.